Walter
DEW

Walter DEW

The Man Who Caught CRIPPEN

Nicholas Connell

SUTTON PUBLISHING

First published in the United Kingdom in 2005 by
Sutton Publishing Limited · Phoenix Mill
Thrupp · Stroud · Gloucestershire · GL5 2BU

British Library Cataloguing in Publication Data
A catalogue record for this book is available from the British Library.

ISBN 0-7509-3803-X

Typeset in 10/12pt New Baskerville.
Typesetting and origination by
Sutton Publishing Limited.
Printed and bound in England by
J.H. Haynes & Co. Ltd, Sparkford.

For Mum

Contents

List of Illustrations

Acknowledgements

I would particularly like to thank Jon Ogan, who lent me his own copy of Walter Dew's autobiography for several years while I was researching and writing this book. I would also like to thank the following for their invaluable help: Maggie Bird, Sarah Bryce, Alex Chisholm, Stewart Evans, Christopher Feeney, Stuart Goffee, Jonathan Goodman, Brian Gravestock, the late Melvin Harris, Peter Lovesey, Gary Moyle, Phil Sugden and Richard Whittington-Egan.

The staff of the following archives and libraries were all unfailingly helpful: the British Library, The British Library Newspaper Library, Churchill Archives Centre (Churchill College, University of Cambridge), Hertfordshire Archives and Local Studies, Hertfordshire Central Resources Library, Islington Central Library, London Metropolitan Archives, Madame Tussaud's Archives, Metropolitan Police Records Management Branch, the National Archives, Northamptonshire County Record Office, Northamptonshire Studies Collection, Tower Hamlets Local History Library, University College London, West Sussex County Record Office and Worthing Library.

The work of Inspector Dew
is worthy of close study.

L.A. Perry MD, 'Crippen',
from *Crime and Detection*, vol. II

Prologue:
Walter Dew's Early Days

So commenced my career in the finest police force in the world.
Walter Dew

Walter Dew, the man who was to capture the most infamous murderer of the early twentieth century, was born on 7 April 1863 at Far Cotton, a hamlet in the parish of Hardingstone, some two miles south-east of the county town of Northampton. Hardingstone had a railway station on the London & North Western line and Dew's Herefordshire-born father, also named Walter, worked as a guard for the railway. His Irish mother Eliza[1] would eventually have ten other children. When Dew was ten years old the family moved to London.

Dew was no scholar. He would later recall that 'I detested school, and was an absolute dud there, and promptly left when I attained the ripe age of thirteen.' He got a job at a solicitor's office off Chancery Lane, the result of which was that Dew frequently had to attend the old Law Courts at Westminster. The job only lasted a year. He left after he 'got fed up'. Despite the boredom that office work brought on he had always enjoyed attending court and he never grew tired of listening to the cases.

The young Dew's next job was as a junior clerk with a large seed-merchants in Holborn. This only lasted for a few months. One lunchtime he spotted a fire on the roof of the Central Criminal Court (the Old Bailey) and rushed off to the fire station and raised the alarm. Dew then stayed to watch the fire being put out, which made him late back to work and resulted in him being sacked. Little could he have envisaged that, some thirty years later in that same court, he would be watched by the eyes of the world when he gave evidence in one of the most sensational trials ever to be held there.

Following in his father's and brother George's footsteps Dew took a job with the London & North Western Railway. He had always loved the railway and it was his ambition to become a guard.[2] Dew stayed with the railway for some years and said that he 'enjoyed every day of it'. When he was nineteen it was suggested to him (it is not recorded by whom) that he

1

should join the Metropolitan Police. This struck Dew as an unusual suggestion as, 'for some strange reason or other, I had an instinctive dread of the London policeman, which lasted more or less until I became one myself'.

Overcoming his fears, Walter Dew applied to join the Metropolitan Police force. He doubted he would be accepted, because he 'was very slim and boyish looking' in those days.[3] However, Dew passed his medical at Scotland Yard and was sworn in and given the warrant number 66711. For his first ten weeks he was forced to stay in seedy digs at a common lodging house while he underwent drill training at Wellington Barracks. He was paid a modest 15s a week, but that rose to 24s when he was posted to Paddington Green police station in X Division, Kilburn, in June 1882.

On 15 November 1886 Dew married coachman's daughter Kate Morris[4] at Christ Church, Notting Hill. They moved to Tinnis Street, Bethnal Green, and would eventually have five children: Walter (b. 1887), Ethel (b. 1891), Stanley (b. 1893), Kate May (b. 1895) and Dorothy Bertha (b. 1903). Another son, Raymond, died in infancy in 1891.

Dew remained at Paddington Green for five years, where hc made a good impression on his superiors. He had quickly taken to his new profession, made numerous arrests and received rewards and commendations from magistrates and judges. Consequently, in June 1887 he was made a plain-clothes detective in the Criminal Investigation Department (CID), where he would deal exclusively with crime, instead of the high-profile public policing duties he had undertaken when in uniform.[5] It was as an officer of the CID that Dew was to play a role in two of the greatest events in British criminal history. The case of Dr Crippen and the hunt for Jack the Ripper.[6]

The young detective was transferred to H Division, Whitechapel. He was somewhat apprehensive about the move:

> From Paddington and Bayswater I was sent to a district which, even before the advent of Jack the Ripper, a year later, had a reputation for vice and villainy unequalled anywhere in the British Isles.
>
> I had attained my first ambition as a police officer, being now a member of the famous Criminal Investigation Department – a detective officer. But the natural elation with which I viewed my promotion was tempered by my knowledge of my neighbourhood to which I had been sent to win my detective's 'spurs'.
>
> I knew that I might have to spend many years there. For myself I did not care so much. My chief concern arose from the fact that I had just married, and the thought of taking my wife to live in that hot-bed of crime filled me with foreboding.

Whitechapel, Spitalfields and Shoreditch were now my hunting-ground, with hundreds of criminals of the worst type as my quarry.

Whitechapel in those days was full of slums in which vice of all kinds was rampant. Sordid narrow streets, still narrower courts, filthy and practically unlighted.

Woe betide any innocent wayfarer venturing alone down any of those dark and sinister passages.

So bad was the reputation of Flower-and-Dean Street that it was always 'double-patrolled' by the police. A single constable would have been lucky to reach the other end unscathed.

Crime was rampant, but it did not go unchecked. A study of the Old Bailey calendar of the time would confirm this. I had the pleasure of seeing scores of them sentenced to long terms of imprisonment and lashes with the cat.

I say I saw this with pleasure, for had I not seen the suffering of many of the victims?

A Home Office report written at the height of the Ripper murders in October 1888 gives a clear indication of what type of area Dew was about to enter:

there has been no return hitherto of the probable numbers of brothels in London, but during the last few months I have been tabulating the observations of Constables on their beats, and have come to the conclusion that there are 62 houses known to be brothels on the H or Whitechapel Divn and probably a great number of other houses which are more or less intermitently [*sic*] used for such purposes.

The number of C.L.Hs. [Common Lodging Houses] is 233, accommodating 8,530 persons, we have no means of ascertaining what women are prostitutes and who are not, but there is an impression that there are about 1,200 prostitutes, mostly of a very low condition.

The lower class of C.L.Hs. is naturally frequented by prostitutes, thieves & tramps as there is nowhere else for them to go, & no law to prevent their congregating there.

The press too highlighted conditions for the poor in Whitechapel. The following is a description of a typical slum area in the district:

A wretched back street is crowded with houses of the most miserable class. Nearly all of them are let out in lodgings, of a single room, or

3

part of a room. Loose women have as free run in these abodes as rabbits in a warren. There is a continual coming and going. Precepts of decency are not observed, the standard of propriety is low, the whole moral atmosphere is pestilential. Poverty in its direst form haunts some dwellings, ghastly profligacy defiles others, and this in street after street, alley after alley, cul de sac after cul de sac, garret after garret, and cellar after cellar. Amid such gross surroundings who can be good? With this atrocious miasma continually brooding over them and settling down among them, who can rise to anything better? Morally these people are not only lost – they are dead and buried.[7]

At this time the population of London that was policed by the 14,000 Metropolitan Police officers was around 5,500,000. H division had over 110,000 inhabitants and 548 officers. Dew was one of the 473 constables in the Whitechapel Division, and was quickly given the nickname 'Blue Serge' by his colleagues, on account of the blue serge suit he habitually wore when he joined H Division. He worked alongside some interesting characters, all under the charge of the head of the Whitechapel Division, Superintendent Thomas Arnold, a veteran of the Crimean War.

The head of the Whitechapel CID since 1878 had been Detective Inspector Frederick Abberline, an officer for whom Dew had the greatest respect. Dew described him as being

portly and gentle speaking.
   The type of police officer who might easily have been mistaken for the manager of a bank or a solicitor. He was also a man who had proved himself in many previous big cases. His strong suit was his knowledge of crime and criminals in the East End, for he had been for many years the detective-inspector of the Whitechapel Division, or, as it was called then, the 'Local Inspector'. No question at all of Inspector Abberline's abilities as a criminal-hunter.

Much to Dew's regret, Abberline was soon transferred to Scotland Yard. He was replaced by Detective Inspector Edmund Reid, who had previously been the Local Inspector in the neighbouring Bethnal Green Division. At 5ft 6in, Reid was the shortest officer in the Metropolitan Police. After a myriad of occupations, including hotel waiter, ship's steward and pastry cook, Reid had joined the police in 1872. In addition to being a renowned detective Reid was also famous as a pioneering parachutist, and the inspiration for the fictional character Detective Dier in a series of books written by his friend, the Scottish author Charles Gibbon, whose work was reputed to be enjoyed by Queen Victoria.

Among the sergeants in the CID was William Thick, 'a holy terror to the local law-breakers', according to Dew. He was known as 'Johnny Upright' because, Dew said, 'he was very upright both in his walk and in his methods'. Another sergeant was Eli Caunter, known as 'Tommy Roundhead'. This came as no surprise to Dew, who observed that Caunter 'certainly had an unusually round head'.

Dew mentioned a further two anonymous colleagues, whom he referred to only by their nicknames. There was 'The Russian', who had 'a very thick, long auburn beard which I am afraid must have been a severe handicap when he was struggling with a prisoner'. Then there was 'The Shah', a 'finely built man with jet black hair and moustache, one of the best-looking police officers I have ever seen. It was his appearance which had earned him his nickname.'

The Beginning of the Red Terror

I knew Whitechapel pretty well by the time the first of the atrocious murders, afterwards attributed to Jack the Ripper, took place. And I remained there until his orgy of motiveless killing came to an end.

Walter Dew

The Metropolitan Police's surviving files upon the unsolved series of Whitechapel murders are now held at the National Archives, in Kew, Surrey. They list eleven murders that took place between 1888 and 1891, more than one of which was committed by the unknown murderer who was to become known as Jack the Ripper. Walter Dew worked as a detective in Whitechapel through the very worst period of the Ripper's reign of terror, a period upon which he commented, 'Life for the police officer in Whitechapel in those days was one long nightmare.'

The first name that appears in the files is that of 45-year-old prostitute Emma Smith. Separated from her family, she lived at a common lodging house at 18 George Street, Spitalfields. In the eighteen months she had lived there, Smith had gained the reputation of one who stayed out all hours, often returning drunk. Dew said of her:

Her past was a closed book even to her most intimate friends. All she had ever told anyone about herself was that she was a widow who more than ten years before had left her husband and broken away from all her early associations.

There was something about Emma Smith which suggested that there had been a time when the comforts of life had not been denied her. There was a touch of culture in her speech unusual in her class.

Once when Emma was asked why she had broken away so completely from her old life she replied, a little wistfully: 'They would not understand now any more than they understood then. I must live somehow.'

Around 1.30 a.m. on the night of 3 April 1888 Smith was attacked in Osborn Street by three men. They robbed and assaulted her, inflicting fearful injuries by thrusting a blunt instrument into her vagina with great force. This ruptured her peritoneum, adding to her injuries of a bruised head and a torn right ear. She managed to drag herself back to her lodging house, from where she was taken to the London Hospital. Smith managed to point out where the attack took place, and said that one of her attackers was a youth of about nineteen years of age. Emma Smith died at the hospital the next day, at 9 a.m., from peritonitis.

Dew was not surprised that such a terrible crime had been committed in the Whitechapel division, but had no idea about what was to follow; nor did the police or the public. 'How could they do so?', Dew asked. 'The crime itself, save for the unusual nature of the injuries, was no novelty in Whitechapel.' He pointed out that 'a single killing in the streets of Whitechapel of that time was not unknown'. The streets were terrorised by the High Rip gang, who extorted money from prostitutes. Smith's fellow lodger, Margaret Hames, had been attacked the previous December, but she had survived and told of her attack at the coroner's inquest on the death of Emma Smith.

The police investigation, under Detective Inspector Reid, was thorough. Dew recalled:

> As in every case of murder in this country, however poor and friendless the victim might be, the police made every effort to track down Emma Smith's assailant. Unlikely as well as likely places were searched for clues. Hundreds of people were interrogated, many of them by me personally. Scores of statements were taken. Soldiers from the Tower of London [which stood within H Division] were questioned as to their movements. Ships in docks were searched and sailors questioned.

There were two issues with the Smith case in which Dew was at odds with the general consensus of opinion. Firstly, there was the question of the motive behind the murder. Inspector Reid and Chief Inspector West both clearly stated in their reports that the motive had been robbery. Mary Russell, the deputy keeper of the lodging house, also testified that Smith told her that she had been robbed before she died. In spite of this, Dew was adamant that robbery had not been the motive.

Dew conceded that the High Rip gang was initially suspected, partly on account of Smith's purse being found empty. However, Dew argued that Smith might have had no money when she had left the lodging house, and having an empty purse was 'far from being a novel experience to women of their type'. If robbery had been the motive, surely the killer would have chosen a different type of victim? Dew's theory is flatly contradicted by the surviving evidence.

The second point of dispute was as to whether Emma Smith was in fact the first victim of Jack the Ripper. Smith's dying statement that she had been attacked by a gang would appear to eliminate her as a possible victim of Jack the Ripper. Dew disagreed. Decades later, in his retirement, Dew said with hindsight, 'some even now doubt that the murder of Mrs. Smith was the handiwork of the Ripper. In some respects the crime differed from those which followed.' Nevertheless, Dew continued, '[i]n its brutality and its lack of motive the murder in Osborne [*sic*] Street had the stamp of the Ripper upon it'.

Dew elucidated his theory:

The silence, the suddenness, the complete elimination of clues, the baffling disappearance all go to support the view which I have always held that Emma Smith was the first to meet her death at the hands of Jack the Ripper.

I have another theory. It is that the Ripper having, like a tiger, tasted blood, remained unsatisfied until his dread knife had cut short the lives of one after another of his victims.

While it seems wholly unlikely that Emma Smith was the first victim of Jack the Ripper, her murder was the beginning of the terrible series of unsolved Whitechapel murders which were to bring panic and fear to London for the next three years.

The next prostitute who became a Whitechapel murder victim was Martha Tabram, on 7 August 1888, the August Bank Holiday. Her body was discovered shortly before 5 a.m. by a labourer named John Reeves, who was on his way to work. She lay on her back in a pool of blood on the first-floor landing of George Yard buildings, formerly a weaving factory but now cheap housing. Dr Timothy Killeen, who lived in nearby Brick Lane, examined the body. Killeen found thirty-nine stab wounds on Tabram. He thought that they had all been inflicted with a knife except for one that had gone through her chest bone. This he attributed to a heavier weapon, a bayonet for example.

The victim was identified as Martha Tabram, or Turner. She had left her husband Samuel Tabram some thirteen years before, and had been living with a man named Henry Turner for twelve years, up until one month before her untimely death. The marital status of the first two Whitechapel murder victims led to Dew revealing his belief that the women separating from their husbands was partially to blame for their downfalls, and thus their eventual deaths. 'How often has tragedy resulted from such separations! I have seen it again and again in the course of my career. All the victims of Jack the Ripper, with the exception of Marie Kelly, were women of this type.' (Kelly was allegedly widowed when her husband died in a colliery explosion.)

Dew also noted that the victims had put themselves in a fatally perilous situation. In the case of Tabram, he believed she had met her killer in the busy main roads of Whitechapel Road or Commercial Street. From there she had led him 'to this backwater known as George Yard to escape the watchful eyes of passing policemen and others'. It was of course natural for the local prostitutes to take their clients to secluded areas to conduct their business. This only made it easier for the Whitechapel murderer to kill and escape undetected. Dew recalled: 'An unlighted alley; the back of premises which could be reached by a passage from the street; an unfrequented court; a dark archway. It was in such spots that all the murders took place.'

Martha Tabram had a companion on the night of her murder, a fellow streetwalker by the name of Mary Ann Connolly who was known as 'Pearly Poll'. Connolly said that Tabram had gone off with a soldier. This seemed promising to Dew, for 'the fact that a soldier would probably have been wearing his bayonet, a weapon with which the injuries might have been inflicted, seemed to point in the right direction'.

An extraordinary series of identification parades of soldiers took place before Mary Ann Connolly at the Tower of London and also the Wellington Barracks, but these led nowhere. Despite adhering at that time to the soldier suspect theory, Dew was quick to defend the reputation of the soldiers at the Tower of London:

It was not the practice of the Tower soldiers to frequent the East End and associate with women of Martha Turner's type. The majority of them had too much decency and too much common sense to penetrate at night into the haunts of Whitechapel. But there were always a few, generally among the younger ones, who were not so mindful as they should have been of their own reputations or of the dignity of their uniforms.

Once again, the police investigation of the murder was a vigorous one. Dew 'played my own small part. At first we seemed to make a little progress. Then we came up against a blank wall.' After the coroner's inquest had returned a verdict of wilful murder against some person or persons unknown, the search for Tabram's killer continued unabated. The efforts of Dew and his colleagues were laborious, their rewards scant.

A significant aspect of Dew's character was that he would always respond to any criticism levelled against either himself or the efforts of the Metropolitan Police in general. This was first evident after the

Tabram murder, and would continue long after his retirement, when he would write to the newspapers defending his conduct in the Crippen case whenever it was brought into question.

In the case of Tabram, Dew's belief that the criticism – from both press and public – that the police had failed to find any clues was 'grossly unfair', was reasonable. His defence was that the police, for 'the sake of their own prestige, quite apart from their natural desire to avenge a heinous crime . . . were determined to succeed'. Dew also pointed out another element 'our critics overlooked'. This was that the detectives of the busy Whitechapel Division were 'already grievously overworked. Other crimes were being committed and other criminals had to be hunted' – a fact that has often been overlooked by subsequent commentators on the case. The Metropolitan Police could not be criticised for any lack of effort in hunting the Whitechapel murderer, but they had never had to investigate a series of murders like these before. Metropolitan Police Commissioner Sir Charles Warren described them as 'unique in the history of our country'.

Dew's only criticism of his colleagues throughout the Whitechapel murders was of their policy 'to keep the Press at arm's length'. It was fine that individual officers were prohibited from divulging information to the newspapers, 'but I have always thought that the higher police authorities in ignoring the power of the Press deliberately flouted a great potential ally, and indeed might have turned that ally into an enemy'.

The press was in agreement with Dew. After one of the later Whitechapel murders the London evening newspaper the *Star* fumed:

> One thing is absolutely certain, and that is that murderers will always escape with the ease that now characterises their escape in London until the police authorities adopt a different attitude towards the Press. They treat the reporters of the newspapers, who are simply news-gatherers for the great mass of the people, with a snobbery that would be beneath contempt were it not senseless to an almost criminal degree. On Saturday they shut the reporters out of the mortuary . . . The constable at the mortuary door lied to them; some of the inspectors at the offices seemed to willingly mislead them; they denied information which would have done no harm to make public, and the withholding of which only tended to increase the public uneasiness over the affair.[1]

The police investigation following the coroner's inquest on Tabram was again painstaking and difficult. Dew remembered:

Police efforts were not relaxed.

It would be impossible to recount here all that was done, the hundreds of inquiries made, the scores of statements taken and the long, long hours put in by us all. No clue was turned down as too trivial for investigation.

We all had heartbreaking experiences, several times I got on to something which looked like a clue, followed it up day and night, only to find in the end it led nowhere.

The murders of Emma Smith and Martha Tabram remained unsolved.

2

Long Days and Sleepless Nights

Whitechapel was harbouring a devil in human form.

Walter Dew

A third Whitechapel murder took place on 31 August. Mary Ann 'Polly' Nichols had separated from her husband some nine years previously and, as in the case of Martha and Samuel Tabram, it had been on account of her drunkenness. She had lived in workhouses and common lodging houses ever since.

Nichols had left her common lodging house around 1.40 a.m. on a quest to find 4*d*, the price of a bed for the night. Her body was found by Charles Cross, a carman, on his way to work shortly before 4 a.m. While Cross went to look for a policeman, patrolling PC John Neil came across the corpse lying in Buck's Row. Her throat had been cut, and when she was examined at the mortuary it emerged that her abdomen had been cut open. Dr Rees Ralph Llewellyn, a surgeon living in Whitechapel Road who examined the body, thought that the weapon used was a 'long-bladed knife, moderately sharp, and used with great violence'.

The murder had taken place in J Division, Bethnal Green, adjacent to Whitechapel Division. Dew described J Division as 'squalid. The spot for such a crime was ideal. Close by were a number of slaughterhouses.' Indeed, three local slaughtermen were questioned after the murder, but were all subsequently released.

Once again the police had few clues to work on. Dew explained the reality of the police's situation:

The hope and ambition of every East-End policeman – myself included – was to catch the Ripper red-handed. This seemed the only way. There was small chance of the killer being caught and convicted through circumstantial evidence. Of such evidence there was virtually none.

Other difficulties presented themselves. Dew pointed out that 'the Whitechapel victims were all strangers to their slayer, and died within a few minutes of their first meeting with him'. In addition, the murders appeared to be motiveless unless, as Dew suggested, for some unknown reason, 'the killer was wreaking his vengeance against a class'.

Scotland Yard was now called in, and they took charge of the whole Whitechapel murder investigations. This was no reflection on the local divisions; Scotland Yard had greater experience in big cases and murder investigations than they had. Three inspectors were sent by the Yard. They were Henry Moore, described by Dew as 'a huge figure of a man, as strong minded as he was powerful physically. He had much experience behind him, and was in every way a thoroughly reliable and painstaking officer.' He was joined by Walter Andrews, 'a jovial, gentlemanly man, with a fine personality and a sound knowledge of the job'. Finally there was Inspector Abberline, making a welcome return to the district he knew so well.

Three murders in such a short space of time in a small area led to the people of the East End becoming extremely uneasy. Dew recalled:

There were definite signs now of panic among the populace. The publicity given by the newspapers and the freedom with which the cases were discussed everywhere caused the actual dangers to be magnified.

A moment's serious thought would have been sufficient to show that the only people to whom the fiend was a menace were the poor women of the streets. The three victims had all been of this class. Those that followed were the same.

But I am afraid that the respectable women of Whitechapel derived small comfort at the time from any such reflection, and everywhere extreme precautions were taken against the Ripper's coming.

As soon as the darkness set in on the night following the Mary Nicholls' [*sic*] murder hundreds of women locked themselves in their homes. Tradesmen made a rich harvest in making houses secure. Courts, which had hitherto remained in sinister darkness, were now illuminated by feeble lanterns.

Dew felt a degree of sympathy for the prostitutes, who were the ones who faced the real danger. 'They were defenceless, not knowing from where the danger would come and unable to seek police protection due to the nature of their work.' Many left the district and Dew remembered that those who remained 'walked about in groups, and made a picture of frightened misery'.

There was one lead that seemed promising. A bootmaker called John Pizer, known as 'Leather Apron', on account of the garment he habitually wore, was reputed to be terrorising and extorting money from prostitutes. Dew described Leather Apron as 'a doubtful character known to the Police. Moreover, he invariably wore boots with rubber soles, this fitting with the popular conception of the silent-working Ripper.' Before his identity became known, the press described this shadowy character in lurid detail. 'His expression is sinister, and seems to be full of terror for the women who describe it. His eyes are small and glittering. His lips are usually parted in a grin which is not only not reassuring, but excessively repellent.'[1] But for the moment Leather Apron had gone to ground. The Whitechapel murderer had once again escaped detection and left no clues. As Dew put it, 'He came, no one knew whence and departed, no one knew whither.'

Dew described the effects the investigation was having on him personally. They must have reflected the feelings of many of his colleagues:

> Those were wretched days for me. The hunt became an obsession. I spent long, long hours on duty, only to return home worn out but sleepless.
>
> Night after night I tossed about on my bed seeing again and again the terrible sights I had witnessed. In this I was not alone. There were dozens of other police officers whose lives Jack the Ripper had made scarcely worth living.
>
> My food sickened me. The sight of a butcher's shop nauseated me.

Unfortunately for Dew there was much worse to come.

Just over one week later, on 8 September, Annie Chapman left her common lodging house at 35 Dorset Street at 2 a.m. Like Nichols, she was in search of doss money and was somewhat the worse for drink. Chapman had separated from her husband four years earlier. By Dew's way of thinking, this fact alone meant trouble. To him, Chapman was 'another woman who had once known respectability and a happy home life [who] met the qualifications which Jack the Ripper required in his victims, and had the bad luck to cross his path early on this September morning'.

Shortly before 6 a.m. her body was found in the back yard of 29 Hanbury Street. John Davis, one of the seventeen inhabitants of the house, made the grim discovery. He hurried to the nearby Commercial Street Police Station to inform the police.

Whitechapel Division police surgeon Dr George Bagster Phillips was called to the scene. Dew knew Phillips well and held him in high esteem, as his thumbnail sketch of the doctor shows. 'He was a character. An elderly man, he was ultra old-fashioned both in his personal appearance and his dress. He used to look for all the world as though he had stepped out of a century-old painting. His manners were charming; he was immensely popular both with the police and the public, and he was highly skilled.'

Phillips found that Chapman's throat had been cut and her body mutilated. The doctor considered that the wounds could have been inflicted by a very sharp knife with a narrow blade, which must have been at least 6–8in long. Phillips also thought that the killer possessed some anatomical knowledge, as Chapman's uterus had been extracted.

Also missing from Chapman were two rings that had been torn from her fingers. Dew refused to believe that this was evidence of the Whitechapel murderer being a thief, a position he was still clinging to after the murder of Emma Smith. He argued, 'there were many other ways in which the loss of the murdered woman's rings might have been accounted for'. Phillips found a small piece of coarse muslin and a pocket comb in a paper case arranged by Chapman's feet. This astonished Dew, who was amazed that 'with every second precious to him, he had stayed to arrange the woman's personal belongings in a neat pile at her feet'.

Once again the Whitechapel murderer had escaped undetected. Dew contemplated the killer's elusiveness:

> In some ways, this was the most daring of all the Ripper crimes. Had either he or the woman given an inkling of their presence in that small yard he could have been caught like a rat in a trap. But again he was true to the Ripper tradition. His deed was done in silence, and not a soul in the building guessed that they would awake next morning to discover the frightful evidence of his coming on their own back doorstep.
>
> But more remarkable than his escape from the house itself is his safe passage through the streets now filled with hunters.
>
> Huge numbers of police, both from the uniformed and plain-clothes branches, were on patrol from dusk till dawn. Yet he must have passed through the ring of watchers, not once but twice. Small wonder that the superstitious-minded began to whisper that such an escape was possible only to a supernatural being.
>
> With luck – and the killer must have had the devil's own luck – a man of his undoubted cunning always had slightly more than even money chance of getting away.

Dew set out on door-to-door enquiries. This was no easy task, and he frequently required the services of an interpreter among the large immigrant population of London's East End. It was during this house-to-house search that Dew and his colleague Detective Thomas Stacey had an encounter with George Cullen, alias 'Squibby', a 25-year-old muscular, tattooed East End street gambler. Squibby was wanted for an assault on a child after a stone he had thrown at a policeman missed its intended target and hit a young girl.[2] Squibby had gone into hiding, but emerged on the day of the Hanbury Street murder only to be spotted by Dew. What happened next demonstrates the mood of the inhabitants of Whitechapel at that time. In Dew's own words:

> Unfortunately for me, 'Squibby's' eyes were as sharp as my own. Recognition was mutual. He knew I would be after him, and was determined to give me a hard chase. He made a sudden dash, dived between the legs of a horse, crossed the road, and ran as fast as his short legs could carry him along Commercial Street, in the direction of Aldgate.
>
> Stacey and I gave chase, drawing our truncheons – plain-clothes men carried truncheons during the Ripper murders – as we went.
>
> The sight of a man running away from the scene of a Ripper crime with police officers in hot pursuit sent the crowd wild with excitement. They jumped to the conclusion that the man on the run was a murder suspect.
>
> 'Jack the Ripper! Jack the Ripper! Lynch him!' The cry was started by a few and taken up by hundreds.
>
> Behind us as I ran I could hear the tramp of hundreds of feet.
>
> Stacey and I dashed in after him. He led us up the stairs and into a bedroom where we grabbed him just as he was making his way through a back window.
>
> I was done in. So was Stacey. Now for a rough time, I thought. 'Squibby' had never been known to be arrested without the most violent resistance.

However, Squibby was terrified of the howling mob that had gathered outside. The trembling Squibby put himself in the hands of Dew and Stacey, who now had to get him back to the safety of the nearest police station.

> I told him we would do what we could, but I have often wondered what would have happened had not a number of uniformed police officers followed and, as I discovered afterwards, with great difficulty held the door of the house in which we were marooned.
>
> Precautions had also been taken against a demonstration of mob law. Urgent messages had been sent to the surrounding police

stations – Leman Street and Commercial Street – and soon reinforcements of uniformed police arrived on the scene.

The baffled crowd became more bloodthirsty than ever. The very precautions the police were taking confirmed them in their conviction that the man whose life they were demanding could be none other than the East End Terror.

Presently, however, the yells of the crowd became more subdued, and I ventured down to the front door of the hovel into which our prisoner had led us. The sight I saw filled me with relief. Scores of lusty policemen were clearing a space in front of the house.

On emerging into Flower-and-Dean Street I realized that our dangers were far from over. At the sight of the little man being shepherded by a posse of police officers the mob seemed to go mad.

They made one mad, concerted rush which threatened for a time to break down the police barrier. Their cries became louder than ever, filthy epithets being intermixed with the demands for 'Squibby's' summary execution.

One thoughtful young constable solved our immediate problem by getting a four-wheeled cab from Aldgate into which we bundled our prisoner and proceeded with the police forming a 'guard of honour'.

At last it seemed that our troubles were over. But, oh dear, no! Several ugly rushes were made at the cab, and more than once it came within an ace of being over-turned.

A big, burly inspector named Babbington came to our rescue. He suggested that we should be much safer on foot than in our precarious vehicle, and with this I agreed. So out we scrambled, just along Spitalfields Market.

The whole of Commercial Street was now packed by a yelling, hooting mob of frenzied people. Some, I have no doubt, regarded the opportunity as a heaven-sent one to have a go at the police.

A lane was formed all the way to Commercial Street police station, and after what seemed to me an interminable time, and likewise I am sure to 'Squibby', we fought our way into the grimy-looking building which for once looked really beautiful to me.

The station is, or was, an island. It was immediately surrounded by the mob, now more infuriated than ever because the man they believed to be the 'Ripper' had been delivered safely at the police station.

Even now they did not abandon hope of taking the law into their own hands. The police station was attacked again and again, and it was only the indomitable pluck of the men in blue which prevented an innocent man being crucified. There were many sore heads in Commercial Street that day.

After many hours, the crowd eventually dispersed. 'Squibby' received a three-month prison sentence, much to his relief. 'I shall be much safer in Pentonville', he said. Dew had never seen anything like the mob he saw on that day. 'Every man and woman in that mob was ready to tear a fellow-creature to pieces because some fool, seeing a man pursued by police officers, had shouted "Jack the Ripper".'

A story appeared in the *Star* newspaper on the day of the murder of Annie Chapman which appears to be a report on the 'Squibby' incident:

A man for whom there has been a warrant out for some time was arrested. In an instant the news spread like wild-fire. From every street, from every court, from the market stands, from the public-houses, rushed forth men and women, all trying to get at the unfortunate captive, declaring he was 'one of the gang,' and they meant to lynch him. Thousands gathered, and the police and a private detective had all their work to prevent the man being torn to pieces. The police barrack doors were closed the moment their prisoner had been brought in, and a number of constables did their duty outside to prevent the mad onrush of the furious crowd. The inspector in charge informed our reporter the man was arrested for an assault on the police. The crowd sighed at hearing the news, but were not persuaded that the person in question had not something to do with the murder.[3]

So one false suspect had narrowly escaped death. The genuine suspect 'Leather Apron' – John Pizer – had also been arrested, but he had provided alibis for the nights of the previous murders, and was released.

Two more likely suspects quickly emerged. On 9 September William Pigott was arrested at Gravesend. He had told locals there that he had walked to Gravesend from Whitechapel, and spoke of his hatred of women. The police found a bloodstained shirt amongst his possessions. Pigott's explanation was that a woman had bitten his hand in a yard at the back of a lodging house in the East End. However, he was eventually exonerated from any involvement in the Whitechapel murders.

Then there was Joseph Isenschmid. He was a 38-year-old butcher from Holloway who was frequently absent from his lodgings in the early hours. Furthermore, Isenschmid had spent ten weeks at the Colney Hatch lunatic asylum the previous year. Abberline was fairly confident of the suspect's validity. He said that, '[a]lthough at present we are unable to procure any evidence to connect him with the murders he appears to be the most likely person that has come under our notice to have committed the crimes'. Sergeant Thick added that Isenschmid was known as the 'mad butcher'. Isenschmid was later eliminated, when further murders occurred while he was detained in a lunatic asylum.

Despite such exciting incidents as the pursuit of 'Squibby', the relentless and futile investigation was taking its toll on Dew, who recalled, 'We *were* hard pressed. Sometimes, as I went wearily about my work, ever seeking the elusive clue that would bring the Killer to justice, I became sick at heart as I wondered how much longer those nightmares were to continue.'

Dew would refer to the Whitechapel murderer as Jack the Ripper throughout his later reminiscences, from the murder of Emma Smith onwards. This was due to faulty memory, for as he admitted, 'After the lapse of so many years I find it difficult to say just when the name of Jack the Ripper became associated with the Whitechapel murders, but it was certainly in the early days of the mystery.' The name of Jack the Ripper did not exist until the Central News Agency received a letter on 27 September 1888. It was written in red ink, and read:

25 Sept. 1888

Dear Boss

I keep on hearing the police have caught me but they wont fix me just yet. I have laughed when they look so clever and talk about being on the right track. That joke about Leather Apron gave me real fits. I am down on whores and I shant quit ripping them till I do get buckled. Grand work the last job was, I gave the lady no time to squeal. How can they catch me now, I love my work and want to start again. You will soon hear of me with my funny little games. I saved some of the proper red stuff in a ginger beer bottle over the last job to write with but it went thick like glue and I cant use it. Red ink is fit enough I hope ha. Ha. The next job I do I shall clip the ladys ears off and send to the police officers just for jolly wouldn't you. Keep this letter back till I do a bit more work then give it out straight. My knife's so nice and sharp I want to get to work right away if I get a chance, good luck.

Yours truly
Jack the Ripper

Don't mind me giving the trade name.
Wasnt good enough to post this before I got all the red ink off my hands curse it. No luck yet. They say I'm a doctor now ha ha.

Dew was sure the letter was a hoax:

> That letter did not deceive me for one moment. I am ready to stake
> my reputation that it was never penned by the man whom the
> signature was supposed to represent.
>
> The man who wrote that letter was illiterate. If you accept it at its
> face value you must rule out at once the theory widely held at the
> time, and accepted in many quarters to-day that Jack the Ripper was
> a man of education and culture.

The view that the 'Dear Boss' letter was fraudulent was shared by several
of the senior officers who worked on the case. Chief Inspector John
George Littlechild of the Special Branch had no hesitation in pointing
the finger at the man who had forwarded the letter to the police, Tom
Bulling of the Central News Agency. Littlechild said, 'With regard to the
term "Jack the Ripper" it was generally believed at the Yard that Tom
Bullen [*sic*] of the Central News was the originator but it is probable
Moore, who was his chief, was the inventor.' Dr Robert Anderson, the
Junior Assistant Commissioner of the Metropolitan Police, described it as
'the creation of an enterprising London journalist'.

The police presence in the East End of London was stepped up.
Hundreds of officers, in both plain-clothes and uniform, swamped the
district. All manner of disguises were employed, including policemen
dressing as women. The early panic among the prostitutes was dying
down. Dew recalled:

> Indeed the conduct of these women throughout the period of the
> crimes was to me one of the most remarkable features of the whole
> drama.
>
> It is true they became panic-stricken following each of the later
> murders. Sheer terror was reflected in their faces as they walked
> about, no longer singly, but in groups.
>
> But soon their courage returned. The groups gave way to couples,
> and then, as time passed with no further evidence of the Ripper, they
> were to be seen venturing once more alone.
>
> Some of them tried to make a joke of the business. They would call
> across the street to me, 'I'm the next for Jack.'
>
> Though much of this was bravado cloaking a secret fear, I had to
> admire their attitude.

3

The Elusive Jack

England had never known anything like it before;
I pray she will never again.

Walter Dew

An awe-struck and bewildered detective constable Walter Dew said of the horrific events of the night of 30 September 1888, 'I am completely mystified as to how the terrible events of that night could have happened. What courage the man must have had, and what cunning to walk into so carefully prepared a trap and to get out again without anyone having the slightest suspicion that he was abroad.'

The Ripper struck twice in one night. The first murder took place in Berner Street. Dew knew the area well:

Berners [*sic*] Street had been reformed. Formerly it had been known as Tigers' Bay and had been the refuge of many of the most desperate criminals of the East End. But the police had combed and cleared it, with the result that it had become a comparatively decent street in which to live.

Some distance along the street was a dark, narrow court, leading to Commercial Road. The court was closed at night by two large wooden gates, in one of which there was a small wicket gate for the use of residents when the larger ones were closed. It was through this wicket gate that the Ripper and the first of his two victims that night passed.

The court had no lamps and was in darkness. On one side were cottages occupied mostly by cigarette makers and tailors. The whole length of the other side was taken up by the rear of a social club known as The Working Men's Educational Club. A back entrance linked the building with the court and was in fairly frequent use.

At 1 a.m. Louis Diemshutz, the steward of the International Working Men's Club (a socialist working men's club) in Berner Street, entered Dutfield's Yard in his pony-drawn costermonger's barrow. Both the gates to the yard were wide open. As the pony entered the yard it shied to the left. Diemshutz looked to his right, where he saw something lying on the ground, but it was too dark for him to make out what it was. When he examined it more closely by the light of a match Diemshutz saw it was the body of a woman, but whether she was drunk or dead, he could not tell. Diemshutz entered the club and told his wife and the members present that there was a woman lying in the yard. He returned with a lighted candle and saw blood by the body of Swedish-born prostitute Elizabeth 'Long Liz' Stride.

The police arrived in the yard, followed soon afterwards by a local doctor, Frederick Blackwell. Blackwell noted that Stride's throat had been cut and her neck and chest were still quite warm. Her legs and face were slightly warm, but her hands were cold. He thought that the murder had taken place some 20–30 minutes before. Dr Phillips arrived shortly afterwards. He thought that the fatal injury could have been inflicted in as little as two seconds.

Dew was moved by the fate of Stride. 'Poor, pathetic thing! Just another unfortunate of the streets whose pinched face and shabby clothing spoke plainly enough of struggling poverty.' Dew observed, 'Traces of prettiness remained in her face, and there must have been a time when she had been exceedingly proud of her curly black hair.' The Ripper had made yet another successful escape. Dew believed that his escape on this occasion must have been an extremely close one. The detective thought that Diemshutz's return to the yard had interrupted the killer, 'for he did not stay to mutilate the body. His blood lust was not satisfied.'

While Dutfield's Yard buzzed with the commotion of the police investigation another murder was taking place in nearby Mitre Square, which was within the boundaries of the City of London, which had its own police force. The victim was prostitute Catherine Eddowes. Dew described the scene of the crime:

> Mitre Square is small as a square, but very much larger in area than the court in Berners [*sic*] Street. Moreover, even in those days, it was well lit. On three sides it was flanked by large warehouses, and on the fourth by two dwelling-houses.
>
> Ironically enough, a police officer lived in one of the houses. He had gone to bed at midnight, worn out by a long day of Ripper hunting, and was doubtless fast asleep by the time the murder was committed, almost under his own window.

The murder of Eddowes was the most dreadful to date. Her throat had been cut and her face mutilated. She had been disembowelled and her intestines had been largely drawn out and placed over her right shoulder. Eddowes' left kidney and uterus had been taken away. Once again the escape of the Ripper astonished Dew. He said it was 'little short of a miracle. Small wonder, when it became known, that there were many among the public ready to ascribe to him powers gained from supernatural sources!'

The City of London's police surgeon, Dr Frederick Gordon Brown, arrived at Mitre Square at 2.18 a.m. He thought that Eddowes had been dead for about half an hour, and that her injuries had been caused by a sharp pointed knife some 6in long. Brown made some contentious observations upon the nature of Eddowes' injuries:

> I believe the perpetrator of the act must have had considerable knowledge of the position of the organs in the abdominal cavity and the way of removing them. It required a great deal of knowledge to have removed the kidney and to know where it was placed. It would take at least 5 minutes.

Now two police forces were hunting the Ripper. Dew wrote of their collaboration:

> A criticism levelled at the police at this time was that following the Mitre Square murder there was little or no co-operation between the City and the Metropolitan police forces. This is sheer nonsense. The two forces worked amicably together in this as in thousands of other cases.
>
> There was never the remotest reason for one body of police to be jealous of the other.
>
> Speaking from my own experience, I can only say that I always found both the detective and uniformed branches of the City police ready and willing to help. Their main purpose, as ours, was to prevent and detect crime.

At 2.55 a.m. PC Alfred Long found a piece of Eddowes' apron at the bottom of the stairs leading to 108–19 Goulston Street, a block of flats. Above it was written in chalk, 'The Juwes are The men that Will not be Blamed for nothing.' This was misremembered by Dew as 'The Jews are the men who will not be blamed for nothing.'

Metropolitan Police Commissioner Sir Charles Warren learned of the existence of the message. Warren explained his subsequent actions:

The most pressing question at that moment was some writing on the wall in Goulston Street evidently written with the intention of inflaming the public mind against the Jews and which Mr. Arnold with a view to prevent serious disorder proposed to obliterate, and had sent down an Inspector with a sponge for that purpose telling him to await his arrival.

I accordingly went down to Goulston Street at once before going to the scene of the murder: it was just getting light, the public would be in the streets in a few minutes, in a neighbourhood very much crowded on Sunday mornings by Jewish vendors and Christian purchasers from all parts of London.

A discussion took place whether the writing could be left covered up or otherwise or whether any portion of it could be left for an hour until it could be photographed, but after taking into consideration the excited state of the population in London generally at the time the strong feeling which had been excited against the Jews, and the fact that in a short time there would be a large concourse of people in the streets and having before me the Report that if it was left there the house was likely to be wrecked (in which from my own observation I entirely concurred) I considered it desirable to obliterate the writing at once, having taken a copy.

Arnold and Warren's fears of public disorder were not misplaced. The locality of the murders was inhabited by Jews of all nationalities, and 108–19 Goulston Street was predominantly occupied by Jews. Arnold said he 'was apprehensive that if the writing were left it would be the means of causing a riot'.

As to whether the message had been written by Jack the Ripper, and had therefore been a clue, Dew was fairly certain that it was not:

Its destruction was certainly unfortunate. We could not afford to lose even the slenderest of clues. But I doubt if it made a lot of difference anyway. There was no reason, so far as I can see, why this particular message should have proved more useful than many others which Jack the Ripper was supposed to have written.

As I have said before, it is questionable whether these messages were the work of the murderer at all. Why should he fool around chalking things on walls when his life was imperilled by every minute he loitered?

Murderers do foolish things, I know, but such an action does not fit into the mental picture I have formed of the character of Jack the Ripper.

The efforts of the Metropolitan Police to catch the killer of Elizabeth Stride were colossal. The members of the International Working Men's Club were immediately searched, their clothes examined and statements taken. Some 80,000 leaflets appealing for information were distributed, in addition to house-to-house enquiries. The local common lodging houses were visited and 2,000 lodgers searched. Eighty people were detained at police stations, and enquiries were made into the movements of around 300 more. An odd assortment of suspects was added to the seventy-six butchers and slaughtermen who were questioned. These were a band of Greek gypsies, three cowboys from a travelling Wild West show, and three insane medical students. The Thames police joined in the hunt, questioning sailors on board ships at the docks and on the River Thames.

Two possible leads emerged. Matthew Packer, an elderly Berner Street fruit seller, had identified the body of Elizabeth Stride at the mortuary as the woman who had been in his shop with a man shortly before she was found murdered. Dew was excited by this possible clue, which 'for a time, raised the hopes of us all'. Packer was interviewed and said that the man with Stride was between twenty-five and thirty years old, and 5ft 7in tall. He had broad shoulders and a rough voice, and wore a long black coat and a soft felt hat. The man bought Stride half a pound of black grapes before they left the shop, and headed in the direction of the socialist club.

Dew was dismayed when, a few days after the murder of Stride, Packer saw the man again pass by his shop. Packer did not give chase or look for a policeman, and the man was lost. Dew described it as 'the most maddening incident of the whole Ripper mystery'. Dew asked the question:

> But was he Jack the Ripper? This is a question none can now answer. One can, however, ask how it came about that a man, who had shown himself to be a master of cunning, should have fallen into the elementary error of risking recognition by passing so soon again along that street and exposing himself to the view of a man whom he must have known linked him with one of his crimes.
>
> It might also be asked why, on that occasion, the Ripper should have departed so far from custom as to purchase fruit for one of his intended victims?
>
> Although it has never been seriously suggested that the Berners [*sic*] Street murder was not a Ripper crime. I confess I am puzzled.

Frankly, I cannot reconcile the buying of those grapes in the company of the woman he was about to kill, and his reappearance a few days later in the same street, with the undoubted cleverness of the Ripper.

At that I must leave it, with the comment that if the shopkeeper was right in his second identification it was about the worst piece of luck the police could possibly have had. This was not the only bad luck we had. I used to feel at times that the fates were conspiring against us and doing everything to assist the man behind the problem which was daily deepening in horrifying mystery.

There had been another sighting of Stride just before she died. A man named Israel Schwartz was in Berner Street around 12.45 a.m. He saw a man stop and speak to a woman who was standing in the gateway to Dutfield's Yard. The man tried to pull the woman into the street, but he turned her round and threw her down to the ground. The woman screamed three times, but not loudly. Schwartz described the man as being thirty years of age, 5ft 5in, with fair hair, a small dark moustache, a full face and broad shoulders.

The City Police also found a witness, this time in connection with the Eddowes murder. Just after 1.30 a.m., commercial traveller Joseph Lawende saw a woman he later identified from her clothes as Eddowes. He saw her in Church Passage, which led to Mitre Square. She was facing a man slightly taller than herself, but Lawende said, 'I doubt whether I should know him again.'

Both Metropolitan and City Police forces were being inundated with letters claiming to have been written by the Ripper. One of the most significant was again forwarded by Tom Bulling of the Central News Agency to the police. The Agency had received it on 1 October. It ran thus:

> I wasn't codding dear old Boss when I gave you the tip. You'll hear about saucy Jacky's work tomorrow double event this time number one squealed a bit couldnt finish straight off. Had no time to get ears for police. Thanks for keeping last letter back till I got to work again.
>
> Jack the Ripper.

The most disturbing communication received throughout the Whitechapel murders was a packet sent to the chairman of the East End Vigilance Committee, George Lusk. On 16 October Lusk opened the package containing a letter and half a kidney. The note read:

From hell

Mr Lusk
  Sir
   I send you half the
Kidne I took from one woman
prasarved it for you. tother piece I
fried and ate it was very nise. I
may send you the bloody knif that
took it out if you only wate a whil
longer

signed Catch me when
you can
Mishter Lusk

Lusk took the kidney to the London Hospital, where Dr Openshaw examined it before declaring it came from an adult human.

The public's alarm continued unabated. Dew observed that:

Panic became more widespread. Rumours became wilder. We worked harder than ever, but except for the fearful evidences of his coming the Ripper remained as phantom-like as ever.

4

13 Miller's Court

The most gruesome memory of my police career.

Walter Dew

Over a month passed, but there were no more murders. Commissioner Sir Charles Warren had resigned his position on 8 November due to disagreements with the Home Office and Home Secretary Henry Matthews. Despite press assertions that his resignation was forced by the Metropolitan Police's failure to catch the Ripper, it seems that Warren would have resigned then and there regardless of the Whitechapel murders. In a private letter to Sir Edwin Chadwick written on 19 November 1888, Warren confided to the sanitary reformer, 'I should not have resigned had I felt I could do my duty in face of the difficulties so constantly placed in my way by Mr Matthews. Mr Matthews' statements in the House about my actions are most untrue; but the public do not want to know the truth, they only want to sacrifice someone.'[1] Warren was replaced by James Monro, a former Assistant Commissioner of the CID. Dew supported his former chief, and thought the torrent of newspaper criticisms of Warren were undeserved.

The all-too-brief hiatus was shattered on 9 November when Thomas Bowyer was sent by his employer John McCarthy to collect the rent from Irish prostitute Mary Jane Kelly, who rented a room from McCarthy at 13 Miller's Court, off Dorset Street. Bowyer knocked on the door of No. 13 at 10.45 a.m. There was no answer. Looking through the room's window, Bowyer saw the hideously mutilated corpse of Mary Kelly lying on the bed. He rushed back to tell McCarthy, who saw the terrible scene himself before sending Bowyer to Commercial Street police station. Inspector Walter Beck was on duty, and was chatting with Dew when Bowyer burst into the station with his terrible news.

'Come along, Dew', said Beck. Bowyer led them to Miller's Court, collecting any available police officers on the way. Dew takes up the story:

> The youth led us a few yards down Dorset Street from Commercial Street, until we came to a court approached by an arched passage, three feet wide and unlighted, in which there were two entrances to houses which fronted on Dorset Street. The place was known as Miller's Court.

Leaving the constables to block Dorset Street and to prevent anyone from leaving the court itself, Inspector Beck and I proceeded through the narrow archway into what might be described as a small square. It was a cul-de-sac, flanked on all four sides by a few mean houses.

The house on the left of the passage was kept by McCarthy as a chandler's shop, while one room of the houses on the right was rented by a girl named Marie Kelly.

The room was pointed out to me. I tried the door. It would not yield. So I moved to the window, over which, on the inside, an old coat was hanging to act as a curtain and to block the draught from the hole in the glass.

It was Inspector Beck who first pushed the coat aside and peered into the little room. 'For God's sake, Dew', he cried, 'Don't look.' But Dew did look. What he saw was described by Dr Thomas Bond, who examined the body in situ after the door had been broken down:

The whole of the surface of the abdomen & thighs were removed & the abdominal cavity emptied of its viscera. The breasts were cut off, the arms mutilated by several jagged wounds & the face hacked beyond recognition of the features. The tissues of the neck were severed all round down to the bone.

The viscera were found in various parts viz; the uterus & kidneys with one breast under the head, the other breast by the right foot, the liver between the feet, the intestines by the right side & the spleen by the left side of the body.

The flaps removed from the abdomen & thighs were on a table.

The bed clothing at the right corner was saturated with blood, & on the floor beneath was a pool of blood covering about 2 feet square. The wall by the right side of the bed & in line with the neck was marked by blood which had struck it in a number of separate splashes.

If the sight of this was not bad enough, Dew suffered further by slipping and falling 'on the awfulness of that floor'. Dew's own description of the room revealed more of its dreadful contents:

I followed the others into the room. The sight that confronted us was indescribable, infinitely more horrifying than what I had seen when peeping through the broken pane of glass into the room's semi-darkness.

I had seen most of the other remains. They were sickening enough in all conscience. But none of the others approached for bestial brutality the treatment of the body of poor Marie Kelly, whom I had

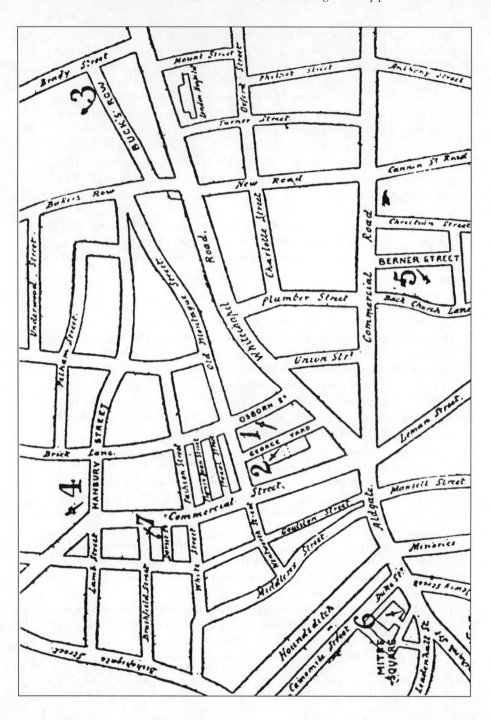

known well by sight as a pretty, buxom girl.

The effect on me as I entered that room was as if someone had given me a tremendous blow in the stomach. Never in my life have I funked a police duty so much as I funked this one.

Whatever the state of the killer's mind when he committed the other murders, there cannot be the slightest doubt that in that room in Miller's Court he became a frenzied, raving madman.

Dew always referred to the latest victim Mary Kelly as Marie Kelly, as had the unfortunate prostitute in her lifetime. The murder seemingly had a greater effect on him than any of the other Whitechapel murders. In addition to the frightful mutilations she suffered, there was also the fact that Dew knew her 'quite well by sight. Often I had seen her parading along Commercial Street, between Flower-and-Dean Street and Aldgate, or along Whitechapel Road.' The shocked detective said, 'No savage could have been more barbaric. No wild animal could have done anything so horrifying.' Decades later Dew could still not forget the horrors of 13 Miller's Court and 'the old nausea, indignation and horror overwhelm me still. Yet my mental picture of it remains as shockingly clear as though it were but yesterday.'

Kelly's eyes were, by Dew's recollection 'wide open, and seemed to be staring straight at me with a look of terror'. The archaic belief that the retina retained the image of the last thing a person had seen led to the police taking the unusual step of photographing Kelly's eyes. Dew described the event:

I do not for a moment think that the police ever seriously expected the photograph of the murderer to materialise, but it was decided to try the experiment.

Opposite: Plan showing the locations of the Whitechapel murders from Emma Smith to Mary Kelly. The original caption reads: 'PLAN OF THE LOCALITY IN WHICH THE SEVEN WOMEN HAVE BEEN MURDERED SINCE APRIL LAST. THE PRECISE SPOT WHERE EACH CRIME WAS COMMITTED IS INDICATED BY A DAGGER AND A FIGURE. 1. April 3.—Emma Elizabeth Smith, 45, had a stake or iron instrument thrust through her body, near Osborn-street, Whitechapel. 2. August 7.—Martha Tabram, 35, stabbed in thirty-nine places, at George Yard-buildings, Commercial-street, Spitalfields. 3. August 31.—Mary Ann Nicholls, 47, her throat cut and body mutilated, in Buck's-row, Whitechapel. 4. September 8.—Annie Chapman, 47, her throat cut and body mutilated, in Hanbury-street, Spitalfields. 5. September 30.—Elizabeth Stride (or Watson), discovered with her throat cut, in Berner-street, Whitechapel. 6. September 30.—Catherine Eldowes, 43, found with her throat cut and body mutilated in Mitre-square, Aldgate. 7. November 9.—Mary Jane Kelly, 25, found with her throat cut and dreadfully mutilated in a house in a court off Dorset-street, Spitalfields. *(The People)*

Several photographs of the eyes were taken by expert photographers with the latest type of cameras.

The result was negative . . . the very fact that this forlorn hope was tried shows that the police, in their eagerness to catch the murderer, were ready to follow any clue and to adopt any suggestion, even at the risk of being made to look absurd.

Dew again commented on the photographing of Kelly's eyes in a letter to a newspaper in the 1940s:

As perhaps the only police officer alive who assisted in inquiries throughout the series of 'Jack the Ripper murders,' I still retain the awful memory of seeing each of the victims [in his autobiography Dew said he had not seen all of the victims].

I was the first officer on the scene at Millers-court. What a fearful shock when I peeped through a window in that small back room!

It was suggested that the mutilations showed evidence of medical skill. I have always maintained that this was not so.

The poor girl Kelly was cut to ribbons as if a raging lunatic had been let loose with a knife. I have always considered that was the last murder committed by Jack the Ripper.

With regard to photographing the retina of the eye to see if it retained the picture of the murderer, Sir Charles Warren, the then Commissioner, visited Millers-court soon after we had the door opened, and at once had the girl's eyes photographed, in my presence, but, of course, without result.[2]

Dew was consistent in his assertions that Kelly was the last Ripper victim, and that the Ripper possessed no medical skill. However, there was another lapse of memory, perhaps more forgivable over fifty years after the event. Charles Warren had not gone to Miller's Court.

Two witnesses provided information which for a while raised hope. On the night of the murder another prostitute who lived in Miller's Court, Mary Ann Cox, said she saw Mary Kelly at around 11.45 p.m. returning home with a man who Cox described as being about thirty-six years of age, around 5ft 5in tall, with a fresh complexion with a blotchy face, and a thick carroty moustache. Dew thought that this man was Jack the Ripper:

In spite of contradictory evidence which came to light later, and in spite of a departure from his method of swift and sudden attack, I think he was, always providing Mary Cox was correct in what she said.

Another witness named George Hutchinson, who was acquainted with Kelly, later said that he had seen her on the night of her murder at about 2 a.m. going towards Thrawl Street. Hutchinson said he had seen a man approaching from the other direction carrying a small parcel in his left hand. Kelly and the man spoke and went off towards Miller's Court. Hutchinson described the man as being between thirty-four and thirty-five, 5ft 6in, with a pale complexion, dark eyes and hair, and a curled moustache. He looked Jewish and surly. Hutchinson said he could identify the man if he saw him again. Dew thought Kelly had died sometime between midnight and 2 a.m. This meant that he thought George Hutchinson was mistaken in his sighting of Kelly.

A further witness claimed to have seen and spoken to Mary Kelly at the much later time of 8.30 a.m. on 9 November, later than the medical evidence would indicate that Kelly was still alive. The witness was Caroline Maxwell, the wife of a lodging house deputy who lived in Dorset Street.

Dew could offer no explanation for Maxwell's story, which she had told the coroner's inquest 'with conviction'. Dew did not believe Maxwell to be a sensation seeker. She seemed 'a sane and sensible woman, and her reputation was excellent'. While Maxwell's alleged sighting was of Kelly throwing up the morning after she had been seen drunk by Cox, Dew could not reconcile the late hour of her sighting, and concluded:

> Indeed, if the medical evidence is accepted, Mrs. Maxwell could not have been right. The doctors were unable, because of the terrible mutilations, to say with any certainty just when death took place, but they were very emphatic that the girl could not have been alive at eight o'clock that morning.
>
> And if Mrs. Maxwell was mistaken, is it not probable that George Hutchinson erred also? This, without reflecting in any way on either witness, is my considered view. I believe that the man of the billycock hat and beard was the last person to enter Marie Kelly's room that night and was her killer. Always assuming that Mrs. Cox ever had seen her with a man.

But nothing came of these potential leads. A pardon was offered to any accomplice of Mary Kelly's murderer who was not directly involved in the murder if their information led to the arrest and conviction of the killer. This was seen as something of an admission of defeat by some – but not to Dew, whose opinion was that 'the step was taken after careful consideration with the definite object of securing vital information which the police were convinced existed. The effort failed, like all the others, but it was none the less commendable for that.'

5

Other Whitechapel Murders

I have never been satisfied that they were the handiwork
of the demon Jack.

Walter Dew

The murder of Mary Kelly convinced Dew that Jack the Ripper was 'being
shielded'. He reached this conclusion after viewing the state of 13
Miller's Court. Dew could not imagine that Kelly's murderer could have
left the room without being

> covered from head to foot with blood. Some of these traces must
> have remained when he reached his house or his lodgings. Yet no
> one came forward to voice the suspicions which such a spectacle
> must have aroused. Proof positive to my mind that the Ripper was
> shielded by someone.

Dew had no qualms about admitting that neither he nor the rest of the
police force had any real idea about the identity of Jack the Ripper.
He admitted that 'Jack the Ripper remained as mythical as ever so far as
the police were concerned. The only certain evidence of his existence was
his fearful crimes.'

Several suspects were arrested after the glut at Miller's Court.
A Swedish traveller named Nikaner Benelius was arrested after entering a
house in Mile End for no apparent reason. He just grinned at the
inhabitant, Harriet Rowe, who alerted a constable who promptly arrested
the Swede. Benelius had previously been arrested in connection with the
murder of Elizabeth Stride, but subsequently released. The Swede had
remained living in the area, staying in a German lodging house despite
having no obvious means of subsistence. Dew told the Worship Street
police court that Benelius 'had been arrested under circumstances which
made it desirable to have the fullest inquiries made as to him'. Although
Benelius's innocence was established it was thought that the erratic
Swede was 'likely to be arrested every time the public attention is strained
to the point of suspecting every man of odd behaviour'.

That the police, and Dew in particular, were still no wiser about the
identity of Jack the Ripper was demonstrated at the trial of the great silk

robbers at the Old Bailey in January 1889. The great silk robbers were responsible for the theft of vast quantities of precious material and goods in the East End of London at the time of the Whitechapel murders. The robbers were eventually caught after an undercover operation led by Inspector Reid. At the trial one of the robbers, Harry Fife, gave an unusual alibi for the night of one of the robberies – he had been at Commercial Street Police Station accusing a man of being Jack the Ripper.

This was indeed the case. The suspect had acted suspiciously in Fife's coffee shop, and was taken to the police station. He was eventually released, the police believing he was suffering from some form of 'religious mania'. Dew suspected at the time that this man was Jack the Ripper, for Thomas Stacey (who shared the 'Squibby' adventure with Dew) testified that 'he was charged with behaving in such a manner that Dew thought he might be the Whitechapel murderer'.[1]

As ever, the Ripper had '[run] the gauntlet successfully, and escaped'. However, despite subsequent murders of prostitutes in the East End, Dew firmly believed that the murder of Mary Kelly was the last to be committed by Jack the Ripper. The 'graduating ferocity' of the murders had surely culminated with the Miller's Court murder, and now 'even the seemingly insatiable monster was satisfied. He came no more.'

While Dew was satisfied that, for whatever reason, the Ripper scare was now over, not everyone else was. There were to be several more unsolved murders of prostitutes in the East End of London, but Dew had by now been transferred to F Division, Paddington, and promoted to the rank of detective sergeant, and took no part in the investigations. On 20 December 1888 Rose Mylett, a prostitute who had left Whitechapel when the Ripper murders began, was found dead in Poplar High Street at 4 a.m. The case was to cause some confusion.

The police surgeon who initially examined the body thought that Mylett had been murdered, although there was no sign of a struggle and Mylett's features were placid. The doctor suggested that the marks around her neck were caused by strangulation with a cord, even though there was no abrasion to the skin around Mylett's neck. After a further medical examination suggested that Mylett had been strangled, Commissioner Monro was in no doubt that 'the case was one of murder – and murder of a strange and unusual type . . . How this murder could have been carried out, without a sign of the <u>ground being disturbed by the struggles of the victim</u>, or of her murderer, I confess is very difficult to understand.'

Assistant Commissioner Robert Anderson examined the body for himself at the mortuary and 'came to the conclusion that the death had not been caused by homicidal violence'. He thought Mylett had died by accidental strangulation while drunk. As far as Dew was concerned, the death of Rose Mylett 'needlessly revived' the panic in the East End of London. The only resemblance to the other murders was that the victim was a prostitute.

A seemingly more likely candidate for a Jack the Ripper victim was Alice McKenzie, who was found at 12.50 a.m. on 17 July 1889, in Castle Alley. She had been fatally stabbed in the neck, and her exposed abdomen had been scored with a zig-zag-shaped cut, probably after death had occurred. Commissioner Monro and Dr Bond were convinced that McKenzie was a victim of Jack the Ripper. Dew was sure she was not. Dew argued his case forcibly, as he had done when he had attempted to make a case for Emma Smith being a Ripper victim. This was the crux of Dew's case.

> The trouble was that people's minds were so dominated by Jack the Ripper thoughts and fears, that they sought to fasten upon him every murder no matter how, where or when it was committed.
>
> Many diabolical murders were committed in the Whitechapel district after the Miller's Court drama. Several of these are still ascribed to the Ripper. People seem to forget that there were plenty of similar crimes in Whitechapel long before Jack the Ripper was ever heard of.

There were similarities with the previous murders, and Dew admitted that Castle Alley was 'just such a place as Jack the Ripper himself might have chosen'. The lack of mutilation could be explained by the suggestion that the killer was disturbed before he could inflict any.

Dew countered these arguments with his interpretation of the fact that a highly polished farthing had been found under McKenzie's body. Dew thought that McKenzie's killer had tried to trick her by offering her the polished farthing, passing it off as a half-sovereign in the poor light:

> This was probably the true explanation, for another woman came forward to say that the offer of a similar coin had been made to her, but she had discovered the trick and had run away. Her description of the man was 'a dark foreigner, speaking good English'.
>
> Jack the Ripper had never been in the habit of decoying his victims with bright farthings. Nor had he ever made the mistake of allowing one of his intended victims to escape.

To conclude his argument, Dew dismissed the similarity of the elusiveness of the Ripper to McKenzie's killer: 'It is true that this murderer succeeded in getting away, but so have many others.'

Dew did not even mention the next Whitechapel murder, disclosed by the discovery of a woman's torso in Pinchin Street on 10 September 1889. The woman had been killed and cut up elsewhere, before the remains were deposited in Pinchin Street. Dew had dismissed a similar case, when a woman's torso was found on 2 October 1888, when New Scotland Yard was being built.

The last Whitechapel murder was that of Frances Coles, whose throat was cut on 13 February 1891 at Swallow Gardens. Dew saw similarities with the McKenzie case, as again 'there was disarrangement of the clothing without mutilation, and again those who attributed the crime to the Ripper argued that he must have been disturbed'. This did not convince Dew.

> There was great excitement. Ripper panic was revived. My view is that this was a false alarm. There was a tendency – and a natural enough tendency – for years for any violent murder which was not followed by a conviction to be laid at the Ripper's door.

A seaman named James Thomas Sadler had been seen in Coles' company on the night she was murdered. He was arrested the next day and questioned. It appeared that the police initially believed, or at the very least hoped, that Sadler and Jack the Ripper were one and the same. Efforts were made to establish his whereabouts on the nights of other Whitechapel murders. These proved that he had been at sea at the time of several of them.

A witness provided Sadler with an alibi for the time of the Coles murder, and he was subsequently released. After his release Sadler stayed in the East End for a time, before reportedly taking to gun-running in South America.[2]

6

Theories and Suspects

I saw so much that was uncanny during the reign of Ripper terror
that it would be in keeping with the whole case were the most
unlikely solution to be the correct one.

Walter Dew

The police had failed to catch Jack the Ripper, but several senior police
officers named suspects who, to their minds, might have been the
Whitechapel murderer. In February 1894 Chief Constable Melville
Macnaghten named three police suspects in response to a series of
articles in the *Sun* newspaper which suggested the Ripper was an
incarcerated lunatic named Thomas Cutbush. Macnaghten dismissed
Cutbush as a viable Ripper suspect, adding that the Ripper had only five
victims: Nichols, Chapman, Stride, Eddowes and Kelly. Macnaghten
noted the cases 'of 3 men, any one of whom would have been more likely
than Cutbush to have committed this series of murders':

1. Montague John Druitt, a 31-year-old barrister and school teacher
whose body was found in the Thames on 31 December 1888. Macnaghten
said he was 'sexually insane and from private inf. I have little doubt but
that his own family believed him to have been the murderer'. Druitt was
dismissed from his teaching post in late November 1888 after getting into
unspecified 'serious trouble' there, but carried on working as a barrister
until shortly before his untimely death. He was the son of a surgeon, and
his mother was in an asylum at the time of the Whitechapel murders.
Other members of his family had committed suicide. In a suicide note
Druitt wrote, 'Since Friday I have felt as if I was going to be like mother.'

2. Kosminski, a Polish Jew from Whitechapel who 'had a great hatred of
women, specially of the prostitute class, & had strong homicidal
tendencies; he was removed to a lunatic asylum about March 1889'.
Macnaghten added there were many circumstances which made
Kosminski a strong suspect. There was an Aaron Kosminski who was sent
to Colney Hatch lunatic asylum in February 1891, before being
transferred to Leavesden Asylum for imbeciles in 1894, where he
eventually died in 1919.

3. Michael Ostrog, a habitual criminal who had frequently been incarcerated in prisons and asylums. At the height of the Ripper murders, the *Police Gazette* reported that '[s]pecial attention is called to this dangerous man'. Macnaghten said that Ostrog 'was said to have been habitually cruel to women, & for a long time was known to have carried about with him surgical knives & other instruments'. It has since been established that Ostrog was in prison in Paris at the time of the Whitechapel murders.[1]

Dr Robert Anderson also had a Polish Jewish suspect, the same Kosminski named by Macnaghten, although Anderson did not name him. In 1895 Anderson had 'a perfectly plausible theory that Jack the Ripper was a homicidal maniac, temporarily at large, whose hideous career was cut short by committal to an asylum'. When Anderson's memoirs were published in 1910, he added

> that the criminal was a sexual maniac of a virulent type; that he was living in the immediate vicinity of the scenes of the murders; and that, if he was not living absolutely alone, his people knew of his guilt, and refused to give him up to justice. And the conclusion we came to was that he and his people were certain low-class Polish Jews; for it is a remarkable fact that people of that class in the East End will not give up one of their number to gentile justice.
>
> Having regard to the interest attaching to this case, I am almost tempted to disclose the identity of the murderer and of the pressmen who wrote the letter above referred to. But no public benefit would result from such a course, and the traditions of my old department would suffer. I will merely add the only person who ever had a good view of the murderer unhesitatingly identified the suspect the instant he was confronted with him; but he refused to give evidence against him.

Chief Inspector Littlechild named Dr Francis Tumblety, an Irish-American quack doctor, in a private letter to the journalist George R. Sims. Littlechild considered Tumblety a 'very likely' suspect. Tumblety was arrested in London for gross indecency on 7 November 1888, but jumped bail and fled to France, before returning to America where he died in 1903. American newspapers featured Tumblety heavily in November and December 1888, but he does not appear to have been mentioned by name in the English press at the time.

The City of London Police also had a suspect they took seriously. He was a man who worked in Butcher's Row, Aldgate, and was kept under careful observation. Although not named, he was described physically as being 'about five feet six inches in height, with short, black, curly hair, and he had a habit of taking late walks abroad. He occupied several shops in the East End, but from time to time he became insane, and was forced to spend a portion of his time in an asylum in Surrey.' As was always the case, 'not the slightest scrap of evidence could be found to connect him with the crimes'.

Dew does not appear ever to have mentioned any of these suspects (and it is not clear whether he had heard of them in 1888). He admitted of the investigation that 'failure it certainly was, but I have never regarded it other than an honourable failure'. Despite this, Dew had no qualms about addressing the question 'Who was Jack the Ripper?' While he could not answer that question, Dew sometimes discussed his views on the type of man he thought Jack the Ripper was, but as he explained, 'I was closely associated with the murders. Yet I hesitate to express a definite opinion as to who or what the man may have been.'

Dew was not alone in admitting defeat. In his retirement, Detective Inspector Edmund Reid said, 'I challenge anyone to prove that there was a tittle of evidence against any man, woman or child in connexion with the Ripper murders.'[2] Upon his retirement in 1893, Superintendent Arnold confessed that he had wanted to retire earlier but had 'remained a few years in the hope of solving the mystery. Anyhow, they all did their best and no-one could do any more.'[3]

Writing in his retirement in the seaside town of Worthing, Sussex, Dew first expressed his puzzlement at how the Ripper managed to gain the confidence of his victims, who were, after all, only too aware that they were likely targets of the Red Terror. Dew speculated that the explanation could have been 'that the man in appearance and conduct was entirely different from the popular conception of him'. That perception was that 'in their midst stalked a human devil who could pass noiselessly among them and murder at will'. Dew elaborated his theory:

Is it not feasible that there was something about him which placed him above suspicion?

Let us assume for a moment he was a man of prominence and good repute locally. Against such a man, in the absence of direct evidence, it is too much to expect that local police officers would hold such a terrible suspicion.

And, assuming this to be the case, the man's amazing immunity can be the more readily explained. The same qualities which silenced the suspicions of his women victims would keep him right with the police officers who knew and respected him.

I am not putting this forward as anything more than a reasonable deduction from the facts as they are known. It is merely one of the many possibilities, though, I must say, far more likely than some of the wild theories that have been advanced.

I cannot conceive any woman at that time accompanying any man of whom she entertained the slightest suspicion into that dark and dismal court off Berners [*sic*] Street into which Mr Diemshitz [*sic*] drove his pony and cart just a few minutes too late.

That was the closest Dew would ever come to offering an identification of Jack the Ripper. He speculated on the Whitechapel murderer's state of mind, and on this subject he was more confident. Dew said that 'one of the strongest inferences to be deduced from the crimes was that the man we were hunting was probably a sexual maniac. This angle of investigation was pursued relentlessly.'

Another angle of investigation was that the Ripper was insane. Dew recalled that '[i]nquiries were made at asylums all over the country, including the Criminal Lunatic Asylum at Broadmoor, with the object of discovering whether a homicidal lunatic had been released as cured about the time the Ripper crimes commenced.' But, as ever, 'No useful evidence was obtained.'

Despite this, Dew was convinced that Jack the Ripper 'at times must have been quite mad. There can be no other explanation of those wicked mutilations. It may have been sex mania, blood lust, or some other form of insanity, but madness there certainly was.' However, even if this was the case it was of no help to Dew, who also thought that 'it is quite possible that Jack the Ripper was quite sane at all other times. There have been plenty of instances of this. Seemingly clever, cultured and normal people can be found in any lunatic asylum – even in Broadmoor – but they are none the less dangerous for that.'

Dew did not accept the theory that the Ripper committed his murders during periods of insanity, forgetting all about them the following morning:

There is a big stumbling block to the acceptance of this theory. It is that the man who committed the Whitechapel murders had with him when he met his victims the weapon – and no ordinary weapon – with which the deeds were done. This surely suggests premeditation and indicates when he set out on his evil excursions it was with deliberate intent.

The fact that the Ripper always worked in the same area, and chose prostitutes as his victims, also indicated to Dew that there was method behind his actions. Why the Ripper murdered prostitutes was a mystery to Dew. For him it was 'one of the questions which will now never be answered'.

Even in Dew's lifetime the theories about the identity of Jack the Ripper were legion, but Dew was not dismissive of the armchair theorists:

> Far be it from me to ridicule the most improbable of them. I saw so much that was uncanny during the reign of Ripper terror that it would be in keeping with the whole case were the most unlikely solution to be the correct one.
>
> He may have been a doctor. He may have been a medical student. He may have been a foreigner. He may even have been a slaughterman, and so on.
>
> Such speculation is little more than childish, for there is no evidence to support one view any more than another.

Dew was certain that the Ripper was not a medical man:

> I never thought he was.
>
> There are many people besides doctors expert in the use of the knife. Why not a butcher, or a slaughterman, or even the proprietor of an East End Stall?
>
> Not even the rudiments of surgical skill were needed to cause the mutilations I saw.
>
> I did not see all the murdered women, but I saw most of them, and all I can say is that if the wounds they sustained are representative of a doctor's skill with the knife, it is a very simple matter to become a surgeon. This is certainly true of the case of Marie Kelly, whose poor body had been hacked about in a manner far more suggestive of a maniac than a man with a knowledge of surgery.

The vexed question of whether Jack the Ripper possessed medical knowledge was always a contentious one. Those who thought that he did not included Detective Inspector Edmund Reid, who said, 'The Ripper was a man with no skilled knowledge – not even the skill of a novice in butchery. In every instance the mutilation was clumsy in the extreme.'[4] Dr Phillips' assistant, Dr Percy Clark, agreed with Reid and Dew. He said, 'In one case there was exhibited a certain knowledge of butchery or of killing animals, judging from the way the body was disembowelled. But there was never any justification for the suggestion that the culprit was a professional man.'[5] Others disagreed. Dr Phillips had thought that the killer of Annie Chapman possessed some anatomical knowledge, and

Dr Brown felt that Eddowes' slayer definitely displayed anatomical knowledge.

Another area of contention was the number of victims that could be attributed to Jack the Ripper. Dew thought that the Ripper's killings began with Emma Smith and ended with Mary Kelly, making a total of seven. Inspector Reid thought there were nine victims, Percy Clark was sure that one man committed three of the murders, but he 'would not like to say he did the others'. Sir Melville Macnaghten opted for five, while Superintendent Arnold went for four.

Dew also believed that the Ripper's guilt was known to at least one person:

> Someone, somewhere, shared Jack the Ripper's guilty secret. Of this I am tolerably certain.
>
> The man lived somewhere. Each time there was a murder he must have returned home in the early hours of the morning. His clothing must have been bespattered with blood.
>
> These facts alone ought to have been sufficient to arouse suspicion, and to cause a statement to be made to the police.
>
> Suspicion, I have no doubt, was aroused, but that statement to the police was never made.

Another certainty, by the time Dew wrote his memoirs in the 1930s, was that the Whitechapel murderer was by then dead:

> There is little doubt now that Jack the Ripper is dead. I often wonder what sort of an end he met – whether it was peaceful or whether he did develop into the stark, raving maniac he must have appeared at the moment of striking his victims down. Somehow I cannot picture such a man on a peaceful death bed.

The identity of Jack the Ripper is as much of a mystery today as it was for Dew and his colleagues in 1888. One thing was certain though: Dew's hunt for Jack the Ripper indelibly affected the young detective:

> Since I left Whitechapel I have avoided the scenes of the Ripper murders as I would a plague. Enough of those terrible scenes remain in my memory without seeking to recall any incident which may have been forgotten.

Harry the Valet

Harry the Valet was a thief with a charming smile
and gentlemanly manners.

Walter Dew

Dew's 'dream as a young detective one day to stand in the witness-box
and give evidence against Jack the Ripper' would never be realised.
However, his career progressed steadily. One journalist put this down in
part to his physical appearance:

> If a swell 'mobman' had to be shadowed the usual order was 'Send
> Dew. He doesn't look like a policeman,' and Dew went into
> fashionable houses, restaurants, and theatres. He mixed in society
> without the slightest difficulty, for no one could suspect the
> faultlessly dressed, military-looking man of being an emissary from
> Scotland Yard. Certainly his appearance has helped him
> considerably.[1]

In October 1898 Dew had just been promoted to the rank of inspector
and transferred to Scotland Yard – an indication of his talent as a
detective – when he was charged with recovering the fabulous collection
of jewellery of Mary Caroline, Dowager Duchess of Sutherland. The
jewels had been stolen in Paris by a notorious continental thief, William
Johnson, known amongst other names as 'Harry the Valet'.

On 9 October 1898 the Duchess of Sutherland was on holiday in Paris
with her brother, his wife and the Duchess's maid and footman. She was
later joined by her husband, the Member of Parliament for Islington
South, Sir Albert Rollit. Amongst her luggage the Duchess had a large
dispatch box with a plain cover, fastened by straps and containing
jewellery that had a value of around £30,000. She also had an unset
emerald and an emerald and diamond ring that she wanted to show a
Parisian jeweller.[2]

The party prepared to leave Paris and return to London on 17
October. The Duchess and her maid packed the dispatch box with the
jewels. It was then locked, and the Duchess left the box on a table in her
hotel room instructing the maid to take it to the Gare du Nord railway

station and await her arrival. When the Duchess arrived at the station, her maid was waiting for her in the first-class carriage with the jewel box. The maid left the carriage to look for her own luggage. Thinking that the carriage door was self-locking, the Duchess also left the carriage to let her party know where she was. She was absent for around five minutes, leaving the train to meet her husband on the platform.

The party settled in their carriage, but as the train pulled away from the station the Duchess saw that her jewellery box was gone. Her husband and brother searched the rest of the carriages in vain, but they did not stop the train. When the train did stop, at Amiens in Northern France, telegrams were immediately sent to Scotland Yard and the police headquarters of Paris and Amsterdam informing them of the apparent theft of the gems. The Duchess and Rollit went straight back to Paris, where they informed the rail authorities of the loss before returning to London and giving a full description of the jewels to Scotland Yard.

Dew was put on to the case along with Inspectors Walter Dinnie and Frank Froest.[3] He began his enquiries by checking which known international crooks had been out of the country at the time of the robbery. Although there was no evidence to indicate the nationality of the thief, Dew felt optimistic that there was a chance that it would turn out to be an Englishman who might be linked to London.

Dew heard that a thief known to operate on the continent had come into some money. That thief was William Johnson – 'Harry the Valet'. The Valet was already known to Dew who described his quarry as 'a thief with a charming smile and gentlemanly manners'. Dew thought the Valet was 'just the type of man for such a job. Handsome, debonair and plausible, no one lacking a knowledge of his past would have taken him for what he was – a clever and audacious criminal. There was something very disarming about Harry. He might easily have been mistaken for a prosperous gentleman farmer.'

The Valet had indeed been abroad at the time of the robbery, returning to England on 22 October. The next day he had visited a general dealer named Levy in Houndsditch, London. Levy had known the Valet for some time by the name of Jackson. The Valet gave Levy eight brilliant cut diamonds, a large pearl and a large emerald, and asked Levy to make them into a ring, a pin and a stud.[4]

The Valet was obviously 'flush'. He began to frequent the Brown Bear public house in Worship Street, where he drank copious amounts of champagne and whisky. The Valet told the landlord Thomas Hinton that he had a lot of gold which was weighing him down. He gave Hinton 300 gold sovereigns in exchange for a cheque made payable to 'H Jones or Bearer'.[5] But to Dew's chagrin, the Valet then went to ground.

The police received a lucky break when an actress went to Scotland Yard to make a statement. Her name was Maude Richardson.[6] Dew gallantly and discreetly referred to her as 'Miss X', while in a later court case she was referred to as 'Mrs Ronald' to protect her identity, for she was described as a woman of means who was married to 'a gentleman of blameless character'.[7]

Her story began in April 1898, when she was living in a hotel in Brighton under the assumed name of Mrs Ronald, where she met the Valet, who told her his name was Williams. He did not tell her what he did for a living. He did no work while he was with her, and Richardson was obliged to pay all the bills at the hotels and pubs where the couple stayed. 'He was like a leech', she said. Richardson moved to London in June; the Valet followed. Richardson went to Ostend in July; the Valet followed. In October the pair went to Paris. Mrs Richardson and the Valet fell out in Paris, and they moved to separate hotels. Soon after 17 October (the day of the robbery), Richardson received a letter from the Valet saying, 'I have everything you require. See me at once', which she tore up. Later the Valet spotted her in a cab and followed her back to her hotel, where he showed her a pearl necklace and a diamond coronet which he told her belonged to the Duchess of Sutherland.

The Valet readily admitted that he had stolen the jewellery. He further suggested that he had help from Sutherland's maid, by saying, 'If you want to get anybody's jewels you have only to get round the maid', but there was never any evidence to support the claim that the maid had been in any way involved in the robbery.[8] Richardson immediately forgave the Valet, and was 'so fascinated by the jewellery' that she wore some of it that night. The Valet was uncomfortable with this and was angered the next morning by Richardson's reluctance to return the jewellery.[9] The Valet took it back by force, which led to Richardson telling a gendarme the Valet had stolen the jewellery. The gendarme did not act; Dew thought this might have been because Richardson was hysterical or had been misunderstood.

Mrs Richardson returned to Brighton after making her statement at Scotland Yard. It was there that the Valet caught up with her on 31 October. Richardson's maid had told the Valet that her mistress had made a statement about him. Richardson tried to claim that she had been to Scotland Yard to make a statement about a man called Halliday, but the Valet did not believe her and physically assaulted her. He said he was going abroad and that she would never see him again.[10]

But the Valet did not go abroad. Instead he returned to London and took lodgings at 5 Cathcart Road, South Kensington, where his landlady was a widow named Sarah Morris. It was here that the police finally found him.

Acting upon information received at 5 a.m. on 28 November, Dew, along with Inspectors Walter Dinnie and Frank Froest, went to 5 Cathcart Road. Inside the house they found Sarah Morris standing outside the Valet's locked door, which she refused to open. There was no answer from behind the door, so they had to break it down.[11] Dew was apprehensive about doing this, for the Valet had a reputation as 'a desperate character, capable of violence if driven into a tight corner' (Richardson had claimed that the Valet had attempted to shoot her). However, he was reassured by the fact that Froest was armed with a gun.

The officers immediately recognised the room's occupant. At the foot of the bed stood Harry the Valet, fully dressed except for his collar.[12] He was unperturbed by their entrance, and Dew was amazed at the man's calmness, later recalling, 'He must have known that if we succeeded in pinning the Paris robbery on to him he would get a long stretch at either Dartmoor or Parkhurst, yet he didn't turn a hair.' Dinnie, who was the senior officer, questioned the Valet:

Dinnie   You know who we are?
Valet   Oh yes.
Dinnie   We are going to arrest you for stealing and receiving her Grace the Dowager Duchess of Sutherland's jewels in October last.
Valet   If I had not been a fool and got drunk you would not have found me here.

He then asked what length of imprisonment he might receive, expecting it to be about a 'fiver', adding that if it had not been for women and drink he would never have been caught.

The Valet was taken to Chelsea police station, where Dew searched him. He found one £200 Bank of England note, one £100 note and two £10 notes, as well as a pearl diamond stud, gold sleeve links and other jewellery with a total value of around £800.[13]

Half an hour after the Valet's arrest, the officers returned to 5 Cathcart Road, where they found a man named Moss Lipman at the door. Lipman had twice visited the Valet during his time at that address, and was charged with being an accomplice of the Valet in the theft of the jewels. Lipman denied any involvement and said he could prove that he was in London at the time of the Paris theft.[14]

Froest searched the house and found a cash box on top of the wardrobe in the Valet's room. Its key was concealed under the bedclothes. The box contained a sapphire ring and other jewellery, although some of it belonged to the landlady and was later returned to her. There was further damning evidence in the room – a diamond stud in the clothes drawer; and in a washstand drawer there was a purse containing four large diamonds and five pearls wrapped in paper.[15] The Valet was tried at the West London police court under his real name of William Johnson. He described himself as a 45-year-old dealer. Dew agreed with the Valet's job description, quipping, 'He was – in stolen property.'

Moss Lipman was in fact the Valet's nephew, and his visits to Cathcart Road had been entirely innocent. This, coupled with the fact that there was no evidence against him in connection with the robbery, led to the charge against him being withdrawn.[16]

At the trial it emerged that the Valet had a lot of previous form. In 1891 he had served four months for stealing a pocket book from a diamond merchant. Five years later he was given six months for the theft of a dressing case at Charing Cross Station, and later he spent fifteen months in a French prison for a theft at Monte Carlo.[17] Maude Richardson appeared to give evidence against the Valet. Her name and address were not disclosed to the court, but were discreetly handed to the magistrate on a piece of paper.[18]

The Valet was under no illusions about his chances at the trial, and had pleaded 'guilty', as he was eventually found. His sentencing was postponed, however, because he refused to disclose the whereabouts of the remainder of the Duchess of Sutherland's jewels. He had earlier been interviewed by Dew while on remand, and he had also refused to talk then. He boasted that he would never say where they were, even under the threat of a five-year prison sentence:

Valet   It would make no difference to me if it was fifty-five years.
Magistrate It would make a considerable difference to you. You decline to tell anything about it?
Valet   (smiling) Yes, my Lord.[19]

The Valet received a seven-year prison sentence. The Duchess of Sutherland was given the £320 found on the Valet, but only between £4,000 and £5,000 worth of her jewellery was ever recovered and returned.[20] Years later Dew saw the Valet again. He was in the dock at the Old Bailey for stealing an empty pocket book from someone he thought was a diamond merchant. He was sent back to prison for five years.

Conrad Harms/Henry Clifford

It did not take me long to make up my mind
that I was up against a criminal of class.

Walter Dew

Dew spent two years as an inspector at Scotland Yard before being transferred to T Division, Hammersmith, in 1900. Three years later he was promoted to Inspector First Class, and shortly afterwards transferred to E Division, Bow Street. He spent a further three years there before returning to Scotland Yard as a Chief Inspector, where he replaced Frank Froest, who had just been promoted to the rank of Superintendent.[1]

In the year before Walter Dew's final and greatest investigation he took on what he believed to be a hopeless case – the hunt for an ambitious fraudster named Friedlauski, who called himself both Conrad Harms and Henry Clifford.[2] The respective paths of Dew and Friedlauski did not cross until 1909, but the crime which led to their meeting may have been conceived as early as May 1906. Using the name Conrad Harms, Friedlauski obtained a personal safe in London at the National Safe Deposit in Queen Victoria Street, and then opened a bank account at Parr's Bank, Notting Hill Gate.

On 1 December 1906 Harms married Edith Kate Garman in London, and the couple lived together as Mr and Mrs Harms. This lasted until August 1907 when Harms's business interests in London failed. According to his brother-in-law, Arthur East, Harms was 'financially broke in London'. He sailed to New York from Glasgow on 17 August on the steamer *Furnessia*, deserting his wife in the process.

Harms was next heard of in New York in January 1909. There he visited J.S. Bache & Co. Bank. Harms spoke to Hugo Jacob Lyon,[3] the manager of the bank's foreign department. He asked Lyon to cash a 1,000 rouble Russian draft; but Lyon refused, as he did not know Harms. Harms told Lyon that he had presented J.S. Bache himself with a letter of introduction in August 1907. But Bache was in Cuba at the time, so he could not confirm this.

Two months later Harms returned to the bank and asked the general manager, Hubert Arthur Hensley, for an advance on a Russian bill. Hensley refused. Later in the day Hensley received a letter from Harms which said that he was in great need. Hensley communicated with his superiors and told Harms to call in at the bank two days later. Harms did so, and was given a cheque for $10, and also offered a position in the bank's foreign department for a salary of $10 a week.

Harms started work as a clerk at Bache & co. on 29 March 1909, and his desk was next to Hugo Lyon's. At the bank the clerks had the authority to draw up bills; they would fill in the counterfoil and then get a senior colleague to sign the bill. One of the banks which Bache were accustomed to draw bills on was the Swiss Bankverein in London.

On 6 May 1909 Lyon had to go to Europe for a number of weeks. Before leaving he instructed Harms to conduct part of his duties at the foreign department. The very next day a bill was drawn up in favour of Parr's Bank Limited, London (where Harms had an account), for £1,637 14s on demand. The bill had been handwritten by Harms and apparently signed by Leopold S. Bache. The counterfoil of the bill was also written by Harms, but it was dated 1 May 1909, for the value of £1 10s 2d. Harms resigned from the bank a week later. He sent Hubert Hensley a note saying that he had accepted a job with a higher salary and left without notice. Harms was already on the brink of being fired 'because the office was not satisfied with his record'.

On 17 May 1909 Parr's Bank in London received a cheque from Harms for £1,637 14s, to be drawn from the Swiss Bankverein. The accompanying letter had been written on 7 May. The cheque was presented at the Swiss Bankverein, who believed it to be genuine, and subsequently the full amount was paid into Harms's account at Parr's Bank.

The end of the month saw Harms back in London. On 31 May he visited the Crown Emporium Jewellery Company in the Strand, where he bought a pair of field glasses. The Emporium's manager, John Chisholm, showed Harms a silver watch. Harms liked it, and asked if Chisholm could get him a similar one in gold. Chisholm said that he could, and told Harms to return the following day.

Before returning to the Emporium the next day, Harms called in at Parr's Bank. He asked for a cheque book and drew out £1,437 3s 11d: two £500 notes, four £100 notes and £37 3s 11d in gold and coins. Harms next went to Hands & co., a moneychangers at Charing Cross. He gave the manager William Ernest Farr a £500 note and asked him to exchange it for £300 worth of German money and £200 in £5 Bank of England notes and gold. Returning to the Crown Emporium, Harms purchased the gold watch for £20. Chisholm did not have enough change for the £100 note which Harms had given him, so Harms paid in gold. Chisholm noticed that Harms had more bank notes in his breast pocket.

Harms left the Emporium and went to another moneychangers. There he bought 4,000 French francs and 800 Belgian francs, which he paid for with two £100 notes that he peeled from a roll. Harms mentioned to Walter Lawlor, who worked at the moneychangers, that he was having difficulty shutting his watch. Lawlor said that he had some knowledge of jewellery and was of the opinion that Harms had been overcharged for the timepiece, and that six or seven guineas would have been a more realistic price to have paid for it.

On 2 June 1909 Hugo Lyon was in Amsterdam. There he received a cable from his bank stating that a forgery had been committed. They had received a letter which read:

Dover, June 1, 1909

Messrs J.S. Bache and Co., New York.

Dear Sirs,

I have taken from you £1,637 14s., but I am willing to pay it in full with interest at 5 per cent. per annum on the following conditions:

(1) You do not prosecute.
(2) You do not let anything transpire in the newspapers.
(3) You do not mention the matter to my friends, Messrs. Blair Brothers, New York, Mr. James Gorman, New York, Messrs. Harry Sutherland and Son, London, Parr's Bank, London; and Swiss Bankverein, London.
(4) You will return this letter after I have paid you in full.

If you agree I will pay as follows: – £100 (cheque enclosed); £150, December, 1909; £200, June 1, 1910; £250, December 1, 1910, £300, June 1, 1911, £350, December, 1911; £287 14s., June 1, 1912.

I think it is better for you to keep the matter quiet, because in case of publicity it will be known that your bookkeeping department did not notice anything 25 days after the cheque was drawn, 15 days after it was honoured by the Swiss Bankverein, and eight days after you had in New York the information of payment. This may injure the name of your firm, as with such a bookkeeping your correspondents and customers would not feel safe. It does not interest you, but I must say I had good intentions when you employed me; but Mr. Woolman let me understand that I shall either be discharged or kept on $10 a week, which was unfair. If you wish to avoid such occurrences in the future it should be arranged that the letter of advices [*sic*] should be written by the bookkeeping department (not by the foreign) from the bill book (not the draft book).

Very truly yours

Conrad Harms[4]

Parr's Bank and Scotland Yard were informed, and Dew was put on the case. He was not optimistic about his chances of catching Harms and '[f]or a long time it looked pretty hopeless. All the information indicated that our man had fled the country.' Dew sensed that Harms was a more intelligent criminal than many of the others he had dealt with over the years. This only added to his bleak prognosis. Dew was 'frankly pessimistic. Unless the man was a fool – which it was pretty obvious he was not – he would long since have crossed the Channel to the Continent.'

Nevertheless, Dew threw himself into the investigation. It was an adage of Dew's that, 'Dogged perseverance had brought far more criminals to book than flashes of genius.' He obtained the numbers of the Bank of England notes in Harms' possession and circulated his description throughout the country, and particularly to all the seaports.

Dew enlisted the help of Sergeant James Berrett, a colleague whom he held in high regard, describing him as 'a splendid chap to have as an assistant. He was always exceedingly painstaking, and never minded how many hours he put in on a job. I am afraid no other sort of man would have suited me.'[5]

Dew's suspicions about Harms's flight abroad were correct. He had gone to Vienna. On 21 June he returned to England, landing at Dover, where he booked into the Dover Castle Hotel under the name of Henry Clifford, with a woman named Frieda Braun. He committed bigamy by marrying Braun at Dover on 24 June, before leaving for London, where they booked into room 442 of the Charing Cross Grand Hotel.

Harms was unaware that returning to London was a dangerous move. Dew and Berrett had spoken to Walter Lawlor, the moneychanger, who suggested that Harms may be returning to the jewellers where he had bought his gold watch to complain about it. The detectives had visited John Chisholm at the Crown Emporium. Chisholm was doubtful that Harms would return after nearly a month, but Dew instructed him what to do just in case he did: 'You must try to keep the man in the shop while you get into touch with Bow Street Police Station. If you can't do this, you must do your level best to get the man's address.' Dew managed to trace a

The young detective constable Walter Dew. *(Thomson's Weekly News)*

Detectives Dew and Stacey in pursuit of East End villain George Cullen, alias 'Squibby'. *(Thomson's Weekly News)*

Dew (seated) and Inspector Beck learn of the murder of Mary Jane Kelly. (*Thomson's Weekly News*)

William 'Harry the Valet' Johnson (left) and his nephew Moss Lipman appearing at the West London magistrates' court. (*Lloyd's Weekly Newspaper*)

James Berrett. *(Stewart P. Evans)*

Superintendent Frank Froest. *(Stewart P. Evans)*

Dr Hawley Harvey Crippen. *(Stewart P. Evans)*

Cora Crippen alias Belle Elmore. *(Stewart P. Evans)*

39 Hilldrop Crescent. *(Jon Ogan)*

FOUND A LOADED REVOLVER IN Dr CRIPPEN'S HOUSE.

Dew and Sergeant Mitchell searching 39 Hilldrop Crescent. *(Illustrated Police News)*

Cora Crippen's remains being unearthed. *(Illustrated Police News)*

The remains of Cora Crippen. *(Stewart P. Evans)*

Dew (far right) in the back garden of 39 Hilldrop Crescent. *(Stewart P. Evans)*

Sir Melville Macnaghten.
(Stewart P. Evans)

Professor Augustus Pepper. *(Illustrated Police News)*

few more of Harms's banknotes, but 'not as much as a hint could we get as to our man's present whereabouts'. The detective was 'on the point of abandoning the inquiry when the miracle happened'.

At 3.30 p.m. on 26 June Harms did return to the Crown Emporium. He produced the gold watch and told Chisholm that it wasn't working properly, and that he had been overcharged. Chisholm told Harms that he needed half an hour to check with his employer if he could offer a refund. Harms returned at 5.45 with Frieda Braun in a chauffeur-driven car. By this time Chisholm had phoned Bow Street Police Station, from where Detective Sergeant Alfred Crutchett and Detective Constable Bishop hurried to the Emporium, where they waited on the stairs for Harms. Upon entering the shop, Harms was approached by Crutchett:

Crutchett   We are police officers and you are very much like the photograph of a man named Conrad Harms who is wanted for forgery.
Harms   My name is Henry Clifford.
Crutchett   It may be unfortunate for you, but you see the photograph is very like you.
Harms   The photograph is very like me – too much like me.

Harms was taken to Bow Street Police Station, where he again claimed to be called Henry Clifford. He added that he had been in England for two days, having come from Vienna. He also claimed to be the son of an English father and French mother, and that he had been born in England but raised in France as well as Germany. When the question of his bigamous marriage was raised Harms said, 'It's all a mistake, my first wife died five years ago.' Among the contents of Harms's pockets was a pistol.

With Harms safely in custody, Dew searched his room at the Grand Hotel, and then his private safe at the National Safe Deposit. The contents of the safe conclusively proved that 'Henry Clifford' was indeed Conrad Harms. It contained a photograph of Harms with his first wife, Edith Garman, Harms's Parr's Bank book, and a passenger list for the *Furnessia* which listed Conrad Harms as a first-class passenger. Dew returned to Bow Street shortly before 8 p.m. and interviewed Harms:

Dew   Mr Conrad Harms?
Harms   No, you are making a mistake. My name is Henry Clifford.
Dew   You are detained here on suspicion of being Conrad Harms, wanted for obtaining £1,600 from Parr's Bank on the first of this month.

Harms	Oh, no. My name is Henry Clifford. I only came from Vienna on Tuesday and was married on Thursday.
Dew	If you are Conrad Harms, as I am convinced you are, you already have a wife in London who you deserted, and therefore you have committed bigamy.
Harms	It's all a mistake, my first wife died five years ago. I do not blame anyone. I am very much like the photograph – too much like it – anyone would take it for me, but my name is Henry Clifford.

Dew pointed out that if 'Henry Clifford' reversed his initials then they could stand for 'Conrad Harms'. Harms countered this by saying that they might stand for anything, but Dew later found nine handkerchiefs with a 'CH' monogram in 'Henry Clifford's' hotel room. Harms would later claim in court that the handkerchiefs were manufactured in Germany, where they would have spelt Conrad with a K.[6] Dew told Harms he would be charged as Conrad Harms. 'You can put any charge you like against me', Harms defiantly replied.

Several witnesses positively identified Harms from a line-up of over a dozen men. He was a distinctive-looking man. Dew described him as a 'dark-visaged, sharp-featured little man'. Hugo Lyon from Bache & Co. Bank identified Harms by 'his look – the expression in his eyes'.[7] Several witnesses also commented on Harms's unmistakable voice. Dew had a grudging admiration for Harms's refusal to admit his true identity, saying that 'when a wanted person is so overwhelmingly identified as this, he or she generally gives in and tries to find some defence other than an alibi. Not so Mr Henry Clifford. In a way I admired him for it. The dice was loaded heavily against him, but he put up a stout fight.'

Harms appeared at the magistrates' court, where he requested that his wife Frieda be allowed to return home to Vienna with the money that had been found on him. Dew opposed this request, and the magistrate turned it down. Dew had already arranged for Frieda to be placed in the care of the Austrian consulate,[8] and would later escort her back to Vienna, to her mother's, where Harms had left a metal box containing more incriminating evidence.[9] Frieda explained through an interpreter that Harms had swiftly seduced her in Vienna. They had journeyed to Dover in order to marry immediately, rather than having to wait in Vienna.

In the face of such overwhelming evidence to the contrary Harms continued to protest that he was another man, named Henry Clifford. Perhaps the most extraordinary example of his deceit came on 2 September. Harms had written the day before to his brother-in-law, Arthur East, from Brixton Prison. In a letter signed 'Henry Clifford',

Harms said that he was Conrad Harms's cousin, and requested that East visit him along with his first wife, Edith Garman. East thought that the handwriting in the letter looked like that of Harms, but disguised. The following conversation took place at the prison:

Harms	I presume you are Mr Arthur James East?
East	Yes Conrad, I am, and I am very sorry for you, old boy, and what is it you have sent to see us for?
Harms	Is this Mrs Harms?
East	You know it is, Conrad.
Harms	I have asked you to come and see me so that you can see the difference between me and Conrad Harms, my cousin.
East	What is the use of talking like that when you know you are Conrad Harms?
Harms	Do you say I am your husband?
Edith	Of course I do, Conrad, and so you are my husband, and why do you ask me such a question causing me pain, as you have already caused me sufficient pain, I am sorry you sent to see me, but I came because the solicitors requested me to do so . . . if I could help you without perjuring myself, I would willingly do so, as I have forgiven you for all.
Harms	You say I am Conrad Harms, your husband, and that I deny, as I am Conrad Harms' cousin.
Edith	I can only say what is true, that you are Conrad Harms, and you know you are.
Harms	Well, nothing further can be said, I am very thankful you came to see me as I asked, but I am very disappointed, as I did not expect such a result.

The trial of the 33-year-old Conrad Harms took place at the Central Criminal Court on 9 September 1909. The charges against him were fraud and bigamy; his defence was one of mistaken identity. Harms, still insisting he was Henry Clifford, said that the real Conrad Harms was an English subject of Jewish descent. He had known Harms for ten years, and there were physical differences between the two. The real Harms was two years older and half an inch taller than 'Clifford' (who stood at a mere 5ft 1½in). Furthermore, 'I have three marks on my face – a birthmark like a hole in the left ear, a mark on the upper lip, and my hair will only part in the middle – photographs produced show that Harms parted his hair on the left'. Harms requested that he be allowed to shave off his moustache to show the jury the mark on his lip, but he was refused permission.

While Harms stoically kept up his pretence about his true identity, he invented a new and epic tale of his past to tell the court, which was totally different to what he had told the police at Bow Street. He now said that he had been born in China. Orphaned at a young age, he remained in China and worked for a druggist before getting a bank job in Shanghai. After other banking positions in the Far East, he then went to Russia, then travelled around Europe and South America. Before Harms came to trial, Dew had found out that his real name was Friedlauski, and that he had been educated in law in Russia and had served in the Manchurian army.

The members of the jury were unconvinced by Harms's story, as was a handwriting expert who compared the handwriting of Harms and Clifford and concluded they were written by the same hand. Harms was found guilty of fraud and bigamy and sentenced to six years' penal servitude, with a recommendation that he would be deported at the end of his sentence.[10]

Harms appealed against his sentence on the grounds of mistaken identity. However, the appeal judge pointed out that the evidence against Harms at his original trial had been 'little short of overwhelming'. Harms's failure to communicate with alleged witnesses who he claimed could prove his identity, despite having frequently been given the chance to do so, also weighed against him.

Dew would later describe Harms as 'one of the cleverest swindlers I struck throughout my police career', and reminisced that 'it was a real pleasure' to bring Harms to justice. He added, with a note of grim satisfaction, 'While he was lovemaking in Vienna, Berrett and I were working early and late in our efforts to trace him and recover the stolen money.'

After his release from prison Harms sought out Berrett and the pair had a long talk together. Harms did not bear any grudge against Berrett, who found the Russian swindler to be a cultured man, and was impressed by the fact that he spoke seven languages. They discussed prison conditions and Harms told Berrett, 'Your prisons are admirable, in a way. But a long term of penal servitude in one will inevitably make a vagrant of a man, even if he was not that way inclined before. There is not enough work to keep prisoners amused. I was not allowed to work a quarter as hard as I wanted to work.'[11]

The Disappearance of Belle Elmore

Strikes and lock-outs, champagne suppers and
unemployed marchers, Chinese labour, tariff reform,
HMS *Dreadnought*, Marconi, Home Rule for Ireland,
Doctor Crippen, suffragettes, the lines of Chatalja . . .
James Hilton, Goodbye Mr Chips

Walter Dew's final and most celebrated case began innocuously enough on 30 June 1910, when he was summoned to the Scotland Yard office of Superintendent Frank Froest.[1] According to one journalist's description: 'Short, thick-set, full-faced, Mr. Froest in uniform looked more like a Prussian field-marshal than anything else. Out of uniform (which he generally was) he was always immaculate in silk hat, patent leather boots, and carrying a carefully rolled umbrella.' Known as 'the man with the iron hands', on account of his incredible prehensile strength, Froest was able to tear packs of cards in two and snap a sixpence 'like a biscuit'.[2]

In the office Dew was introduced to John Edward Nash, a theatrical manager, and his wife, a music hall artist professionally known as 'Lil Hawthorne', both acquaintances of Froest. There was nothing to indicate the magnitude of what was about to unfold. Dew later recalled, 'I certainly had no suspicion of the bigness of the case when the name of Crippen was first mentioned at Scotland Yard'; he would later describe the events that were to follow as 'the most intriguing murder mystery of the century'.

The Nashes told Dew they had returned home to London from America to hear that their American friend of Polish descent, Mrs Cora Crippen, was dead. Cora had been the honorary treasurer of the Music Hall Ladies' Guild, a charitable organisation for members of their profession who had fallen upon hard times. The Guild met every Wednesday at Albion House, a large block of flats in New Oxford Street. Cora had been professionally known as 'Belle Elmore', but her stage career as a music hall artiste had been a dismal failure. Mr Nash believed her American husband of seventeen years, Dr Hawley Harvey Crippen, was a dentist with some kind of American qualification. At this time Crippen was in partnership with dentist Dr Gilbert Rylance, and they worked together as the Yale Tooth Specialists. Rylance and Crippen had gone into business together in 1908, and in March 1910 had entered a fresh arrangement whereby Crippen put £200 into the business and the pair would each take a 50 per cent cut of the profits. Up until November 1909 Dr Crippen had also been engaged at £3 a week as manager of Munyon's Remedies, a mail-order patent medicine company which he had previously worked for in America and Canada, becoming their agent, and forsaking his salary for a commission. He had stopped working for Munyon's on 31 January, but carried on working on the third floor of the same building – coincidentally, Albion House.

Dr Crippen was not a stage performer, but like his theatrical associates was also called by another name; to his friends and acquaintances he was known as Peter. The Crippens lived at 39 Hilldrop Crescent, Camden Town, in north London. Crippen had told the Nashes that Cora had left England for America on 2 February, and died there on 23 March, although several cheques had been presented during that period bearing her signature.

Dew was initially nonplussed. The cheques could easily have been signed by Cora before she left for America, or been forged. The story he had heard was 'a somewhat singular one, although', he mused, 'having regard to the Bohemian character of the persons concerned, is capable of explanation'. Nevertheless, Dew knew that the matter did require clearing up, as '[t]he whole circumstances, one must admit, are mysterious, and this being so the persons referred to, the others, have made various enquiries with a view to clear the matter up but without any good result, nor can they discover any trace of Mrs Crippen going by any ship'.

Despite the apparently mundane nature of the inquiry, Dew did not hesitate in taking it up:

> Without a second's hesitation I replied: 'I think it would be just as well if I made a few inquiries into this personally.'
>
> Why did I not suggest that the inquiry should be handed over to the uniformed branch or given to a subordinate?
>
> Well, my experience as a police officer had taught me that it is better to be sure than sorry.
>
> Supposing I had considered myself too big for such an apparently trivial job.

If I had turned the inquiry down all that could have happened was the transfer of the matter to the uniformed branch for the routine inquiries into an ordinary case of a missing person.

Then only in the event of some suspicious circumstances coming to light, would the case have been referred back to the Yard.

Dew set about making his enquiries. He first spoke to the members of the Music Hall Ladies' Guild, and took a large number of statements from Cora's friends. The members of the Guild all told a similar story.

Paul Martinetti, a retired music hall artist, and his wife Clara had known the Crippens for some eighteen months. On 31 January Dr Crippen had called at their address in Shaftesbury Avenue to invite them to dinner that night. Despite Paul having been unwell earlier that day, they accepted the invitation and arrived at Hilldrop Crescent at about 8 p.m. At some time during the evening, Paul went to the lavatory; the lavatory window was open, and he consequently caught a chill from the draught.

Clara Martinetti saw nothing unusual in Cora's behaviour that night other than that she complained of a headache, for which Dr Crippen had given her something. She described her friend as 'very jolly . . . she was nice'. The Martinettis left Hilldrop Crescent around 1.30 a.m. It was the last time they, or anyone else (besides Dr Crippen), would ever see Cora Crippen alive.

The next morning Dr Crippen called at the Martinettis' flat at around midday, to see how Paul was. Clara told him that her husband was still in bed. She then asked after Cora, and Crippen said, 'Oh, she is all right.' Crippen visited again about one week later, by which time Clara Martinetti had heard from the secretary of the Guild, Melinda May, that Cora had apparently gone to America. Clara expected Cora to send her a card from her ship but nothing arrived either from the ship or from New York. When Clara told Crippen this he told her that his wife was not stopping at New York, but heading straight to California.

At the Music Hall Ladies' Benevolent Fund's ball on 20 February, Clara saw Dr Crippen with his typist, 27-year-old Ethel Le Neve, who was wearing a brooch that looked very similar to one she knew Cora possessed. Crippen visited the Martinettis once again after the ball and Clara repeated her concern that she had not heard from Cora. Crippen professed to be as surprised as she was. He did, however, have some worrying news: he said that he had heard from his relatives in America that Cora was very ill, and that there was something the matter with one of her lungs, but he had also heard from Cora to say that she was 'not as bad as they say'.

The Martinettis received a letter dated 20 March, which read:

Dear Clara and Paul,

Please forgive me not running in during the week but I have been so upset by very bad news from Belle that I did not feel equal to talking about anything. And now I have just a cable saying she is so dangerously ill with double pleuro-pneumonia that I am considering if I had not better go over at once. I do not want to worry you with my troubles, but I felt I must explain why I had not been to see you. I will try and run in during the week and have a chat. Hope both of you are well. With love and best wishes.

Yours sincerely

Peter.

After a meeting of the Guild on 23 March, Clara Martinetti, along with fellow Guild member Annie Stratton, went downstairs to find Dr Crippen at the entrance door. He said that he had received a cable saying Cora was dangerously ill, and he expected another any minute to say that she had died. Furthermore, he said that if he were widowed then he would go to France for a week for a change of air.

There was worse news to follow. On Thursday 24 March Clara Martinetti received a telegram from Victoria Station, which read, 'Belle died yesterday at six o'clock. Please 'phone to Annie [Stratton]. Shall be away a week. Peter.' When Clara later went to offer her condolences to Dr Crippen at Albion House, he informed her that Cora had died at Los Angeles with his relations. He subsequently told her that Cora was going to be cremated, and that her ashes would be sent to London.

Crippen had a son from his previous marriage to Charlotte Bell, which had taken place in San Diego in 1887 and had ended with the death of his wife in 1891 or 1892 from apoplexy (according to newspaper reports, she had been buried on 26 January 1892). When the son, Otto Hawley Crippen, was contacted in Los Angeles his answers to the Guild's questions must only have heightened their confusion and suspicion:

The death of my step mother was as great a surprise to me as anyone. She died at San Francisco and the first I heard of it was through my father who wrote to me immediately afterwards. He asked me to forward all letters to him and he would make all the necessary explanation. He said he had, through a mistake given out my name as my step mother's death place. I would be very glad if you find out any particulars of her death if you would let me know of them, as I know as a fact that she died in San Francisco.

Even more worrying news came from America. Following an enquiry from the Guild to the Los Angeles Chamber of Commerce, they were told that no one of the name of Crippen had died there in the month of March, although a man named Crippen had died in April.

Louise Smythson, a member of the committee of the Guild, had known the Crippens for around fifteen months. She had last seen Cora Crippen at the Guild meeting on 26 January, when she seemed to be in perfect health and high spirits. She had also seen Dr Crippen at the ball on 20 February, where she had asked him about Cora. Crippen was initially vague, saying he had heard from his wife somewhere 'up in the wilds of the mountains of California'. When pressed later for an address, he gave Smythson his son's address in Los Angeles. When she asked where Cora died, Crippen brusquely told her that it was irrelevant, as she was dead, and anyway the Guild meant nothing to Cora's American friends.

The secretary of the Music Hall Ladies' Guild, Melinda May, had known Cora Crippen for some two years. Like Louise Smythson, she had seen Cora at the meeting on 26 January, but noticed that she was unusually absent from the 2 February meeting. Melinda May went round to 39 Hilldrop Crescent, where she was greeted by Ethel Le Neve, who handed her a pass-book, a paying-in book, a cheque book, a letter to Melinda and a letter to the committee. The letter to Melinda May was not in Cora's handwriting. It read:

> 39 Hilldrop Crescent, February 2nd
>
> Dear Miss May,
> Illness of a near relative has called me to America on only a few hours' notice, so I must ask you to bring my resignation as treasurer before the meeting to-day, so that a new treasurer can be elected at once. You will appreciate my haste when I tell you that I have not been to bed all night packing, and getting ready to go. I shall hope to see you again a few months later, but cannot spare a moment to call on you before I go. I wish you everything nice till I return to London again. Now, good-bye, with love hastily,
> Yours, Belle Elmore, p.p. H.H.C.

The letter to the committee was also not in Cora Crippen's hand:

> 39 Hilldrop Crescent, London, N.
>
> To the Committee of the Music Hall Ladies' Guild.
>
> Dear Friends,
> Please forgive me a hasty letter and any inconvenience I may cause you, but I have just had bad news of the illness of a near relative and at only a few hours' notice I am obliged to go to America. Under the circumstances I cannot return for several months, and therefore beg

you to accept this as a formal letter resigning from this date my hon. treasurership of the M.H.L.G. I am enclosing the cheque book and deposit book for the immediate use of my successor, and to save any delay I beg to suggest that you vote to suspend the usual rules of election and elect to-day a new honorary treasurer. I hope some months later to be with you again, and in meantime wish the Guild every success and ask my good friends and pals to accept my sincere and loving wishes for their own personal welfare.
Believe me, your [*sic*] faithfully,
Belle Elmore.

A new treasurer was elected that afternoon. When Melinda May saw Dr Crippen on 23 March he told her that Cora was very ill, and that he was waiting for worse news.

Dr John Herbert Burroughs was the honorary physician to the Guild and his acquaintance with the Crippens stretched back to 1902. He described Cora as being 'a vivacious woman, I should say about thirty years of age, bright and cheerful, a very pleasant woman generally. She was very fond of dress, and dressed very well indeed. At times she wore a quantity of jewellery. As far as I know she was in the very best of health. She was a stoutish woman.' Cora was in fact thirty-four years old, which made her Dr Crippen's junior by fourteen years. Like the other members of the Guild (eight or nine usually attended the meetings), Burroughs last saw Cora Crippen alive in January. He heard of her death via the Martinettis, and sent Dr Crippen a letter of condolence:

Dear Peter
Both Maud and myself were inexpressibly shocked and astounded to learn of poor Belle's death. We hasten to send our very heartfelt condolences on your great loss. As two of her oldest friends, why ever did not you send us a line? Do please give us some details of how and where she died. Maud is very much upset, and so anxious to hear. Only quite casually we heard she had suddenly left for America, and were daily expecting a letter or a card from her. Maud could not understand it, as Belle always wrote her on such important occasions, so could only think Belle wanted to cut all her old friends. And now to learn she is no more. It is all so sudden, that one hardly realises the fact. We should so like to send a letter of condolence to her sister, of whom she was so fond, if you would kindly supply her address.
Yours sincerely,
J.H.B.

Crippen replied on black-edged mourning paper:

My Dear Doctor,
I feel sure you will forgive me for my apparent neglect, but really I
have been nearly out of my mind with poor Belle's death so far away.
She was not with her sister, but out in California on business for me,
and, quite like her disposition, would keep up when she should have
been in bed, with the consequence that pleuro-pneumonia
terminated fatally. Almost to the last she refused to let me know
there was any danger, so that the cable that she had gone came as a
most awful shock to me. I fear I have sadly neglected my friends, but
pray forgive, and believe me to be most truly appreciative of your
sympathy. Even now I am not fit to talk to my friends, but as soon as I
feel I can control myself I will run in on you and Maud one evening.
I am, of course, giving up the house, and every night packing things
away. With love to both, and again thanking you for your kindness, I
am, as ever, yours,
Peter.

Besides the members of the Guild, Crippen had also communicated
with Cora's family in America. Cora's younger sister, Theresa Hunn,
known as Tessie, had first met Dr Crippen in 1892 or 1893. Tessie's half-
sister Louise Mills showed her a black-edged letter she had received from
39 Hilldrop Crescent:

My dear Louise and Robert,
I hardly know how to write to you of my dreadful loss. The shock to
me has been so dreadful that I am hardly able to control myself. My
poor Cora is gone, and, to make the shock to me more dreadful, I
did not even see her at the last. A few weeks ago we had news that an
old relative of mine in California was dying, and, to secure important
property for ourselves, it was necessary for one of us to go and put
the matter into a lawyer's hands at once. As I was very busy, Cora
proposed she should go, and as it was necessary for some one to be
there at once, she would go straight through from here to California
without stopping at all and then return by way of Brooklyn, and she
would be able to pay all of you a long visit. Unfortunately, on the way
my poor Cora caught a severe cold, and not having while travelling
taken proper care of herself, it has settled on her lungs, later to
develop into pleuro-pneumonia. She wished not to frighten me, so
kept writing not to worry about her and it was only a slight matter,
and the next I heard by cable was that she was dangerously ill, and

two days later after I cabled to know should I go to her I had the dreadful news that she had passed away. Imagine if you can the dreadful shock to me – never more to see my Cora alive nor hear her voice again. She is being sent back to me, and I shall soon have what is left of her here. Of course, I am giving up the house; in fact, it drives me mad to be in it alone, and I will sell out everything in a few days. I do not know what I shall do, but probably find some business to take me travelling for a few months until I can recover from the shock a little, but as soon as I have a settled address again I will write again to you. As it is so terrible to me to have to write this dreadful news, will you please tell all the others of our loss. Love to all. Write soon again, and give you my address probably next in France.
From Doctor.

There was nothing in Crippen's behaviour since Cora's disappearance and supposed death to cause any undue suspicion. Between February and June Crippen had been attending work as normal and had been 'working very hard indeed'. However, on 2 February he visited Attenborough's pawnbroker's shop in Oxford Street, and asked the manager Ernest Stuart for a loan against a diamond ring and diamond earrings. Stuart considered the items to be worth £100, and agreed to an £80 loan against them. One week later Crippen returned to Attenborough's with a diamond brooch and six diamond rings, for which he was given a loan of £115.

Crippen had given notice to his landlord that he was going to leave 39 Hilldrop Crescent. The house was to play a pivotal role in the story. It was owned by Frederick Lown, who had let it to Dr Crippen for a three-year period in September 1905. After three years the arrangement continued on a yearly basis at the rental price of £52 10s per year. On 16 March 1910 Crippen had told Lown that he wanted to leave Hilldrop Crescent, as he had been left some property in America, and that his wife had already gone there. Crippen agreed to vacate the property on 24 June, but shortly before that date he asked Lown if he could stay until 29 September. Lown asked after Cora Crippen, and was shocked to hear Crippen tell him that his wife had died in America.

Dew also learned that, after he had told Cora's friends that she was dead, Crippen had journeyed to Dieppe, where he had stayed for several days with Ethel Le Neve under the names of Mr and Mrs Crippen. Dew needed to know more and admitted to himself that, 'taken as a whole, my inquiries had yielded little. I was no nearer solving the problem I had set myself.' In a report written on 6 July, Dew wrote that he thought it necessary to interview Dr Crippen himself.

Doctor Crippen

His was that rare thing in English annals, a *crime passionel.*
Filson Young, The Trial of Hawley Harvey Crippen

At this point of his investigation Dew did not harbour the grave doubts of Cora's friends about her apparent death, but he did have some suspicions:

> Mrs Crippen appears to have been a great favourite with all whom she came into contact with, always cheerful, and apparently in excellent health, and does not seem to have expressed any intention of leaving England, to her most intimate friends.
>
> . . . there are most extraordinary contradictions in the story told by Crippen, who is an American citizen, as is Mrs. Crippen, otherwise Belle Elmore.
>
> From the action taken by the various friends of hers there can be but little doubt that Crippen has heard, or will soon hear, of the enquiries that have been made and, without adopting the suggestion made by her friends as to foul play, I do think that the time has now arrived when 'Doctor' Crippen should be seen by us, and asked to give an explanation as to when, and how, Mrs. Crippen left this country, and the circumstances under which she died, which resulted in him causing the advertisement mentioned to be published.
>
> This course, I venture to think, may result in him giving such explanation as would clear up the whole matter and avoid elaborate enquiries being made in the United States.

The 'advertisement mentioned' was an obituary notice that had appeared in the theatrical newspaper the *Era,* on 26 March. It was brief, reading, 'Elmore – March 23, in California, U.S.A., Miss Belle Elmore (Mrs H.H. Crippen).' Crippen had sent the newspaper a 10*s* postal order to insert the obituary, but the cost was only 1*s* 6*d*, so the remainder was returned to Crippen. Further and fuller obituaries appeared on 7 April in the *Music Hall and Theatre Review* and the *Stage*. These were of a more affectionate nature, and were possibly placed by the Guild.

On 8 July, at around 10.00 a.m., Walter Dew, accompanied by Detective Sergeant Arthur Mitchell, made an unannounced visit to 39 Hilldrop

Crescent – what was to be the first of many visits to the quiet, leafy crescent off the Camden Road. Dew described the house as 'rather a large semi-detached dwelling of the old type standing well back from the road and partially screened from the street by overgrown trees'.

They were admitted into the house by Crippen's seventeen-year-old French servant girl, Valentine Lecocq. Ethel Le Neve came downstairs a few minutes later, and Dew saw that she was wearing a brooch that would later be identified as one that had belonged to Cora Crippen. Dew thought that Le Neve 'was not pretty, but there was something quite attractive about her'. He also considered her to be 'a nervous sort of girl'. (Her real surname was Neave, but she always went under the name of Le Neve.) The inspector found Le Neve unhelpful, and got the feeling that she wanted to get him out of the house. She explained that Crippen was not in, and that she was Crippen's housekeeper. When Dew asked her if she was in fact Miss Le Neve she admitted to it, but 'became a little agitated', asking if the detectives could return later.

Dew insisted that she took him and Mitchell to Crippen, but again she was reticent and offered to telephone him. This was not good enough, and finally Le Neve went with Dew and Mitchell by tram car and cab to Crippen's office at Albion House. Dew had been reluctant to leave Le Neve alone, fearing she might telephone Crippen and warn him of their arrival as they made their way to his office. Le Neve went upstairs in a lift to fetch Crippen, while Dew waited downstairs at a point where no one could leave the building without him knowing about it.

Crippen greeted the deputation, and the detectives (but not Le Neve) went into his room. Dew's immediate impression of Crippen was that he was 'an insignificant little man'. Dew introduced himself and Mitchell, and explained that his wife's friends were not satisfied with his story concerning her death and that his own enquiries resulted in him feeling the same way. Crippen said, 'I suppose I had better tell the truth', and immediately confessed: 'The stories I have told them about her death are untrue. As far as I know she is still alive.' Dew suggested he make a full statement, including a history of his life, which Crippen willingly did. Sergeant Mitchell took down the following:

I am forty-eight years of age. After being questioned by Chief Inspector Dew as to the statements made by me that my wife, known as Belle Elmore, is dead, I desire to make a voluntary statement to clear the whole matter up.

I was born at Cold Water, Michigan, U.S.A., in the year 1862, my father's name being Myron Augustus Crippen, a dry goods merchant. My mother's name was Andresse Crippen, *née* Skinner.

My mother is now dead, but my father lives at Los Angeles, Cal.

I was educated first at Cold Water, Indiana, and California, and then attended the University at Michigan until I was about twenty, and finished my education at the Hospital College at Cleveland, here I took the degree of M.D.

I came over to England in 1883, and attended various hospitals to see the operations, and returned to the States, and was assistant for three of four months to Dr. Porter, of Detroit. After that I went to New York and took a degree in specialist eye and ear work at the Ophthalmic Hospital. This would be in 1885.

After then I returned to Detroit, where I remained about two years as assistant to the same doctor. I then went to San Diego, where I practised as an eye and ear specialist for about two years. Before going to this place I was married to a lady named Charlotte Bell, of New York, and she accompanied me to San Diego.

We then came to New York. I have had only one child by my first wife. He was born at San Diego about 1887 or 1888, and his name is Otto Hawley Crippen. He is now married and lives at Los Angeles.

My first wife died, so far as I can remember, in 1890 or 1891. We were living at Salt Lake City, where I was practising as an eye and ear specialist. She was buried at Salt Lake City in my name.

After this my son went to live with his grandmother, my mother, until she died. I then went to New York, and went as an assistant to Dr. Jeffrey, of Brooklyn, and I lived with him.

About 1893, while with Dr. Jeffrey, I met Belle Elmore, who was being attended by him. Her name at that time was Cora Turner. I forget where she was living, but she was living alone. She was only about seventeen years of age, and I, of course, was about thirty.

She, at this time, was living under the protection of a man named C.C. Lincoln, a stove manufacturer, of Water Street, New York. She had been living with him, but he had given up his house and had taken a room for her and was paying all her expenses.

I took her to several places for some weeks, as I was very fond of her, and one day she told me Lincoln wanted her to go away with him. I told her I could not stand that, and would marry her right away, and a few days after this I married her at a minister's house at Jersey City. I forget his name and the name of the street.

I had been married to her some little time when she told me her name was not Turner, but Kunigunde Mackamotzki. She said her mother had been married twice, and her name was then Marsinger, and she was living in Brooklyn. Her mother had been dead some years. My wife told me her father was a Russian Pole and her mother was a German.

Her stepfather, so far as I know, is still living, and resides at Forrest Avenue, Brooklyn.

Her parents were in rather ordinary circumstances, but she had a good education, and spoke German well.

After getting married to her we went to St. Louis, where I practised as consulting physician to an optician in, I think, Olive Street. His name was Hirsch, I think.

We stayed there about a year, and we returned to New York, where I took a position as consulting physician to the Munyon Company. We lived in the office at East Fourteenth Street.

I was in New York for only a few months when the company transferred me to Philadelphia. I was there with my wife for about a year, and was then transferred to the firm's place at Toronto, where I managed their business. I forget where I lived, but we were there only six months, and then returned to Philadelphia.

I was there some time and while there, about 1899, my wife, who had a good voice, went to New York to have her voice trained, as she thought of going in for grand opera.

I paid all her expenses, and occasionally visited her at New York, and then in about 1900 I came to England alone, where I was manager for Munyon's at their offices in Shaftesbury Avenue, and I lived at Queen's Road, St. John's Wood.

It was in April I came over, and she joined me in August, as she wrote and told me she was giving up her lessons in grand opera, and was going in for music hall sketches. To this I objected, and told her to come over here. She came, and we went to live at South Crescent.

When she came to England she decided to give sketches on the music hall stage, and adopted the name of 'Macamotzki,' but she did not make anything at it. She gave a sketch at the Old Marylebone Music Hall, but it was a failure, and she gave it up.

After this she did not do anything in it for two or three years, until I had to go to America about two years after coming here. My firm sent for me, and I became manager in Philadelphia.

When I left England my wife and I were living at, I think, 62 Guildford Street, and she remained there while I was away. I remained in Philadelphia from November till the following June, and sent my wife money regularly.

When I returned I found she had been singing at smoking concerts for payment, and that an American music hall artiste, named Bruce Miller, had been a frequent visitor to her house.

She told me that this man visited her, had taken her about, and was very fond of her, also she was fond of him.

I may say that when she came to England from America her manner towards me was entirely changed, and she had cultivated a most ungovernable temper, and seemed to think I was not good enough for her, and boasted of the men of good position travelling on the boat who had made a fuss of her, and, indeed, some of these visited her at South Crescent, but I do not know their names.

I never saw the man Bruce Miller, but he used to call when I was out, and used to take her out in the evenings.

When I returned to this country, I did not take up my position at Munyon's but went as manager to the 'Sovereign Remedy Company,' 13 Newman Street.

They failed about eight months afterwards, and I then went as physician to the Drouet Institute, Regent's Park, and afterwards at 10 Marble Arch, and they also failed.

From there I took a position with the Aural Clinic Company, 102 New Oxford Street, where I remained until they failed in about six months.

I then went back to Munyon's, 272 Oxford Circus, as manager and advertising manager.

I removed to Albion House as manager about eighteen months ago, after which I took it on as an agency, but as it did not pay, I, in February last, handed it over to the company again, but for the last two years I had been running the Yale Tooth Specialist Company, with Dr. Rylance as partner, and am still doing so.

I ran what I termed the Imperial Press Agency, in connection with Munyon's, because by so doing I got their advertisements inserted at a reduction.

At the present time I am interested in an ear-cure business, called the 'Aural Remedy,' at Craven House, Kingsway, and I work at an address in Vine Street.

I did not think anything of Bruce Miller's visiting my wife at the time.

After returning from America we went to live at 34 Store Street for about a year. During this time she adopted the stage name of 'Belle Elmore,' although she had had it in her mind when she came over, but I persuaded her to use the other name.

She got an engagement at the Town Hall, Teddington, to sing, and then from time to time she got engagements at music halls. She went to the Oxford as a comedienne, and was there about a week.

She also went to the Camberwell, and also at a hall at Balham. She also sang at the Empire, Northampton, and various towns.

She would probably go away for about two weeks and return for about six weeks, but used to earn very little.

We remained at 34 Store Street for some time, and went to 37 same street for about two years, and about five years ago, in, I think, 1905, removed to 39 Hilldrop Crescent, for which I pay £50 a year.

It is quite four years since she ever went out at all to sing, and, although we apparently lived very happily together, as a matter of fact there were very frequent occasions when she got into most violent tempers, and often threatened she would leave me, saying she had a man she could go to, and she would end it all.

I have seen letters from Bruce to her, which ended 'with love and kisses to Brown Eyes.'

About four years ago, in consequence of these frequent outbursts, I discontinued sleeping with her, and have never cohabited with her since.

She did all the housework herself, with the exception of having a charwoman in occasionally.

About two years ago she became honorary treasurer of the Music Hall Ladies' Guild, and was here every Wednesday.

I never interfered with her movements in any way; she went in and out just as she liked, and did what she liked; it was of no interest to me.

As I say, she frequently threatened to leave me, and said that if she did she would go right out of my life, and I should never see or hear from her again.

On the Monday night, the day before I wrote the letter to the Guild resigning her position as treasurer, Mr. and Mrs. Paul Martinetti came to our place to dinner, and during the evening Mr. Martinetti wanted to go to the lavatory. As he had been to our house several times, I did not take the trouble to go and show him where it was. After they had left my wife blamed me for not taking him to the lavatory, and abused me, and said, 'This is the finish of it. I won't stand it any longer. I shall leave you to-morrow, and you will never hear of me again.'

She had said this so often that I did not take much notice of it, but she did say one thing which she had never said before, viz., that I was to arrange to cover up any scandal with our mutual friends and the Guild the best way I could.

Before this she had told me frequently that the man she would go to was better able to support her than I was.

I came to business the next morning, and when I went home between five and six p.m. I found she had gone.

I realised that she had gone, and I sat down to think it over as to how to cover up her absence without any scandal.

I think the same night, or the next morning (Wednesday) I wrote a letter to the Guild saying she had gone away, which I also told several people.

I afterwards realised that this would not be a sufficient explanation for her not coming back, and later on I told people that she was ill with bronchitis and pneumonia, and afterwards I told them she was dead from this ailment.

I told them she died in California, but I have no recollection of telling any one exactly where she died.

Some one afterwards asked me where my son lived, and I told them.

I then put an advertisement in the *Era* that she was dead, as I thought this would prevent people asking a lot of questions.

Whatever I have said to other people in regard to her death is absolutely wrong, and I am giving this as an explanation.

So far as I know, she did not die, but is still alive.

It is not true that she went away on legal business for me, or to see any relations in America.

I did not receive any cables to say that she was ill, and it is not true that she was cremated at San Francisco, and that the ashes were sent to me, or that she sailed from Havre.

So far as I know, she has no claim to any title.

I have no recollection of telling any one my son was with her when she died.

We had a joint account at the Charing Cross Bank, subject to the signature of either, but it pleased her to think she was signing cheques and she also did so, and several blank cheques were always already signed by her, and some of them have been changed by me since her departure, and there is one here now (produced).

When my wife went away I cannot say if she took anything with her or not, but I believe there is a theatrical travelling basket missing, and she might have taken this with some clothes.

She took some of her jewellery, I know, with her, but she left four rings behind – three single stone (or solitaire) diamonds, and one of four diamonds and a ruby and a diamond brooch.

She had other jewellery, and must have taken that with her.

I have never pawned or sold anything belonging to her before or after she left.

Everything I have told you is true.

I do not know what clothes, if any, she took away; she had plenty.

Whenever we quarrelled, and she threatened to leave me, she told me she wanted nothing from me.

I have bought all her jewellery, and, so far as I know, she never had any jewellery presents, and I do not know that she ever had any money sent her, except that Bruce Miller used to send her small amounts on her birthday and at Easter and Christmas, to purchase a present.

She suffered from bilious attacks, and I have given her medicine for that – homeopathic remedies.

It is true that I was at the Benevolent Fund dinner at the Criterion with Miss Le Neve, and she wore the brooch my wife left behind. She has also worn my wife's furs.

Miss Le Neve has been in my employ, and known to me through being employed by the firms I have worked for, for the past eight years, and she is now living with me as my wife at Hilldrop Crescent. I have been intimate with her during the past three years, and have frequently stayed with her at hotels, but was never from home at nights.

After I told people my wife was dead Miss Le Neve and I went to Dieppe for about five days, and stayed at a hotel there (I forget the name, but the proprietor's name was Vacher) in the names of Mr. and Mrs. Crippen.

My belief is that my wife has gone to Chicago to join Bruce Miller, whose business on the music hall stage is a musical instrument turn, but I think he has now gone into another business, and has speculated and made money. Mr. Didcot was his agent when he was over here.

I shall, of course, do all I can to get in touch with her, so as to clear this matter up.

She has a sister named Louise, whose name is Mills, living with her husband, who is a soapmaker living at Brooklyn. They live with my wife's stepfather, Mr. Haaranger.

I do not know where any of her other relations live.

I cannot tell you how you can find or trace her, except as I have already said.

I will willingly go to my house with you to see if I can find any letters which may throw any light on the matter, and I invite you to look round the house, and do whatever you like in the house.

This is all I can tell you.

Any notes that I have changed through any one in this building were in connection with my business.

This statement has been read over to me. It is quite correct, and has been made by me quite voluntarily, and without any promise or threat having been held out to me.

This lengthy statement took around six hours to compile, partly due to the fact that it was taken between Crippen's consultations and tooth-pulling appointments. Indeed, by lunchtime barely the introductory part of the statement had been taken, so Dew and Mitchell asked Crippen to join them for lunch at a small Italian restaurant close to Albion House. Crippen polished off a beefsteak 'with the relish of a man who hadn't a care in the world'. After lunch they returned to the office, where Crippen finished his statement. The statement was read back to him, and he signed each page.

Dew made it clear that at this time the question of arresting Dr Crippen 'did not enter my mind'. He had only interviewed Crippen in order to get his explanation about Cora. Dew was not entirely satisfied with the story, saying, 'I cannot say that for a moment I considered his statement a reasonable one. I did not absolutely think that any crime had been committed. I was not satisfied with his statement.'

Despite his doubts over the statement Dew was struck by Crippen's conduct, and would often comment on his 'cool and collected' manner:

His replies came freely. There was no hesitation. From his manner one could only have assumed that he was a much maligned man eager only to clear the matter up by telling the whole truth.

I was impressed by the man's demeanour. It was impossible to be otherwise. Much can sometimes be learned by an experienced police officer during the making of such a statement.

From Dr. Hawley Harvey Crippen's manner on this, our first meeting, I learned nothing at all.

With hindsight, Dew thought that Crippen must have been expecting a call from the police at some time and that he had thought out his story in advance of that eventuality. Dew considered Crippen's statement had been 'an ingenious story. Half of it was true and half of it was false.' Contradicting himself slightly, Dew admitted that he had in fact learnt one thing about Crippen: he was an 'accomplished liar', as his statement had been so different to the story he had told Cora's friends. But as Dew pointed out, 'you can't charge a man with being a liar. My job was to find out if he was telling the truth now. Somehow I did not think he was.'

Dew also asked Le Neve for a statement, and she readily agreed to give one. Like Crippen, there was nothing suspicious about her manner at the time, although she was slightly embarrassed about admitting the nature of her relationship with Crippen:

I am a single woman, twenty-seven years of age, and am a shorthand typist. Since the latter end of February I have been living at 39 Hilldrop Crescent with Dr. Crippen as his wife, I have been on intimate terms with Dr. Crippen for two or three years.

In the early part of February I received a note from Dr. Crippen, saying Mrs. Crippen had gone to America. I know Mrs. Crippen. She treated me as a friend.

About a week after he had told me she had gone to America I went to Hilldrop Crescent to put the place straight, as there were no servants kept; but at night I went to my lodgings. I did this daily for about a fortnight. The place appeared to be quite all right and quite as usual. He took me to the Benevolent Fund Dinner, and leant [*sic*] me a brooch to wear. Later on, he told me I could keep it.

Afterwards he told me his wife was dead. I was very much astonished, but I do not think I said anything to him about it. He gave me some furs of his wife's to wear, and I have been living with him ever since as his wife. My father and mother do not know what I am doing, and think I am a housekeeper at Hilldrop Crescent.

There was possibly a greater element of suspicion in Dew's mind after taking Le Neve's statement, for he observed that 'Miss Le Neve has not told me she thoroughly believed what Dr Crippen has told her.' Nevertheless, Dew was sure she knew nothing herself, for 'there was nothing in Miss Le Neve's manner which gave rise to anything in the nature of suspicion'.

Dr Crippen was absent when the interview with Le Neve took place. Dew stated that he did not see Crippen again until 6.00 or 6.30, so the Le Neve interview took place prior to that time. The manageress of Munyon's Remedies, Marion Louisa Curnow, stated that on that day Crippen called in on her at around 4.30 with regard to two envelopes he had asked her to store in her safe at the beginning of March. They were marked 'Dr. Crippen' and 'Dr. Crippen, personal'. Crippen said to Curnow, 'If any one should ask you, know nothing,' or 'say nothing', adding 'and if anything happens to me please give what you have there to Miss Le Neve'. Curnow replied, 'all right'. One of the envelopes later proved to contain deposit notes with the Charing Cross Bank for £600 and insurance receipts worth £300. In the other envelope was a watch and brooch.

Dew wanted to make a search of 39 Hilldrop Crescent, 'to see if we could find any papers which would throw any light on her movements'. Crippen consented to the request, saying that Dew was welcome to search the house any time he liked. There was no time like the present, so all four of them went to Hilldrop Crescent, and on the way there Dew had much to contemplate:

I was trying to get the hang of a case which was becoming more difficult at every turn.

I certainly had no suspicion of murder. You don't jump to the conclusion that murder has been committed merely because a wife has disappeared and a husband has told lies about it.

But he had lied. I couldn't get this fact out of my mind, and I was determined, if humanly possible, to find out why he had gone to such lengths to throw dust into the eyes of Belle Elmore's friends.

Dew was accompanied by Crippen, who was being 'absolutely courteous and polite', as his house was being searched. They went through all the rooms in the house, many of which were still adorned by pictures of Cora. Dew observed that '[t]he rooms were in good order as a dwelling house would be . . . there was nothing in the house to attract attention'. They then went out to the garden, and finally the coal cellar, whose evenly laid brick floor was covered with dust that did not appear to have been disturbed for years. Mitchell searched through the rafters of the house, but found nothing. Everything appeared to be in perfect order except for some rolled up carpets and packed boxes; but these could be explained, as Crippen had given notice that he was going to move anyway.

Dew had no particular reason for looking in the cellar at that time, other than wanting to make an examination of the whole house. It was reached from a passage which led from the kitchen to the back door. Crippen and Le Neve stood watching in the doorway while Dew and Mitchell poked around.

After searching the house, Crippen and Dew went to the breakfast room. Dew asked about the jewellery Cora had left behind, and Crippen produced three rings and a rising sun brooch. Crippen was apparently being very helpful, and asked what he could do to help find Cora. Would advertising be a good idea? Dew thought it would, and Crippen said he would place adverts in several American papers. He took a piece of paper and, with Dew's help, composed the following message:

'Mackamotzki'
Will Belle Elmore communicate with H.H.C. or
Authorities at once.
Serious trouble through your absence. $25 reward
Anyone communicating whereabouts to —

Dew and Mitchell finally left Hilldrop Crescent at 8.00, after the inspector told Crippen, 'Of course I shall have to find Mrs. Crippen to clear this matter up.' It was the last time Dew was to see Dr Crippen and Ethel Le Neve for some months.

The Remains

How dull the murders are getting nowadays. Not a patch on the old
domestic poisoning dramas, Crippen, Seddon, Mrs Maybrick;
the truth being, I suppose, that you can't do a good murder unless
you believe you're going to roast in hell for it.

George Orwell, Coming up for Air

Despite having just finished a long and gruelling day's investigation, Dew
was unable to sleep:

> I was dog tired, yet sleep I could not. My mind refused to rest. The
> events of the day kept cropping up.
> What was behind it all? There was something, I now felt sure.
> Crippen had a secret which he was cunningly trying to hide. There
> would be no rest for me until I had found out.

The day after interviewing Crippen, Dew circulated a description of Cora
Crippen as a missing person throughout the Metropolitan Police district,
and continued with his enquiries. On Monday 11 July Dew and Mitchell
returned to Albion House again to see Crippen, but neither he nor Le
Neve was there.

Dew and Mitchell then went to 39 Hilldrop Crescent and were let in by
the French maid and Mrs Long, the wife of one of Crippen's employees.
The detectives searched the property again but this time they made some
startling discoveries. In the wardrobe of the first-floor bedroom Dew
found a fully loaded revolver, while Mitchell found a box containing
forty-five cartridges that fitted the revolver. Dew did not know how long
Crippen had possessed the gun, but it did not appear to be new.
According to Dew the revolver had not been there during his initial
search when Crippen was present. He came to the dramatic conclusion
that Crippen had the gun in his pocket at the time, and would have used
it had the detectives discovered anything. Dew, who was a keen gardener
while off duty, then dug up the garden and re-examined every room in
the house and the coal cellar, but found nothing suspicious.

Dew ascertained that the day after he had interviewed him, Crippen
had left Hilldrop Crescent at around 8.30 a.m., followed by Le Neve

about an hour afterwards. They had both gone to Albion House as usual. Neither of them had any luggage besides Le Neve's reticule bag. Later in the morning Crippen sent one of his employees, William Long, out of the office to purchase a suit of boy's clothes, boots and hats. Crippen had visited a neighbouring office and exchanged a cheque for gold to the value of £37. At about 1 p.m. Crippen and Le Neve left the office unseen, leaving behind them Crippen's suit of clothes and Le Neve's hat. Long had asked Crippen if he was in any trouble. 'Only a little scandal', was Crippen's reply.

Crippen's disappearance suggested only one thing to Dew:

My quarry had gone, but the manner of his going pointed to guilt.

My view was that a completely innocent man with nothing to fear would have seen the thing through. A man of Crippen's calibre would certainly have done so. I had already seen enough of him to know that he was not the type to do anything foolishly rash.

Here was the real clue.

His decision was a sudden one. Of that I felt convinced. A fair deduction seemed to be that he had been scared by the events of Friday.

Crippen's maid, who had only been employed at Hilldrop Crescent for about a month, had received a letter from Crippen telling her not to be alarmed, and that he and Le Neve had gone to the theatre. The maid had no friends in London, and was sent back to France the next day. She was later interviewed by the French paper *Le Matin,* whom she told that she had believed that Crippen and Le Neve were man and wife.

Dew circulated descriptions of Crippen and Le Neve to domestic and foreign ports, requesting that they keep a look-out for the pair but not arrest them. He then sent out enquiries throughout London to find out if any cabmen or carmen had removed boxes or packages from 39 Hilldrop Crescent since 31 January. The following day Dew and Mitchell carried out a further search of 39 Hilldrop Crescent, but again without result.

On 13 July came a discovery which turned Dew's investigation from one of trying to establish the fate of Cora Crippen to what would turn out to be one of the most sensational criminal cases of the twentieth century. With Crippen absent, Dew now had the opportunity to search 39 Hilldrop Crescent without 'Crippen at my elbow to hamper me and perhaps throw me off the scent'. Dew was now beginning to consider the possibility that Cora had been murdered, but the house had yet to yield any clues other than the discovery of the advertisement Crippen had written on 8 July, but had not sent to any newspaper.

Dew was again suffering from the same exhaustion he had experienced twenty-two years earlier, while hunting Jack the Ripper. Both he and Mitchell were 'completely fagged out' after making inquiries around Camden Town. He wanted to go home and sleep for twenty-four hours, but could not give up the search for Cora Crippen until the case was resolved. The day began, once again, with Dew searching 39 Hilldrop Crescent, examining the floors and digging up more of the garden. He also decided to make a more thorough search of the cellar. The cellar held a 'peculiar fascination' for Dew. 'Maybe it was my sixth sense', was the only explanation he could offer. Dew takes up the tale:

> I got a small poker with a sharp point and Sergt Mitchell and I probed all over the cellar. We found that between some of the bricks of the cellar floor the poker went in pretty easily. We then removed several bricks and found a flat surface of clay. I got a spade and, after digging 2 or 3 spadefuls, I dug up what appeared to be some human remains. I had to desist on account of the terrible smell for a time.

Despite the hideous stench, Dew 'was now as excited as I ever allowed myself to be. I knew that I was on the eve of a great discovery.' Dew and Mitchell fortified themselves with brandy and returned to their grim task:

> The remains which I found there were not in an advanced state of decomposition, some portion of them were decomposed, some were quite firm. They were of a brownish colour, but when cut they were quite fresh.

The remains were covered in a large quantity of lime, some of which was coarsely granular while some had set in hard lumps like concrete. Whoever had put the remains there had made a simple blunder. The lime, mixed with water, had acted as a preservative rather than a destroyer of the flesh.

Dr Crippen's disappearance was now explained. Amongst the remains were a lady's hair-curling pin with light and dark dyed hair attached, portions of ladies' undergarments, a portion of a man's pyjama shirt, and a piece of coarse string. It was that which was not found that made the discovery all the more shocking. The head, hands, feet, bones and teeth were missing. To Dew's mind the remains had 'every appearance of a calculated plot to destroy all signs of identity'. Dew had 'that strange hunch . . . that what we had found represented all that remained of the once charming and vivacious Belle Elmore'.

Dew immediately sent for the local divisional police surgeon, Dr Thomas Marshall, and informed Sir Melville Macnaghten, who was now the Assistant Commissioner of the CID, of the find. Macnaghten filled his pockets with cigars, grabbed Superintendent Froest, jumped into a car and sped to Hilldrop Crescent, where he handed the cigars out to the officers. 'I thought they might be needed by the officers – and they were!'[1] (Dew was a smoker). Dr Marshall arrived at around 5.40 p.m., when the remains were partly exposed. He thought they were human but did not make a proper examination that day. He merely returned at 9 p.m., when the remains were uncovered, and just touched the surface of them. Dew ordered the photographing of the remains, and then covered them up.

Macnaghten and Froest had a look around the house. Macnaghten was surprised to see on the dining room sideboard bottles of whisky, claret, sherry and chartreuse. He observed that Crippen's chair at the head of the table was only some fifteen or twenty yards away from where the remains lay, and later commented, 'How, for five long months, good digestion could have waited upon appetite in such circumstances has always been a marvel to me!'[2] The house was locked up for the night and guarded by the police, but the outside world was beginning to hear about what had transpired. The following morning *The Times* reported:

> Some persons who were passing the house last night were attracted by several slight explosions, and it then became known that the police were taking flashlight photographs of a body which is said to have been in the cellar for some months.

As the crowds began to gather the local newspaper sent their reporter to investigate 'The Green Crescent of the Crime', which he thus described:

> Hilldrop-crescent is a quiet suburban place although in the inner ring of the Metropolis; and, reasoning superficially, it would be the last spot one would have dreamt of for the stage of a sordid murder. The exterior aspect of the quiet residential streets speaks of respectability: and in the placid atmosphere of well-to-do Suburbia the tokens of the grim deed seized the heart with a greater shock than they would have done in the denser and darker neighbourhood that lies not far away.
>
> For this secluded crescent is situated just off the bustle and roar of several busy thoroughfares, and a stone thrown in any direction would fall in the thick of clustering human hives. It is no more than five minutes from Holloway-road with its ceaseless traffic; it is close

to Caledonian-road with its constant goings-to-and-fro; on the other side the huge glass palaces rattle on their way to Tottenham Court-road. In a word, it nestles serenely in a back-wash of the whirling waters of the modern Babylon.

It is this strange contrast of peacefulness and quietude with the hurrying stretch of main thoroughfares that bound it and the network of mean and squalid streets that surround it, that seems to intensify the horror of the crime committed in its smug and snug precincts.

The crescent, then, is hidden away in the district which abounds in leafiness, and although not far off is a very different world of bricks and mortar, so cosily shut in is the essentially middle-class part that one can almost forget the grime and the encircling gloom.

Here it was – in this unlikely quarter – that the corpse of a beautiful woman was dug up.

Here it was that last night, as indeed all through the day, a knot of people stood shuddering, and conversing almost in whispers.

Here it was, in this grccn and salubrious road, that a garden gate was guarded by two stalwart men in blue – the guardians of a terrible interior that no prying eyes were permitted to look upon.

Here it was that detectives silently came and went; here came eminent professors and official photographers; and here came a coffin to bear away a woman's mangled remains.

It stands up, does that ill-fated house, behind large, spreading trees that almost conceal its frontage. In the sunshine of a summer day the green foliage gave almost a gay appearance to the scene.[3]

The remains were removed the next day under the supervision of Dr Marshall and Dr Augustus Pepper, a consultant surgeon from St Mary's Hospital. They were placed in a coffin and taken to the mortuary. Two local police constables, Frederick Martin and Daniel Gooch[4] of Y Division, Highgate, had helped Dew unearth the remains and place them in the coffin. In recognition of their conduct during this unpleasant task, Dew spoke to Macnaghten, who promised them a 10s bonus.

Dew made a further discovery that would later prove to be vital. In a box under the bed in the first-floor bedroom there were two suits of pyjamas and one odd pair of pyjama trousers. The jackets bore the label of 'Shirt-makers, James Brothers (Holloway), Limited, Holloway, N'. The house and its key were then placed into the possession of the coroner's officer.

Dew had noticed a raised heap at the end of Crippen's garden that was covered with garden litter and flower pots. He started digging and found a layer of clay similar to that which he had found when digging up the cellar. Dew thought he had discovered the clay that had been excavated from the cellar in order to hide the remains, but upon further examination he found that the clay was a normal feature of the garden and could be found throughout.

The news of the discovery of the remains was met with disbelief by the Crippens' friends and neighbours, who perceived Hawley and Cora to be a most devoted couple. Crippen had told Dr Rylance the story that Cora had gone to America on family business, and that she had later died. On 9 July Rylance had received a letter from Crippen which read, 'I now find that in order to escape trouble I shall be obliged to absent myself for a time.' Once the remains had been discovered the press interviewed Rylance, who told them:

> A more humble, unassuming little man I have never met, and to me it seems unthinkable that he would have committed so dastardly a crime.
>
> In my judgement he was a smart man and a wonderful organizer, very exact, with fine business methods; in fact, one could not have desired a straighter representative.
>
> Of late, I had observed that he looked worried. He had, of course, his bright moments, but generally he appeared to be distressed and perturbed by something or other, and I came to the conclusion that it was due to financial troubles.
>
> His wife was a woman of charming manners. I frequently saw her here. What passes my understanding is how Crippen could have thrown her over in favour of his typist. It was a strange infatuation. She had little to recommend her so far as I noticed. The typist was a delicate woman. She was always ailing, and was jocularly known in this building as the woman who always answered inquiries with the same remark, 'Not very well, thank you.'[5]

Miss Gillatt, a neighbour, who lived at 40 Hilldrop Crescent, revealed:

> We first missed Mrs. Crippen some time last February. My sister met Mr. Crippen about that time, and he told her she had gone to America and that he intended to give up the house.
>
> Both Mr. and Mrs. Crippen used to spend a great part of their time in the garden. He always seemed exceedingly fond of her, and used to follow her round in quite an adoring way.[6]

Another acquaintance stated that Crippen's devotion to Cora 'was remarkable'.[7] But Dew had already learned that, after seventeen years of marriage, '[q]uarrels between them . . . were not infrequent'. These rows had been going on for some time. A Mr Richards had stayed at 39 Hilldrop Crescent during a period when the Crippens were taking in lodgers. He had witnessed 'several domestic eruptions of rather a one-sided nature. Mrs. Crippen, excitable and irritable, chiding her husband; Crippen, pale, quiet, imperturbable.'

There was immediate concern that Crippen and Le Neve may have fled the country. Cablegrams were quickly sent out to various countries. The one sent to Ottawa, Canada gave full physical descriptions of the pair:

Wanted for murder and mutilation of a woman Hawley Harvey Crippen alias Peter Crippen alias Francke, an American age fifty, 5 feet three or four, complexion fresh, hair light brown inclined sandy, thin bald on top, scanty straggling moustache, eyes grey, bridge of nose flat, false teeth, wears gold rim spectacles, may be wearing brown jacket suit marked Baker and Grey, round flat hat, Horne Bros. inside, wears hat back of head, rather slovenly appearance, throws his feet out when walking, slight American accent, very plausible and quiet spoken, speaks French and shows his teeth when speaking; and Ethel Clara Leneve [*sic*] travelling as his wife, age 27, height five feet five, complexion pale, hair light brown, large grey eyes, good teeth, good looking, medium build, pleasing appearance, quiet subdued manner, looks interested when in conversation, is reticent, walks slowly, probably dressed blue serge skirt, ditto three quarter jacket suit, large hat or may be dressed in boys dark brown jacket suit, grey hard felt hat, native of London, shorthand writer and typist.

The description of Le Neve was later amended when it was discovered that, far from having good teeth, Le Neve was the possessor of about twenty false teeth.[8] Further descriptions of the wanted couple appeared in newspapers in Spain, Sweden and Grand Canary, where large numbers of British steamers called.

The descriptions also appeared in the British press, leading to numerous false sightings covering the length and breadth of England. Reports came in from London, Edinburgh, Aberdeen, Manchester and Birmingham, to name but a few.[9] Dew himself recalled one 'humorous' incident:

On two occasions a gentleman who was unfortunate enough to resemble Crippen facially, was brought to Scotland Yard on suspicion of being the wanted man. On the first occasion he took the experience in good part, but when the same thing happened a second time he was highly indignant, and said it was getting a habit.

Having 'done everything possible to set the police forces of the whole world on the hunt for the missing couple', Dew 'took on the almost equally big task of searching for evidence that would satisfy a jury that the woman who had met her fate in that gloomy looking house in Hilldrop Crescent was indeed Crippen's wife'. Dew was convinced that the remains were Cora Crippen, for she was missing, and her husband had lied about her disappearance, and had subsequently fled. On 16 July Dew appeared at Bow Street Police Court to apply for a warrant against:

HAWLEY HARVEY CRIPPEN and ETHEL CLARA LE NEVE, alias, NEAVE, for having on or about the 2nd day of February 1910, at 39 Hilldrop Crescent, Camden Road, in the said County and district, wilfully murdered one CORA CRIPPEN otherwise BELLE ELMORE, supposed to be the wife of HAWLEY HARVEY CRIPPEN, and that they did mutilate and bury some of the remains in the coal cellar at the above address.

12

The Hunt

We sought him here, we sought him there,
Detectives sought him everywhere.
Is he in heaven, or hell, maybe,
The dem'd elusive Dr. C.

Sir Melville Macnaghten

Dew sensed the enormity of the Crippen case. He set out to track down Dr Crippen with the same fervour he felt as a young detective hunting Jack the Ripper. He later recalled:

As the man in sole charge of the biggest murder mystery of the century, I felt that Dr. Crippen had thrown out a challenge. I was ready to accept it.

I gave every ounce of effort. For sixteen – sometimes more – hours out of every twenty-four, I was directing the police campaign to track Crippen down.

The first sitting of the coroner's inquest on the remains found by Dew at 39 Hilldrop Crescent was held on 18 July at the Chapel of Ease, Holloway Road, Islington, but this location proved to be too small for such an event and resumed inquests were held at the Central Library in Holloway Road. Frequent heavy showers failed to deter large numbers of curious onlookers who lined the approach to the coroner's court and mortuary. Amongst those attending the hearing were Ethel Le Neve's mother and a number of actresses who were connected to the Music Hall Ladies' Guild.

His Majesty's Coroner for the district of Islington, Dr Danford Thomas, swore in a jury to investigate the cause of death of 'some human remains now lying dead', which they viewed through a glass screen. Dr Thomas explained that the remains were believed to be those of Cora Crippen, adding that an adjournment would be necessary as there was not a great deal of evidence to be put before them at this instance; but the police had the matter of finding Dr Crippen in hand, and the analysis of the remains was still in progress.

Walter Dew gave his evidence. He outlined the extent of his investigations, including the discovery of the remains. He ended by saying that the police 'had not lost one minute, and search was being made everywhere for Crippen'. Dr Thomas heaped praise on Dew for making the find, saying, 'Many a man might have gone into that cellar and made no discovery. It had to remain for a detective with a genius for his work to go a step further, and it is due to the keenness of the inspector that this ghastly affair is brought to light.' Describing Dew as a genius was an overstatement. He certainly had been tenacious, and if the Nashes had visited their local police station, rather than Scotland Yard, the outcome of the investigation could have been different. There had been an element of luck in Dew's discovery. If Crippen had not aroused suspicion by fleeing, or if he had filled the cellar with coal, Dew may not have been so diligent in his search. Things may also have been different if Crippen had left Hilldrop Crescent on 24 June, as he had originally agreed with his landlord.

Dr Marshall detailed the preliminary findings of the medical analysis. He thought that the remains were female, but could not at this point prove it because 'the perpetrator of the outrage had tried to obliterate not only all evidences of identity but all traces of sex'. Marshall thought that the cadaver was dissected in the cellar where it was found, 'and whoever did it must have taken his time about it, for it was a most deliberate and long process'.

As he promised, Dr Thomas adjourned the inquest until Monday 15 August. The main difficulty faced at this stage was establishing that the pile of flesh was in fact Cora Crippen. Here Dew had a lucky break. Outside the inquest he overheard Clara Martinetti say that Cora had undergone a serious operation, and had quite a large scar on the lower part of her body, which she had seen. Amongst the remains there was a piece of skin bearing the mark of what could have been an operation scar.

Dew thought it was 'more than probable' that sooner or later Le Neve would try to communicate with her parents, who also lived in Camden Town, or her sister in Tottenham. He considered that Crippen might try to write to his employee William Long, who, Dew had discovered, had withheld the information from him for three days that he had bought a suit of boy's clothes at Crippen's request.[1] With this in mind he asked the Home Office to direct the postal authorities to look out for letters going to their addresses, and forward them on to him under a Home Office warrant, later adding telegrams to his request. Scotland Yard had by now offered a reward of £250 for information leading to the arrest of Crippen and Le Neve.

It was at this time that Dew's conduct in the case so far was brought into question for the first time. A question was put to the Home

Secretary, Winston Churchill, by another Member of Parliament, who wanted to know '[i]f he can state who is responsible for allowing Dr. Crippen to get out of the hands of the police . . . [and whether] it was in consequence of the pressing inquiries that caused Dr. Crippen to vanish'.[2] Scotland Yard gave their answer, saying that until the discovery of the remains it had simply been a missing person case, of the sort which numbered around 100 a week in London alone. It was not until there was evidence of foul play that the house could be searched more thoroughly.[3]

Dew later responded angrily to the criticism:

> I came in for criticism. Certain people with no knowledge of police procedure and less of the law blamed me for allowing Crippen to go. I ought to have arrested him, they said. Ridiculous!
>
> There was up to this time no shred of evidence against Crippen upon which he could have been arrested or even detained. Futile to talk of arresting a man until you know there has been a crime.

It was not until a fortnight later that Churchill responded to the question, which he dismissed as unfair, Dew being engaged on special duty at the time and therefore unable to defend himself.[4]

Now the events at Hilldrop Crescent were publicly known, rumours spread like wildfire. When a German named John Evert committed suicide at a Finsbury boarding house, word spread that he was fact been Dr Crippen.[5] When a young woman committed suicide at Bourges on 13 July, a theory emerged from Paris that she was Ethel Le Neve.[6] Furthermore, several American newspapers reported that Scotland Yard were investigating the death of Crippen's first wife, but nothing seemed to come of this. The Crippen case dominated the newspapers. Melville Macnaghten recalled that 'no case has ever fascinated the British public, and, indeed, engaged the attention of the whole world, in quite the same way the case of Dr. Crippen did'.[7] Dew agreed:

> There has never been a hue and cry like that which went up throughout the country for Crippen and Miss Le Neve. The newspapers were full of the case. It was the one big topic of conversation. On the trains and buses one heard members of the public speculating and theorizing as to where they were likely to be.
>
> All the elements to fire the public imagination were present. They were intrigued by the relationship between the doctor and his former secretary; repelled by the gruesome find in the coal cellar, and mystified as to how the victim had met her death. Every day that passed increased the fevered interest in the hunt.

The Times referred to Crippen as 'Dr' Crippen – rather than Dr Crippen – in their coverage. There was some doubt as to the validity of Crippen's medical qualifications. Dew referred to Crippen as a doctor because he had found a diploma at 39 Hilldrop Crescent, which had been issued ten years to the day that Dew interviewed Crippen, and read:

> Presented and Registered in the Office of the Clerk of the County of King's by Hawley H. Crippen, as his authority to practice physic and surgery, this 8th day of July 1900. This will certify that the within diploma is from a reputable Medical College, legally chartered under the laws of the State of Ohio.

This was good enough for Dew, who pointed out that the diploma proved Crippen 'was not drawing on his imagination in describing himself as a doctor, at any rate, so far as the U.S.A. was concerned'. Crippen's American qualification would not, however, allow him to practise as a doctor in England.[8]

More sightings of the fugitives came pouring in from all over the country, and also the continent. Remembering that, to his annoyance, his superiors had not asked for press help during the Whitechapel murders, Dew determined to follow his instincts and do the opposite. Dew made an appeal to the French newspaper *Le Matin* for 'the Press to give us its assistance'.[9]

More false sightings were reported. Mr Newton, a costumier with premises at Great Portland Street, reported that a man answering Dr Crippen's description had entered his shop 'and said he wanted to purchase a lady's costume and under clothes which he said was for himself'. A man fitting Crippen's description had been spotted in the south of France before crossing the frontier to Spain (provisional arrest and extradition orders had already been issued in France, Spain and Portugal). He was also 'seen' in Cardiganshire and Willesden.[10] Perhaps the strangest 'sighting' was of the couple in a small town on the south coast getting into a hot air balloon.[11]

All the reports of the public's sightings were in vain. In 1910 it was not necessary to have a passport to travel to much of the world, and Crippen and Le Neve were in Europe by 10 July. On that day they had booked into the Hôtel des Ardennes in the Rue de Brabant in Brussels, Belgium. Later enquiries ascertained that they had arrived around lunchtime and stayed there until 18 July. Crippen signed the visitor's register 'John Robinson, age 55 Merchant born in Quebec Canada last place of residence, Vienna'. The hotel's proprietress signed the book on behalf of Le Neve under the name of 'John Robinson Junior', for the typist was now masquerading as a boy. The only luggage they brought with them was a small basketwork trunk. To the staff at the hotel they appeared to be two people travelling for pleasure. They spent most of their time in their room, only leaving it for about two hours a day.

The story Crippen told the hotel staff was that he was a merchant travelling with his sick son, and that his wife had died two months previously. Le Neve spoke only in whispers, which Crippen explained by saying that 'he' was deaf and suffering from an affliction of the throat. He added that they had come from Quebec and planned to go to The Hague, Rotterdam and Amsterdam, and spend a few days in the Cambre Forest before returning to Quebec. Other enquiries elicited that Crippen had said he was going to go to Vilvorde, near Brussels, for the benefit of his son's health.

On 13 July – the day Dew discovered the remains at Hilldrop Crescent – Crippen called in at the office of M. Baur, an agent of the Red Star shipping line. He asked for a second-class cabin in a ship bound for Canada. The only one that carried second-class passengers was the steamer *Montrose*, which was due to leave Antwerp on 3 August. Crippen (still using the name 'Robinson') did not book it there and then, but returned the next day. Then he was told that he could get an earlier berth by booking a ship that went via England to Canada, but he declined and booked a cabin on the *Montrose*, a 5,000-ton steamship that travelled at a speed of 13 knots.

Crippen made another visit to Baur on 15 July. He was then informed that the *Montrose* was now sailing early, on 20 July. Crippen collected his two tickets for cabin no. 5, which cost 275 francs each (a total of around £22). Crippen paid with English gold. He then asked Baur if he could recommend someone in Brussels who might lend him some money, but Baur declined to give him that information.

The *Montrose* arrived at Antwerp on 15 July, where it moored at the CPR wharf on the riverfront. The vessel had first been launched in 1897, and was initially used to transport troops to the Boer War. By 1910 the *Montrose* had the reputation of being a modest and reliable ship. Its captain, Henry George Kendall, had sailed from the Millwall Docks in London the day before. He had been given a full description of Dr Crippen by the Thames Police, which also included the detail that Le Neve may be dressed as a boy.

The passengers for the *Montrose* (all second and third class) boarded the ship on 20 July between 8.30 and 10.00 a.m. There were in all 20 second-class passengers, 246 third-class, and a crew of 107, making a total of 373 souls on board. Kendall did not notice anything untoward about any of the passengers; that was until he went ashore and bought a continental edition of the *Daily Mail* that contained photographs and descriptions of Dr Crippen and Ethel Le Neve.

Kendall's suspicions were aroused within three hours of the start of the voyage, when he saw Mr and Master 'Robinson'. Crippen had signed the manifest 'John Philo Robinson, age 55, Merchant, American, of Detroit, Michigan U.S.A.' Le Neve was described as 'John George Robinson, age 16, single, Student'. 'Mr Robinson' was clean-shaven, but had several days of growth on his chin. When the captain 'saw the boy squeeze the man's hand I thought it strange and unnatural, and it occurred to me at once that they might be Crippen and Le Neve'. Kendall wished them the time of day, and observed them keenly. Already he felt 'quite confident' that they were the fugitives, but he did not do anything else at that point as he wanted to make sure he hadn't made a mistake.

The following day Captain Kendall shared his suspicions, in strict confidence, with his chief officer, Alfred Henry Sergent, and instructed him to join him in collecting any English newspapers on the ship which mentioned the North London cellar murder. On 22 July Kendall engaged Crippen in conversation on the subject of sea-sickness amongst passengers and the remedies used for curing it. Crippen's answer included some medical terms for certain remedies. This convinced Kendall that 'Robinson' was a medical man.

In addition, 'Robinson' fitted two of the points of description of Dr Crippen. The bridge of his nose was flat, and there was a deep mark on his nose as if caused by the wearing of spectacles. Also, Kendall heard 'Robinson' speak in French to the French passengers. This 'positively convinced' Kendall that his suspicions were justified. Kendall told Crippen stories he hoped would make him laugh out loud, to see if Crippen would open his mouth wide enough for Kendall to ascertain if he had false teeth. Kendall tested Crippen two or three times by calling after him 'Mr Robinson', to which Crippen did not respond. It was only when Kendall repeated his call and Le Neve prompted him that Crippen responded, explaining that the cold weather had made him deaf.

Kendall now made a historic decision. He instructed his Marconi wireless operator to send the following message:

Montrose.130 miles West of Lizard.
Have strong suspicion that Crippen London Cellar
Murderer and accomplice are amongst saloon passengers.
Moustache shaved off, growing beard. Accomplice dressed
as boy, voice, manner and build undoubtedly a girl.
Kendall.

The wireless telegraph had come into existence in the late nineteenth century, and by the twentieth century it was possible to send messages over ever-increasing distances. Before this it had been necessary to send transatlantic messages via underwater cables that linked Britain and America. Ironically, Crippen would often sit on deck and look up at the wireless aerial, listening to the cracking electric spark messages being sent by the operator. He once commented, 'What a wonderful invention it is!'

Kendall continued to keep the pair under observation. He noted that Le Neve

has the manner and appearance of a very refined, modest girl. She does not speak much, but always wears a pleasant smile. She seems thoroughly under his thumb, and he will not leave her for a moment. Her suit is anything but a good fit. Her trousers are very tight about the hips, and are split a bit down the back and secured with large safety pins.

He continually shaves his upper lip, and his beard is growing nicely. I often see him stroking it and he seems pleased, looking more like a farmer every day. The mark on his nose has not worn off since coming on board.

He sits about on the deck reading, or pretending to read, and both seem to be thoroughly enjoying all their meals. They have not been seasick, and I have discussed various parts of the world with him. He knows Toronto, Detroit, and California well, and says he is going to take his boy to California for his health (meaning Miss Le Neve). Has in conversation used several medical terms. Crippen says that when the ship arrives he will go to Detroit by boat, if possible, as he prefers it. The books he has been most interested in have been

'Pickwick Papers.'
'Nebo the Nailer' (S.B. Gould)
'Metropolis.'
'A Name to Conjure With.'

And he is now busy reading 'The Four Just Men,' which is all about a murder in London and £1,000 reward.

The 'Robinsons' dined at the Captain's table, where Le Neve's table manners were

most lady like, handling knife and fork, and taking fruit off the dishes with two fingers. Crippen kept cracking nuts for her, and giving her half his salad, and was always paying her the most marked attention . . . and the more I saw of them the more I was convinced and I sent a further Marconi to Liverpool when in Mid Atlantic, saying that I was fully convinced as to the identity, passengers not suspicious am keeping everything quiet.

Dew, exhausted by the relentless and as yet unsuccessful hunt for Crippen, received the 'electrifying' news of Captain Kendall's suspicions one evening in a telegram from the Liverpool police. As Dew read the contents 'a wave of optimism swept over me. My fatigue instantly vanished.' Dew rushed from his Scotland Yard office and jumped into a cab that took him to the residence of Assistant Commissioner Sir Melville Macnaghten. Dew handed Macnaghten the telegram, which he read with raised eyebrows. Macnaghten asked:

'What do you think?'
'I feel confident it's them.'
'So do I. What do you suggest?'
'I want to go after them in a fast steamer. The White Star liner *Laurentic* sails from Liverpool to-morrow. I believe it is possible for her to overtake the *Montrose* and reach Canada first.'
'Here's your authority, Dew, and I wish you all the luck in the world.'

Despite endorsing Dew's voyage, Macnaghten was only too aware of the risks it entailed. Dew knew every detail of the case and had spoken to Crippen. His absence could create problems, '[b]ut a decision had to be arrived at . . . the die was cast, the Rubicon was crossed. If the coup happened to come off, well and good, but, if otherwise, why, then, the case would have been hopelessly messed up, and I didn't care to dwell on the eventualities of its future.' The Assistant Commissioner's spirits were somewhat dampened when he arrived at Scotland Yard the next morning and asked Superintendent Froest, 'Well, what do you think of last night's decision?' Froest was unimpressed by Macnaghten's 'sanguine view' of the chances of the Marconi message being correct, although Chief Constable Sir Edward Henry shared Macnaghten's optimism.[12]

The Chief Constable of Liverpool had booked Walter Dew onto the steamer *Laurentic* under the name of 'Mr Dewhurst'. The ship was going to sail from Liverpool at 6.30 p.m. on 23 July, a whole three and a half days after Crippen and Le Neve had departed for Canada. The *Laurentic* could travel at about 3.5 miles per hour faster than the *Montrose*, and sailed directly to Quebec. She was due to arrive there on 31 July, a good couple of days before the arrival of *Montrose*. Dew did not even tell his wife about his mission, named 'Operation Handcuffs'. He just told her that he had to go abroad 'on a matter of great urgency'. This was not unusual, for Dew never discussed any of his cases with his family. His daughter Kate would later recall that her father 'was usually very reluctant to give any information or express any opinion on the work on which he was engaged'.[13]

Dew journeyed from Euston Station to Liverpool, where he was met by a Liverpudlian police officer wearing a red rose in his coat for identification. News of Dew's imminent departure had leaked and a number of reporters and photographers assembled on Prince's landing stage, but he managed to slip quietly on board and evade the gathered pressmen.[14]

While Dew was steadily gaining ground on the *Montrose* he made numerous attempts to contact Captain Kendall via the Marconi wireless, but his messages failed to get through. Somehow, the passengers on the *Laurentic* suspected that the broad-shouldered man with the merry eyes and large grey moustache was a Scotland Yard man. Dew 'made every possible effort to hide his identity. It was soon discovered, however, but by tacit consent of everyone his incognito has been respected.' Dew said nothing, and kept himself to himself, giving every appearance of being 'an Englishman out for a little pleasure jaunt'.[15] Nevertheless, Dew admitted, 'I had a most pleasant voyage'.

Captain Kendall, meanwhile, continued his observations of Crippen and Le Neve. Crippen was very relaxed, and he and Le Neve spent one night in the saloon

> enjoying songs and music, he was quite interested, and spoke to me next morning, saying how one song, 'We All Walked Into the Shop,' had been drumming in his head all night, and how his boy had enjoyed it, and laughed heartily when they retired to their room. In the course of one conversation he spoke about American drinks, and said that Selfridge's was the only decent place in London to get them at.

Kendall sensed an almost sinister hold Crippen had over Le Neve:

> At times both would sit and appear to be in deep thought. Though Le Neve does not show any signs of distress, and is, perhaps, ignorant of the crime committed, she appears to be a girl with a very weak will. She has to follow him everywhere. If he looks at her she gives him an endearing smile, as though she were under his hypnotic influence.

As the voyage progressed Crippen became more and more restless. He asked Kendall where the ship stopped to be met by the pilot boat, how he came off, and how far it was from the pilot station to Quebec, and said he was anxious to get to Detroit. Crippen told Kendall that he was thinking about settling down in California on a fruit farm.

Newspapers had been full of the story of the Atlantic chase, and Captain Kendall had been sending back regular wireless messages to the *Daily Mail* that told of his progress and investigations, which were being eagerly read. John Edward Nash, who had originally reported Cora Crippen's disappearance, was elated and declared that the 'fact that Inspector Dew has gone is splendid. This means almost certainly that Crippen will be caught.'[16]

Back in London Superintendent Froest was keeping his feet firmly on the ground, at least publicly. In a statement Froest pointed out the realities of the situation, which were in stark contrast to the press excitement over the chase, which was seen as a prelude to the inevitable capture of the fugitives. Froest said:

> He [Dew] will leave the details of the arrest to the Canadian police, who will of course, make their own arrangements. His position during the proceedings in Canada, which are identical with the proceedings which are taken for extradition orders in other countries, will be first to identify the people and then to wait until they are handed over into his custody by the Canadian police. He will act exactly as a foreign officer does who is in this country waiting for the extradition of a criminal for whom he has been seeking. These proceedings will naturally take some considerable time, and it is not possible for Inspector Dew to arrive back in this country in time for the adjourned inquest, which is fixed for August 15. That is, of course, if he can identify the people. Speaking for myself, I am keeping a perfectly clear mind on the subject. We have so many houses built with cards which fall down when the last of the pack is placed on top, and for this reason we are pursuing every clue which comes to us, just as if the Montrose incident had never occurred. Investigations are being made in London and elsewhere by detectives with a view to building up the story of the crime which is, owing to several aspects of the mystery, somewhat incomplete.[17]

It was not just the newspaper-reading public who were eagerly following Dew's transatlantic chase. Late on 30 July Home Secretary Winston Churchill requested an update on the case, which was delivered to him at St James's Palace.

Dew's fears that the *Montrose* had beaten him to Canada were unfounded. As well as the assurances of the *Laurentic*'s captain, there was the sight of a pilot cutter coming out to meet the steamer at Father Point filled with press reporters and photographers. Dew surmised it never would have been there had the *Montrose* already arrived. To his annoyance, they cried 'Three cheers for Inspector Dew!'[18]

Dew's relationship with the American and Canadian press would always be an uneasy one, principally because he steadfastly refused to tell them anything. Dew saw this as 'upholding the prestige of British justice and British police methods'. Questions were met by blunt responses such as 'Let me alone', 'I don't know anything about it', and 'I do not want any pictures taken at all'.[19] The newsmen could not understand Dew's reticence. 'They do things very differently in America', Dew sighed. 'I prefer the British way.'

13

The Capture

> . . . one of those episodes that no novelist would dare to make up,
> such as Crippen's flight across the Atlantic
> with his mistress dressed as a boy.
> *George Orwell, 'Decline of the English Murder'*

Father Point was a desolate outpost on the St Lawrence River, consisting of some wooden shacks, a wireless station and a lighthouse. As Dew had no power of arrest in Canadian waters he was met by Inspectors McCarthy and Dennis of the Quebec City Police. He was put up in one of the shacks where he sleeplessly awaited the arrival of the *Montrose* amid the din of the lighthouse foghorn and the rowdy singing of the journalists congregated in the other huts.

On 31 July 1910, Dew borrowed the uniform of a pilot before being rowed up to the *Montrose* accompanied by the pilot and Inspectors McCarthy and Dennis. Crippen was still blissfully ignorant of what was about to happen, allegedly commenting to the ship's doctor, 'There seem to be a good many pilots in the boat doctor', when he saw Dew's boat approaching the *Montrose*.[1] Captain Kendall had been forewarned by wireless about what was going to happen, and he was waiting for Dew on the bridge, where the pair shook hands.

While making his way towards the Captain's cabin, Dew caught sight of and instantly recognised Dr Crippen, despite his now being clean-shaven and not wearing glasses. Crippen, like Dew in his Whitechapel days, was wearing a blue serge suit under his tweed coat:

> Presently only a few feet separated us. A pair of bulgy eyes were raised to mine. I would have recognized them anywhere.
>
> The little man was Crippen. I thrilled with the realization that this was no wild goose chase after all. My search was ended. Miss Le Neve, I felt certain, would not be far away.
>
> During my long career as a detective, I have experienced many big moments, but at no other time have I felt such a sense of triumph and achievement.

Crippen was brought by McCarthy and Dennis into the captain's cabin, where Dew confronted him with the words 'Good morning, Dr. Crippen; I am Chief Inspector Dew.' Crippen simply replied 'Good morning, Mr. Dew.' Dew continued, 'You will be arrested for the murder and mutilation of your wife, Cora Crippen, in London, on or about the 2nd of February last.'

Dew recalled:

Even though I believed him to be a murderer, and a brutal murderer at that, it was impossible at that moment not to feel for him a pang of pity. He had been caught on the threshold of freedom. Only twelve hours more and he would have been safely at Quebec.

Macnaghten spoke of the confrontation between Dew and Crippen as being on a par with that of Henry Morton Stanley and Dr David Livingstone, some forty years previously in Africa.[2] Livingstone had embarked on an African expedition in 1866 and was not heard of for years. The editor of the *New York Herald* dispatched journalist Stanley to find out what had happened to Livingstone. Stanley set out in 1871 and eventually tracked down Livingstone eight months later, greeting him with the immortal question, 'Dr. Livingstone I presume?'

Dew was joined by Chief Inspector McCarthy, who cautioned the now speechless Crippen. Inspector Dennis then searched Crippen and found several items from Cora Crippen's jewellery collection. There were also two printed cards bearing the name 'E. Robinson & Co., Detroit, Mich. Presented by Mr John Robinson.' On the back of one was written, 'I cannot stand the horror I go through every night any longer and as I see nothing bright ahead and money has come to an end I have made up my mind to jump overboard tonight – I know I have spoil [*sic*] your life – but I – I hope some day you can learn to forgive me. With last words of love, your H.' On the back of the other card was written, 'Shall we wait until tonight about 10 or 11 o'clock? If not, what time?'

Dew thought the writing was that of Dr Crippen, and believed that they showed he would have committed suicide before the *Montrose* reached Quebec. Dew found Crippen's explanation of the cards unsatisfactory:

He stated that two days before his arrival at Quebec, the Quartermaster of the 'Montrose', approached and showed him an unsigned letter, in which it said that the Police were going to arrest him on his arrival at Quebec, and he (the Quartermaster) offered to hide him amongst the cargo till all was quiet, and then at Montreal would facilitate his escape. Crippen alleged that it was arranged that Miss Le Neve should remain on board, as it was not supposed that Police wanted her, and that the cards found on him when arrested, in which he had written, that the horror was too much and that he intended jumping overboard etc, were written by him as part of the plot, and would have been produced by Miss Le Neve, when Police came on board.

He further said that the Quartermaster was going to make a splash in the water at night, and then tell the Captain that he (Crippen) had jumped overboard.

Dew left Crippen with McCarthy and entered cabin no. 5, where he saw Ethel Le Neve reclining on a settee. Her appearance had also altered since Dew had last seen her. Dew said to her with his 'characteristic lisp',[3] 'Miss Le Neve', to which she replied, 'Yes'. Dew identified himself and told her the charge she was facing. Le Neve did not reply, but became agitated and faint. Dew left Le Neve with a stewardess and then returned to the captain's cabin to remove Crippen to another cabin. Crippen suddenly said, 'I am not sorry; the anxiety has been too much.' McCarthy handcuffed Crippen, explaining, 'We must put these on, because on a card found on you you have written that you intend jumping over-board.' Crippen replied, 'I won't. I am more than satisfied, because the anxiety has been too awful.'

Dew made a further search of Crippen and found even more jewellery concealed about his person. Crippen asked Dew how Le Neve was. 'Agitated,' Dew replied, 'but I am doing all I can for her.' Crippen replied, 'It is only fair to say that she knows nothing about it; I never told her anything.' Le Neve said as much herself. She had not seen any newspapers on the voyage thanks to the efforts of Captain Kendall and Chief Officer Sergent. 'I assure you Mr Dew,' she said, 'I know nothing about it, I intended writing to my sister when I got to Quebec.'

As soon as he could Dew sent a telegram to Scotland Yard. 'Crippen and Leneve [*sic*] arrested wire later Dew.' The following day he sent another, 'Confirming former cable arrest made, arrive Quebec midnight Sunday. Suggest matron and Mitchell, Crippen threatened suicide, writing soon. Dew.'

The arrest of Crippen was the first instance of a murderer being captured largely thanks to wireless telegraphy, but in 1845 John Tawell had become the first murderer to be caught by a normal telegraph. He was observed getting onto a train at Slough after murdering his mistress. A telegraph was sent to Paddington station, and the police were waiting for him when he arrived.

The Times explained the importance of the wireless in the Crippen case:

In the absence of wireless telegraphy the fugitives would have reached Canada in comparatively favourable circumstances. There would have been no apparatus of detention ready for their arrival. No doubt the captain's suspicions would have been made known in the proper quarters, and means might have been found to keep them under observation for a time. But there would have been no means of absolute identification, and the action of the authorities would plainly have been very much hampered. Wireless telegraphy enabled the captain, without altering his course, and without giving the alarm to the fugitives, to communicate his suspicions to his owners, who promptly handed them on to Scotland Yard.[4]

The *Montrose* arrived in Quebec early on the morning of 1 August. As with all the events surrounding the case, a crowd had gathered, this time numbering around 500. Amid the flashes of camera lamps they saw a handcuffed Dr Crippen, holding his head down low, following Walter Dew down the gangplank. Ethel Le Neve followed, her boy's attire replaced by ill-fitting garments that belonged to the stewardess of the *Montrose*. Crippen and Le Neve were taken to the city gaol.

In his report on the arrest of Crippen and Le Neve Dew insisted, 'Whatever may have appeared in the press to the contrary I may say that my identity was not known until about a day before my landing at Father Point.' He was dismayed by the behaviour of the press, who were hungry for a story:

I was absolutely mobbed. Cameras were thrust in my face and I was practically at their mercy. I was importuned to say something, but I need hardly say that I refused.

In passing I cannot refrain from saying that the whole affair was disgraceful and should and could have been avoided and I was fearful lest this should in any way mar the success of my mission.

Dew further revealed that he found it 'difficult to believe that any person with an average amount of intelligence could ever have believed her [Le Neve] to be a boy'. Dew requested that he be allowed to have a free hand when it came to arranging the return voyage. He said that Crippen would never be left alone (no doubt fearing he may try to attempt suicide) and expressed concern that heavy bribes may be offered by the press to the matrons in order to get to Le Neve. Dew emphasised that Crippen and Le Neve would be kept entirely apart.

At the initial Police Court hearing a crowd of 3,000 women blocked the entrance to the court in the fight for admission. All the available seats were occupied by women, with forty or fifty others standing. Crippen's physical appearance came as a disappointment to the expectant spectators. He was not 'the hypnotic marvel which cabled stories had held up. Instead, the cringing figure with stooped head gave the lie to expectations. Crippen whined where criminals with more backbone would have answered smartly and posed serenely. He rolled his swollen eyes and twitched his head.'[5] Le Neve was no more inspiring. She 'leaned weakly upon the arms of her guards like one who had risen from a sick bed', before fainting and being carried out.

The hearing itself was merely a formality. Crippen confirmed his name and acknowledged he knew Le Neve and the reason they were there. He also stated that he was an American citizen, and that he would not fight extradition. The 1881 Fugitive Offenders Act meant that fugitives from British justice wanted for offences carrying a sentence of twelve months or more could be arrested on a warrant in any part of the British dominions. When caught, the fugitive would appear before a magistrate and if the evidence presented 'raise[d] a strong or probable presumption that the fugitive committed the offence', they would then be sent to prison for fifteen days to allow them to appeal, before being extradited. This is what happened with Crippen, and it meant that he and Dew would miss the resumed coroner's inquest in London.

Dew had anticipated a stay in Canada after Crippen's arrest. The intensity of the Canadian public's feelings of revulsion towards Crippen came as a surprise to him:

I had plenty of opportunities for sensing public opinion in Quebec. The people there were incensed against Crippen. They looked upon him as a monster in human form. By some he had already been judged and found guilty. The ghastly murder and mutilation of Belle Elmore, followed by his flight from justice with Miss Ethel Le Neve as his companion, had roused public feeling against him to fever pitch.

It was the same the world over. I have never known anything like it. Only those who can remember the case and the intense excitement and bitterness it engendered, can have any conception of the widespread antipathy towards the little man who was now in my charge.

Another rumour emerged on 4 August that Crippen had confessed to the murder of his wife. Dew stoutly denied this, saying 'there is not an iota of truth in the rumour'. Froest described the rumour as 'absolutely untrue', and the Canadian Provincial Premier, Sir Lomer Gouin, described the stories as 'tissues of lies'. They were; and this would later prove costly for the newspapers that had made the claim. This story had followed hotly on the heels of a bogus report that Dew had been sent a telegram from Scotland Yard saying that the remains had been positively identified as being female. An 'absolute invention', was the exasperated Froest's response. Dew had not received any communications from Scotland Yard, and they had not had any more from Dew.[6]

The foreign journalists were bemused by Dew's reluctance to talk to them. At one point he warned them, 'If you chaps don't stop pestering me about this confession business I'll have to leave town.'[7] However, Dew's success had put him in a state of high spirits. He reportedly 'delighted the pressmen by abandoning a little of his reserve' and told them he thought Le Neve knew nothing of Cora Crippen's death, and that he 'had been absolutely fascinated by Crippen'.[8] Nevertheless, the constant harassment from the press was wearing Dew out:

> My first and most pressing bother was the newspaper men. When they came on board the *Montrose* they began to badger me to be allowed to interview and photograph the prisoners.
>
> I flatly refused and, because of my attitude, I am afraid I became somewhat unpopular. They seemed to think they should be allowed to carry on just as they would have done in the United States. I had very different views and expressed them pretty strongly.
>
> All they got from me was that the suspected passengers had been identified as Crippen and Miss Le Neve, and had been placed under arrest.

As there was some time to spare before Crippen was due to reappear in court, Dew allegedly took the opportunity to escape journalistic attention by visiting the Niagara Falls with Captain Kendall.[9] The trip caused much comment, and many could not believe that such an astute officer as Dew would be relaxing before the Crippen case had closed. It was suggested that Dew was in fact secretly arranging the return trip to England, ensuring that it would be carried out with the utmost discretion. Dew did not mention a trip to the Niagara Falls in his memoirs.

More bizarre stories were emerging. Le Neve was offered £200 a week to star in a twenty-week tour, which included a music hall sketch called 'Caught by Wireless'. Crippen was offered a massive £1,000 a week for another twenty-week engagement if he was acquitted.[10] At this time one of the most bizarre stories concerning Dew's investigations emerged from Buffalo, New York. It was reported that Dew's wife Kate had expressed the opinion that Belle Elmore was still alive, and that the whole Crippen case had been arranged as an advertising stunt.[11] Stranger still, Dew was reported as saying that the remains had not even been identified as human, let alone female. If Cora Crippen were to have reappeared alive, she would have been a great attraction on the stage, and could have named her price.[12]

Detective Sergeant Mitchell had left Liverpool, and was making his way to Quebec aboard the *Lake Manitoba* to deliver extradition papers.[13] He was accompanied by two stern-faced wardresses from Holloway Prison (there were no police matrons), Miss Stone and Miss Foster, to accompany Ethel Le Neve back home.

When Mitchell was reunited with Dew on 14 August he handed him a letter from Chief Constable Bigham of Scotland Yard. Dew replied to Bigham, saying that he had received the two cables that the letter referred to. One of the cables appears to have contained instructions from Home Secretary Winston Churchill, for Dew wrote:

> The wishes of H.M. Secretary of State were anticipated by me, and I would remark that I have always made it a practice to treat prisoners with courtesy & consideration no matter what their position in life.
>
> If I have erred in this case it has been on the side of consideration and humanity, and at great cost to my own personal convenience & comfort.

Churchill had also expressed a desire that Crippen and Le Neve should be protected from the reporters and photographers. Dew was very pleased to report that 'so far as I am personally concerned I succeeded in preventing all annoyance from these people, and I also think succeeded in preventing their photographs being taken, but no one except myself can ever realise at what a cost this was done'.

Dew went on to inform Bigham that he was 'devising a scheme' to get the prisoners back to England, as he was concerned about the strength of feeling the Canadians had against Crippen. They saw him 'as a monster in human form', and this jeopardised Dew's chances of bringing him back home safely:

> This of course will depend to some extent on the Police here, to whom sooner or later I must divulge my plans, but bluntly speaking, I don't trust them too much in respect to reporters, however, I shall do my best to avoid publicity and annoyance to fugitives.

Dew signed off by thanking Bigham for communicating with his wife on his behalf. The Canadian journalists hoped that Sergeant Mitchell might be more forthcoming than Dew, but their hopes were dashed when Dew told them in no uncertain terms that 'Mr. Mitchell is acting under my instruction, and I have instructed him not to discuss the case'.[14] Mitchell remained silent.

The adjourned coroner's inquest went ahead in London as planned on 15 July without Dew, Crippen or Le Neve. Also absent was the original coroner, Dr Danford Thomas, who had recently died. He had been suffering from ill health and decided to take a holiday during the adjournment of hearings, but died suddenly at the coastal town of Hastings. It was agreed that the assistant coroner Walter Schroder should replace him. Frank Froest appeared and said that he could not predict exactly when Dew and Mitchell would return with the prisoners, but that it would probably be in about three weeks' time, and suggested that the inquest be adjourned until then. While Crippen was under arrest in Canada a friend of his had obtained the services of solicitor Arthur Newton, who had previously represented Crippen in a less serious matter in 1906. Newton suggested a month's adjournment. Travers Humphreys, of the Director of Public Prosecutions' office, agreed with this, as did Schroder, who set a date of 12 September at the Central Library, Holloway Road.[15]

Travers Humphreys' junior, Cecil William Mercer, constructed the case against Crippen. Years later Mercer wrote a series of books under the pseudonym Dornford Yates. Several were written as conversations between a local magistrate named Berry and a barrister (Mercer) called Boy. In 'As Berry and I Were Saying', Mercer wrote about his experiences in the Crippen case. Mercer's conclusions are interestingly at odds with those of many subsequent commentators on the case, who have portrayed Crippen as a poor, hen-pecked husband with a monstrous and overbearing wife who made his life unbearable and drove him to murder:

> Attempts have actually been made to palliate the crime. What is the truth? It was the sordid and barbarous murder by her husband of the Honorary Secretary (or Treasurer) of the Ladies' Music Hall Guild, to whom her many women-friends were deeply attached. Crippen had fallen for his typist: but, because a man falls for his typist he doesn't have to murder his wife. I have read that Mrs. Crippen led him a dog's life. Of that, there is not a tittle of evidence. She certainly had her interests, and he had his. What was their private relation, nobody ever knew.[16]

Dew's plan to leave Canada unseen was successful. Dew's 'neat little scheme' involved boarding a small steamer at a wharf which would meet the liner *Megantic* downstream. There was one small mishap as Crippen walked the gangway between the steamer and the *Megantic*, handcuffed and with his hat pulled down over his eyes. He walked into one of the ropes holding the gangway. It struck him on the chin and jerked him backwards, but fortunately Dew caught him before he fell into the sea.[17] On 20 August four people boarded the White Star liner *Megantic* under false names. Inspector Dew was Silas P. Doyle, Dr Crippen was Cyrus Field (Dew remembered the name as 'Nield'), Ethel Le Neve was Miss J. Byrne, and Sergeant Mitchell was F.M. Johnson.[18] On board, Dew read Crippen and Le Neve the warrant that charged them both with the wilful murder of Cora Crippen; Le Neve was also charged with being an accessory after the fact to that murder. After hearing the charge again, Crippen simply said 'Right', while Le Neve said 'Yes'.

One American newspaper, perhaps frustrated by Dew's refusal to speak to the press, launched a scathing attack on the departing detective:

> That ridiculous Inspector Dew has taken his two prisoners and departed. Atlas with the weight of the universe on his shoulders was never more impressed with the importance of his job than Mr. Dew has been for the last twenty days. Pomposity and overwhelming conceit apparently pass at Scotland Yard for cleverness and efficiency.
>
> Dew has been very funny while in America. And he has done a good service in destroying that traditional American awe and reverence felt for Scotland Yard and London police methods in general.[19]

Dew described the return voyage aboard the *Megantic*:

> Crippen ate well and apparently slept well. I found him a good conversationalist, able to talk on almost any subject. For the most part we confined ourselves to general topics – books, the weather, the liner, the progress we were making, and so on – but several times every day he asked about Miss Le Neve.
>
> One would never have guessed from Crippen's demeanour and manner, on that homeward voyage, that he was under arrest for murder, and that he had on his conscience a burden which few men could have borne without wilting.
>
> The more I saw of this remarkable man the more he amazed me.
>
> I was greatly impressed on the voyage home by the unswerving loyalty of Crippen to Miss Le Neve.
>
> Every morning he asked first thing how Miss Le Neve was. He never seemed to care much what happened to himself, so long as her innocence was established.

One incident sticks out in my memory. When off the coast of Ireland we ran into a heavy storm. Most of the passengers became ill, including my girl prisoner.

Crippen was a good sailor. He remained unperturbed through it all, or would have remained unperturbed had he not learned of Miss Le Neve's condition. The news that she was seasick caused him great concern. He told me the best remedy was champagne, and that the patient should lie flat.

For a moment it didn't strike me that he had it in his mind that champagne should be given to Miss Le Neve.

He saw this, and looked pleadingly at me as he said: 'Oh, Mr. Dew, please give her a little champagne and I will be eternally grateful to you.'

Dew obtained a bottle of champagne, which restored Le Neve immediately. Crippen 'was like a dog in his gratitude. He could scarcely have expressed greater pleasure had I told him that he could go free.'

Crippen never showed the slightest sign that he might lose his nerve as the ship neared England. Dew did not even notice any sign of depression, which might have been expected:

His nerves must have been made of iron. Except that he was under constant supervision and was handcuffed when he was taken out for exercise, he lived the life of a normal passenger.

He mystified me. He seemed quite happy. He gave no trouble, and never once tried the patience of Sergeant Mitchell or myself.

The impression he gave me was that of a man with a mind completely at rest. Most of his time he spent reading. I used to fetch his books myself from the ship's library, being careful, of course, never to get him one with a crime or murder plot. He loved novels, especially those with a strong love interest.

Sergeant Mitchell also found Crippen an easy prisoner to deal with. 'He chatted with me from time to time on various matters', Mitchell recalled, reporting that throughout the voyage Crippen 'seemed quite bright + jolly'.

Dew kept a close watch on Crippen during the return voyage, and several times he saw his prisoner stripped. To his surprise the diminutive Crippen was strongly built, and Dew was relieved that his prisoner was so well behaved. Dew was not a physical coward but he told Cecil Mercer, 'Well, I'm a much heavier man, but I should have been very sorry to have had to take Crippen on.'[20]

Crippen never mentioned his wife, and never showed any animosity towards his captor. Dew recalled, 'He was intelligent enough to realize that I had only done my duty.' He was often asked in later years why he treated Crippen with such kindness after his arrest. Dew did not consider that he had shown Crippen any more consideration than he had hundreds of other prisoners throughout his career. Dew thought that it was his duty to consider a prisoner innocent until he or she appeared before the proper tribunal and was found guilty. Despite this, Dew had 'never wavered from the opinion that Crippen was guilty'.

Dew also spent a lot of time during the return voyage with Ethel Le Neve, who had fully recovered after the initial shock of her arrest. He made frequent visits to her cabin every day to see if there was anything she wanted. He found her 'almost as calm and collected as Crippen himself'. Le Neve showed great composure throughout the journey. Dew thought that this was because she had a clear conscience, and that '[h]er fortitude was born of the knowledge of her own innocence and her faith in the integrity of the British Justice to which she was being surrendered'. Le Neve had protested her ignorance of the murder of Cora Crippen to Dew. When the detective asked her if she had not seen a letter her father wrote in the newspapers, she said that she had not seen any newspapers since leaving London, and that she had intended to write to her sister as soon as she and Crippen reached Quebec.

Le Neve did cause Dew a few problems on the return voyage. He told Cecil Mercer that, while Crippen was pining for Le Neve in his cabin on the opposite side of the ship, she was enjoying herself, joking and flirting with the ship's crew. In the end Dew had to move Le Neve to a less accessible cabin.[21]

Le Neve would later reveal that Dew became sea-sick as well during the rough weather near Ireland. She found Dew's manner to be very paternal, and she and Crippen referred to him affectionately as 'father'. Le Neve also said that Dew had a curious way of saying 'Ah', which he often did 'as though he knew so much more than I did'.[22]

On 24 August Dew took a handcuffed Crippen on to the deck to allow him some exercise. The prisoner asked Dew for 'a favour but I will leave it for Friday'. Dew told Crippen that he could give an answer then and there as well as he could on Friday, so Crippen explained his request. 'When you took me off the ship I did not see Miss Le Neve. I don't know how things will go, they may go all right or they may go all wrong with me. I may never see her again and I want to ask you if you will let me see her – but I won't speak to her. She has been my only comfort for the last 3 years.' Dew considered the request to be a 'delicate matter', but did allow him to see but not talk to her, on a train from Liverpool to London after the boat had docked.

As the *Megantic* approached the Liverpool landing stage, the waiting crowds spotted Dew on the deck smoking a cigar and chatting with Inspector Duckworth of the Liverpool Police, who had gone out in a boat to meet Dew. The sight of Dew indicated that Crippen and Le Neve were still aboard, and that they had not been surreptitiously landed already. The crowd thought that Dew would not emerge with his prisoners until late in the afternoon, but when a military and civic reception began to welcome the disembarking Canadian passengers and members of the Queen's Own Rifles, Dew rushed Crippen and Le Neve down the gangway surrounded by police officers. One newspaper described it as 'a very neatly contrived manoeuvre'.[23] The representative of the *Liverpool Courier* managed to get close enough to observe Crippen's pale, thin face and the stubbly growth of a sandy moustache.[24]

Dew was 'in the best of spirits' upon his return to England. Not only had he dramatically captured Crippen and Le Neve; he had left behind the American journalists and was reunited with the English media, who reported:

His [Dew's] comments on the methods of the American journalists with whom he came in contact were highly amusing, and there was no little feeling in his tone when he remarked, 'It is quite a pleasure to meet English Pressmen, for they are gentlemen.'[25]

Magistrates and Coroners

... when she thought of the dreadful wickedness of
that little American doctor who dismembered his wife
the tears actually came into her eyes.
George Orwell, Coming up for Air

The train carrying Dew, Crippen and Le Neve from Liverpool arrived at London's Euston Station, where Crippen was greeted by boos and jeers from a waiting crowd who clearly loathed him as much as the Canadian public had. He and Le Neve were whisked off to Bow Street Police Court for two nights, until the Monday sitting of the court, when they were to appear before Mr Marsham, whom Dew described as 'a giant of a man with a ruddy face and an old-fashioned style of dress which gave him the appearance of a prosperous farmer. One of the finest gentlemen I have ever met.'

An anonymous Bow Street gaoler later recalled Crippen's time there:

[Crippen] looked tired and jaded, completely worn out, but conscious of the great ordeal which he knew he must face once he was in the grip of the police.

I spoke to him about his journey, and he told me how glad he was in one way to have all the anxiety ended. But he never complained through all the monotony of the police-court proceedings, which lasted for many weeks. He was very keen to know what kind of treatment he might expect in Brixton Prison, and afterwards during his various visits to Bow Street he never once complained of the routine or the food or sleeping accommodation. In fact, he declared that the governor and warders did everything possible for his comfort and convenience. He had a great partiality for tea, and he always looked forward to this each afternoon of the Magisterial hearing.[1]

Dew breathed a sigh of relief after handing the prisoners over. He had achieved his goal of capturing the fugitive Dr Crippen and Ethel Le Neve. While his 'personal responsibility was over', he knew that his connection with the case was far from ended. However, there was a brief period of celebration as Dew received a letter of congratulation from Chief Constable Bigham, and was enthusiastically received by Sir Melville

Macnaghten. Dew's 'best welcome of all' came from his family, whom he rushed home to see.

Crippen's solicitor, Arthur Newton, was a well known figure in legal circles. Travers Humphreys described him as 'a public school boy, very good-looking, with a charming manner and considerable gifts of advocacy based upon an extensive knowledge of the world rather than a knowledge of law'.[2] He added that Newton possessed a 'scheming brain', and usually got what he wanted 'by fair means or otherwise'.[3]

Newton had been avidly following the story of the North London murder in the newspapers, when he realised the missing suspect was a former client of his. Crippen had failed to make much of an impression on Newton back in 1906, when he had represented him in a trivial matter. Newton remembered Crippen as a 'short, insignificant figure, with weak, goggly eyes, protected by gold-rimmed glasses, and a rather hesitating manner'.[4]

Newton was reunited with Crippen at Bow Street. As a lawyer, Newton was naturally familiar with the Bow Street Police Court, but being a somewhat unscrupulous character, he also had a more intimate knowledge of that establishment than most, for in 1890 he had been tried there on charges of conspiracy to defeat the ends of justice. Newton had attempted to prevent three telegraph boys from testifying that Lord Arthur Somerset had committed acts of gross indecency with them at a male brothel in Cleveland Street, London. He was ultimately sentenced to six weeks' imprisonment.[5]

His client had aged markedly. The first words Crippen said were, 'I want you thoroughly to understand, Mr Newton, that my first anxiety is for Miss Le Neve. She is dearer to me than anything in the world, and, if it becomes necessary, I would sacrifice myself to save her. She knew nothing whatever about the matter.' Newton replied, 'I am assuming, Dr. Crippen, that you are quite innocent.' Crippen responded 'Certainly. But don't forget, whatever happens, your first thought is to be for Miss Le Neve.' Newton went to see Le Neve, whose appearance came as something of a disappointment, for '[s]he was not a beautiful woman, and I could see nothing in her to account for her strong hold on the affections of Crippen. She completely convinced me that she knew nothing, and that she believed that Belle Elmore had gone to America, as Crippen had told her.'[6]

A crowd numbering hundreds had gathered outside the court, many of them women and young girls. Only a handful managed to gain entrance, for the court was a small one that lacked a public gallery. The spectators had to stand behind a barrier at the back of the court. Dew was amazed at the crowds the case attracted everywhere, commenting, 'No other murderer's personality had been quite so magnetic as that of Dr. Crippen.'

It was a puzzle to Dew why people should wait for hours for the merest glimpse of a prisoner or the chance of a scant scrap of information. Dew had 'never been able to understand the mentality of such people', and personally 'detested the atmosphere and surroundings of criminal courts, and always made a point of getting away at the first possible moment'.

This initial hearing was a formality, in order to have Crippen and Le Neve remanded until a later date. Travers Humphreys, representing the Director of Public Prosecutions, asked Mr Marsham if he would adjourn the hearing for eight days, to which he readily consented. Humphreys also pointed out that the likelihood was that Ethel Le Neve would only be charged as accessory after the fact. Walter Dew, sporting a healthy sun-tan from his ocean voyage, gave evidence concerning his arrest of Crippen and Le Neve, and their return voyage aboard the *Megantic*. He entered the witness box and 'proceeded to open his Gladstone bag and produce a notebook and documents. He gave his evidence in so quiet a tone as to be almost inaudible at times in some parts of the court.'[7]

After the hearing the waiting crowds surged forward, towards the public door, desperate to hear of what had happened, while more than one cinematograph camera recorded the events. The prisoners were hastily removed from the court by a side door, to be taken away by taxicab. Crippen's destination was Brixton Prison, while Le Neve was taken to Holloway Prison.[8]

The amazing interest the case was attracting, both at home and abroad, was partly explained in a *Times* editorial:

It is due in part to the fact that Scotland Yard took the whole world into its confidence with unprecedented thoroughness. It enlisted not only the services of the official police of other countries, but also the formidable though unofficial detective service supplied by the extensive publicity afforded by the Press.

The other reason for the keen interest with which this chase has been followed is the unprecedentedly large part played in the capture by wireless telegraphy. The ordinary telegraph has enormously increased the difficulties of fugitives from justice. It has frequently confronted an escaping criminal with a detective and a warrant just when he thought that he had baffled pursuit. But it could never have accomplished what has been done in this case by wireless telegraphy.[9]

Filson Young, who edited *Trial of Hawley Harvey Crippen* for the Notable British Trials series, published in 1920, proffered another explanation of the appeal of the case. This was the paradox of Crippen's character. On the one hand, he was utterly devoted to Ethel Le Neve, and regarded as a most kindly and mild-mannered man by those who knew him. On the other hand, he had just been arrested for a cold-blooded murder that was leaving the newspaper-reading public aghast. Young observed, 'There are two sides to the story – the physical, which is sordid, dreadful, and revolting, and the spiritual, which is good and heroic.' Furthermore, it was the newspaper 'silly season'. Summer was traditionally a quiet period for the press, so they used the Crippen story to fill their pages, allowing their readers to know everything about the hunt for Crippen, while Crippen and Le Neve were blissfully unaware of what was happening.

Dew had his own theory to explain the unusual interest the case was attracting:

> Think of the circumstances! The callous way in which the Doctor killed his actress wife, and the mutilation of her remains; the part played by Miss Ethel Le Neve, the 'other woman' in the case; the flight of the couple with the girl dressed as a boy, and their dramatic arrest on the other side of the Atlantic.

While Dew had been chasing Crippen and Le Neve across the Atlantic, investigations into the events at Hilldrop Crescent continued unabated. The drains and sewers of No. 39 were checked for human remains, but none were found. The building, now under the constant supervision of a plain-clothes officer, had become something of a tourist attraction, with scores of people filing past all day, while those with cameras took commemorative snapshots.

A statement was made at the end of July by metal-worker Frederick Evans, who lived in Brecknock Road, Camden Town. Evans was 'fairly sure' that it was on the night of 4 February that he was returning home from the Orange Tree public house in the Euston Road. At around 1.20 a.m. he heard 'a terrible screech which terminated with a long dragging whine', which emanated from the direction of Hilldrop Crescent. Evans' first thought was of the Whitechapel murders, despite the fact that it was over two decades since the case that had caused Dew such misery. Evans' back garden was some 3 to 4 yards away from that of the Crippens, and they frequently used to hear Cora singing. The Sunday after he had heard the screams Evans smelled burning from the garden of No. 39, which continued for several days.

Crippen had certainly been busy burning something. Islington dustman William Curtis recalled that, for three weeks from mid-February, he had to remove an unusually large amount of rubbish from 39 Hilldrop Crescent. The first week it consisted of burnt paper and women's clothing. In later weeks he removed quantities of a light white ash that was not paper ash, nor was it from a fire grate. Curtis was given a 3*d* tip by a woman he thought might have been Ethel Le Neve.

A similar story emerged from the Crippens' neighbour at 36 Hilldrop Crescent, Franziska Hachenberger. She was 'certain that when I heard the screams at the back of Hilldrop Crescent, [it] was either on the early morning of the 1st or 2nd of February last . . . It was an awful scream, it was not easily forgotten.' Her father had also heard the scream, which he thought had happened at around 2 a.m.

Other people in the neighbourhood reported strange goings on. Lena Lyons and her lodger May Pole lived at 46 Brecknock Road, which overlooked 39 Hilldrop Crescent. They both thought they heard two gunshots around seven o'clock one morning, either at the end of January or the beginning of February.

The re-adjourned magistrates' court hearing took place on 6 September. Dew arrived wearing a long grey overcoat and carrying a brown leather bag. The court was so crowded that he had to search for a vacant seat.[10] Detailed medical evidence was put forward, firstly by Dr Pepper, who thought that the remains found at Hilldrop Crescent were those of a human female in the prime of life and stout of build. The remains, he said, bore signs of an operation in the form of a scar.

Dr William Willcox, senior Home Office scientific analyst, told the court that he had detected traces of an alkaloid poison in all of the organs he had been given to examine. He determined through his tests that the poison was hyoscine, amounting to just under one-third of a grain.[11] Hyoscine was usually given in doses of one one-hundredth or one two-hundredth of a grain as a last resort to quieten someone who was delirious, suffering from delirium tremens or acute forms of insanity. Willcox thought that whoever had given the victim the fatal dose of hyoscine must have administered a very large dose for so much to have remained in the body after such a long period.

It had been ascertained that on 19 January 1910 Dr Crippen had purchased five grains of hydrobromide of hyoscine at Messrs. Lewis and Burroughs chemists, in New Oxford Street, saying it was for 500 individual doses. This was a vast quantity, and there was no reason why someone in Crippen's position would require it under normal circumstances. The poison was virtually tasteless, and could easily be put into food. Once consumed in a large dose the poison would almost instantly put a person into a stupor, and possibly make them delirious. They would then become paralysed and comatose, before death followed within hours.

Dew briefly appeared and gave more evidence, and produced some jewellery he had found on Crippen's person, before the case was adjourned until the next day. The large crowd outside the court booed and shouted at the prisoners when they left.[12]

The next day Walter Dew took to the witness box once again to tell the court about his initial enquiries and interviews with Crippen and Le Neve at Albion House. His evidence was interrupted for over an hour when children's cases were being held in the second court. The Juvenile Offenders' Act provided that when the Children's Court was sitting no charge against an adult could be heard in the same court.[13]

Between magistrates' hearings the coroner's inquest was resumed at the Central Library in Holloway Road. However, this new, larger venue made it difficult for everyone present to hear the evidence being given. Evidence was heard from several members of the Music Hall Ladies' Guild before a further adjournment of one week was given.[14]

Amongst those watching the proceedings at the next sitting of the magistrates' court on 14 September was actor H.B. Irving, the son of the late Sir Henry Irving.[15] At the hearing the evidence was of a more gruesome nature, as Dr Pepper gave a detailed description of what Dew called 'those terrible remains':

At the examination on July 15 he found one portion of skin 11in. by 9in., with some subcutaneous fat. The lower portion of the piece of skin was in his opinion from the upper portion of the abdominal wall, and the upper portion from the chest. There was also a piece consisting of the covering of the lower part of the back and buttocks, a large piece from the upper part of the back, and a further piece measuring 7in. by 6in., which was from the lower part of the abdominal wall, and upon the skin of which there was a mark. There was also a piece of skin 15in. long, with fat and muscle attached, from the hip, and another piece of skin, with fat and muscle, from the thigh. There were several other smaller pieces. There was nothing except the hair which could be identified as coming from the scalp, or from the forearms, from the leg below the knee, from the hands, or from the feet. There was no trace either of the genital organs or of bone. There was one large mass, which comprised the liver, the stomach, the gullet, the lower 2½ in. of the windpipe, two lungs, the heart intact, the diaphragm, the kidneys, the pancreas, the spleen, all the small and the greater part of the large intestines. All this mass was removed in one piece.

Pepper was asked whether he thought the mutilations could have been done by someone without anatomical knowledge or training. Pepper was sure that 'he must have had real anatomical knowledge or have been accustomed to the process of evisceration of animals'.[16]

The penultimate hearing took place two days later. Crippen's lawyer Arthur Newton questioned Dew about his intention to arrest Crippen. Dew explained that at their first meeting at Albion House he had no intention of arresting him. If he had he would not have put a number of questions to Crippen, which he did.

Newton	Did the question of whether you arrested him or not depend on the answers he gave to your questions?
Dew	The question of arresting him did not enter my mind. I went there for information.
Newton	From 'Dr.' Crippen's manner and from the details which he gave you at that time did you believe his statement?
Dew	No, not altogether.
Newton	Did you in substance believe it?
Dew	No, otherwise I should not have searched his house.
Newton	The search took place with his consent?
Dew	It did. I could not have gone to the house without his consent.
Newton	At any rate, after the statement he had given you and after the search did it then occur to you to arrest him?
Dew	I could not arrest him.
Newton	On the face of it, speaking generally, did you not at the time consider the statement a reasonable one?
Dew	No, I could not say I did not absolutely think that any crime had been committed. I thought it my duty to continue my inquiries, and I did so because I was not satisfied with his statement. I wanted to keep a perfectly open mind and to satisfy everybody – both 'Dr.' Crippen and the public.[17]

The final hearing at Bow Street magistrates' court took place on 21 September. The crowds still milled around, awaiting the appearance of the prisoners. On this day Le Neve was taken to court in a four-wheeled cab, accompanied by a warder. She was spotted by a group of women who 'screamed out at the prisoner, and one of the knot pursued the cab to the gates of the station, shrieking opprobrious epithets. Miss Le Neve hid her face behind an open umbrella.'[18]

While that was going on an auction was being held, in Oxford Street, of nearly 100 lots of furniture from 39 Hilldrop Crescent, as Crippen was desperate for money to pay his legal fees and, remarkably, considering the position he was in, anxious to pay the landlord of 39 Hilldrop Crescent the back rent he owed. The sale-room was crowded, and all of the 1,000 catalogues had been snapped up an hour before the sale began. It was a good-natured sale, with much banter and flash-photography taking place. Some lots achieved higher prices than expected, thanks to their infamous association. The highest bid was 14 guineas for a cottage pianoforte.[19]

Dew took the stand for the last time in the magistrates' court witness box to tell the court of some measurements he had made at the request of Dr Pepper, with regard to the dimensions of the cellar of 39 Hilldrop Crescent. In summing up his decision the magistrate, Sir Albert de Rutzen (who had replaced Mr Marsham), concluded that there was no doubt whatsoever that Crippen should stand trial for the charge against him. The case of Le Neve was more difficult. However, he considered there was enough evidence of Le Neve's complicity (which could have meant only that she knew of the murder, rather than having taken part in it) to allow a jury to decide her fate. They were, therefore, committed to trial. Arthur Newton said that both Crippen and Le Neve would plead not guilty when the time came.

Crippen's decision to plead not guilty may have sealed his fate, for there was an alternative. As soon as Newton had been retained by Crippen, he had wanted to offer the brief to Edward Marshall Hall, a charismatic parliamentarian whose forays into the criminal courts often attracted publicity. He had a commanding presence and 'a passion for showing off, tempered by an attractive simplicity . . . combined with a love of the marvellous, which made him on questions of fact somewhat of an impressionist. But there was about his personality something which even his most austere critics found hard to resist.'[20]

Marshall Hall was convinced he could prove Crippen's innocence of the charge of murder if the accused man would only admit to everything except intent to murder, thus resulting in a conviction for manslaughter. Marshall Hall's biographer set forth the potential defence:

Crippen, in order to spend the night with his paramour, whether at home or elsewhere, drugged his wife with a new and rare drug of which he knew little, and of which he had lately purchased five grains. To be on the safe side he gave her a large dose, which turned out to be an overdose; or perhaps his continual dosing of her necessitated a big dose to ensure unconsciousness. In the morning he found his wife dead, and in a panic he made away with the remainder of the hyoscine, and with all a surgeon's skill cut up her body, rising above his inexperience with the inspiration of despair. Then, hurriedly wrapping the flesh in an old pyjama jacket of his own, he buried it in quicklime, thinking it would thus be destroyed; as a matter of fact the quicklime had the reverse effect, and preserved the remains. Then he proceeded to write to a number of his friends a transparent tissue of lies. Crippen admitted that Miss Le Neve had slept at Hilldrop Crescent on February 2nd. Might she not have slept there on one or both of the previous nights, and frequently before that, while his wife was drugged with hyoscine and unconscious?

Unfortunately for Crippen, Marshall Hall was on holiday abroad throughout the magistrates' hearings, and Crippen had firmly instructed his solicitor that his plea would be not guilty. Marshall Hall knew that this 'would be disastrous'. He thought that Crippen would not have agreed to his line of defence anyway, as it could have made Le Neve an accomplice if she had been in the house with him as Cora Crippen lay dying or dead. Crippen would never allow any suggestion of guilt on the part of Le Neve.[21] Newton would have to find a defence team who were willing to try to convince a jury that Crippen knew nothing of the remains found at 39 Hilldrop Crescent.

At another sitting of the coroner's court, on 19 September, Dr Willcox repeated his evidence concerning hyoscine. After Dew had been cross-examined by Newton about his initial search of Hilldrop Crescent, a juror rose and said he would like to ask Dew why it was that he did not have any means to stop Crippen fleeing. The coroner said that was not a question for the jury. Dew responded by saying that he was quite happy to answer it for 'many attacks have been made on me. I shall only be too willing to answer.' The coroner reiterated that the question was not appropriate. Dew said that he had a perfect answer to the juryman's question. There was no question of a crime having been committed at that time. However, the coroner quashed the enquiry and dismissed Dew from the witness box.[22]

Dew was interviewed by the *Penny Illustrated Paper* after the abortive question from the juror. Dew explained that he 'wished to give the information to a juror who was evidently unacquainted with the whole facts of the case. It was with no desire to offer an explanation to the public in answer to the scurrilous attacks – personal attacks – that have been made upon me in various sections of the Press. The police can afford to take no notice of such attacks.'[23]

On 23 September Dew visited Bath to conduct a lengthy interview with a Mrs Jackson, who lived in Great Stanhope Street. Mrs Jackson kept a lodging house for music hall artists, and Cora Crippen had stayed there in 1900 and 1902. During her 1902 visit Cora had told Jackson that she had undergone an operation in America on her womb. Dew was not impressed with Jackson, whose husband had served a three-month prison sentence fourteen years previously for keeping a brothel in Oxford Street. He had been defended by none other than Arthur Newton. Immediately after being seen by Dew, Jackson ran to the papers to tell them about her interview.

Meanwhile, at Brixton prison Arthur Newton's young clerk let slip to the chief warder that Newton had brought an agreement for Crippen to sign, which sold the rights for the story of his life to an American newspaper. This was the means by which Crippen was going to pay his legal fees (it has also been suggested that it would have helped Newton pay off his horse-racing debts). There was more chicanery involved. Newton had held several interviews with Crippen, supposedly in order to prepare his defence, but one of Newton's clerks had also been present and taken down Crippen's life story in shorthand. The interviews took place within sight, but out of hearing, of the prison staff.

The matter was put before Winston Churchill. The Home Secretary considered that there had already been such immense publicity and sensationalism surrounding the case that the publication of Crippen's memoirs could hardly add to it. Therefore, with regard to the publication of Crippen's life story he ordered that they should 'not fetter the accused on grounds of taste', and that, as the money would be used for his defence, the story could be sold. Newton's misuse of his position was a different matter altogether. Churchill advised that Newton must be censured for his improper conduct in using the interviews granted for legal business covertly to obtain a narrative for publication.

Another of Newton's clerks had interviewed Crippen, and was struck by the man's character:

> And yet, feeling convinced that he was a liar and a murderer, I could not help feeling sorry for him. Looking at him and listening to his slow, hesitating, nervous speech I simply could not visualise him as a cold-blooded assassin.
>
> There he was, a little sandy man with drooping moustache and gold-rimmed glasses, blinking at us and stammering with thin fingers playing at his upper lip.
>
> You would have taken him for a timid, kindly little shop-walker, ready to serve you with the utmost politeness, but always, in the back of his mind, thinking of his neat little suburban home and the neat little wife waiting to greet him there.
>
> Always apologetic, always deferential, he contrived to remain aloof from the actual drama and terror of the case. To all outward appearance he might have been a client slightly perturbed at the prospect of a summons for riding a bicycle without a light.[24]

Dew giving evidence at the coroner's inquest. *(Illustrated Police News)*

Scotland Yard's wanted poster for the fugitives Crippen and Le Neve. *(Notable British Trials)*

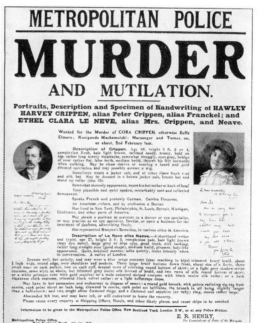

Dew (represented as Sherlock Holmes) being mocked in the American press for not preventing Crippen's escape. *(Cleveland Plain Dealer)*

Dew boarding the *Laurentic* in pursuit of Crippen. *(Illustrated Police News)*

Captain Kendall observing the 'Robinsons' aboard the *Montrose. (Illustrated Police News)*

The *Montrose*'s wireless in action.
(Illustrated Police News)

A typically inaccurate depiction of Dew arresting Crippen and Le Neve. *(The Fifty Most Amazing Crimes)*

Dew escorting Crippen off the *Megantic* at Liverpool. *(Jon Ogan)*

Crippen and Le Neve appearing at Bow Street magistrates' court. *(Jon Ogan)*

The Central Criminal Court where Crippen and Le Neve stood trial. *(Hertfordshire Archives and Local Studies Stg 00016)*

Judge Lord Alverstone. *(Notable British Trials)*

Richard Muir, counsel for the Crown against Crippen. *(Notable British Trials)*

Alfred Tobin, counsel for Crippen's defence. *(Notable British Trials)*

Dew outside the Old Bailey during Crippen's trial. *(Stewart P. Evans)*

Dew outside the Old Bailey. *(Stewart P. Evans)*

F.E. Smith, counsel for Ethel Le Neve's defence. *(Author's collection)*

Dr Crippen's execution at Pentonville Prison.
(Illustrated Police News)

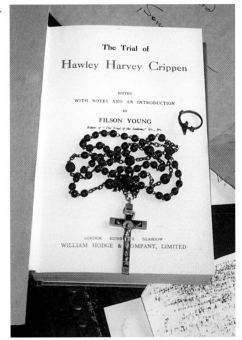

The rosary held by Crippen and the ring he
wore when he was executed. *(Richard
Whittington-Egan)*

Walter Dew in his retirement. *(Jon Ogan)*

Walter Dew at the gate of the 'Wee Hoose' in Worthing. *(Thomson's Weekly News)*

The coroner's inquest to establish what caused the death associated with the remains finally concluded on 26 September. In his summing up, the coroner addressed several questions that the case had raised. Were the remains human? Yes. What was the sex of the remains? The medical evidence could give no decisive opinion. What was the identity of the remains? Unknown, but the fact that they were found at 39 Hilldrop Crescent, combined with Cora Crippen's disappearance and Dr Crippen's subsequent actions, was very suggestive that they were those of Cora Crippen. The jury left to consider their verdict at 4.37 p.m. They returned at 5.20, and returned a verdict of murder against Dr Crippen. They were of the opinion that the remains were those of Cora Crippen, and that she had died as a result of poisoning by hyoscine.[25] This meant he could now be committed for trial.

The name of Bruce Miller had been raised at the very outset of the investigation, when Crippen had told Dew that he believed his wife had left him for Miller. Now residing in East Chicago, Miller appeared to be a little anxious that the impending trial of Dr Crippen would lead to his relationship with Cora Crippen being publicly examined. Miller had already been interviewed in America by the Pinkerton detective agency, at the request of Superintendent Froest. In a personal letter to Walter Dew the retired music hall performer seemed very reluctant to get any more involved than he had to:

Yesterday I made a short statement to the Pinkerton Agcy, and while I do not wish to ignore them in any way, under the circumstances I do not think a personal letter will do any harm.

Miss Elmore and I were the best of friends and I have watched the case with the most intense interest, never suspecting that I would be mentioned in it in any way, until the newspaper men came to see me and then I said as little as possible. However there has been little discression [*sic*] used in quoting my statements, though they have said nothing that will really do any harm.

If Dr Crippen has only made the charge that Miss Elmore eloped with me, I do not see that I would be of any service in the case, as I have not seen her for six years, and as I have been in this place during the past four years, proof of this could be had without my presence.

If on the other hand he makes any attempt to defame her character on my account, there is nothing he can say that I am not willing to face him in, but I do not think he will make any further charges because he well knew of our friendship, and, while he never took the pains to meet me even when he was in the house, and has delivered some of my letters to her in person, and that I have always written to her at their residence and have often recd a reply, from the provences [*sic*], some one must have forwarded them to her, and they were undoubtedly in his possession first.

Besides I have photographs of Miss Elmore that he took of her with a kodak, and according to her statements, he knew that I have them. Again while I was playing in the provinces, I was taken ill, and wrote to her and mentioned what the trouble was and in her reply she told me that the Doctor told her to tell me to take certain remedies.

Now, while I will acknowledge that I thought a great deal of her, and we were the very best of friends, she was always a lady to me in every respect and I always treated her as a gentleman should.

As you no doubt was one of the first to go through the house, you no doubt found my little cards, candy boxes &c. with my name on, and when I left there were two of my photos enlarged and hanging on the wall in her parlor [*sic*]. Now that Dr. Crippen knows all this I do not think that when his trial comes up that he will mention my name again, and I do not think that you will want me in the case either.

If I am wanted, I regret that on account of a big real estate deal that I have on, that my thirty days option will not be up till October 14th and it will perhaps take a few days to close up after that, it looks to me at the present time, impossible to get away before about the 20th of October, but if things progress favourably and I can leave before, I will do so.

Financially, I can hardly afford to leave, as I will have to drop my fall work in the way of building and wait until Spring, and I am making about $10,000.00 a year, you can see what that means to me. However I am willing and ready to stand up and defend the character of a most honourable woman, and a good friend.

Now, if I should come I would like to come into the country incog. And have a consultation with yourself and the prosecuting Attorney before anyone is aware that I am there, then I will act strictly to your advice.

You have won my admiration in this case to such an extent that I trust [you] as a friend, and know that you will protect me in this to the best of your ability.

Before the trial of Dr Crippen and Ethel Le Neve took place, the issue of the reward for his capture had to be resolved. Captain Kendall of the *Montrose* had made a claim for the £250 that was offered. Dew thought that Kendall's claim could not be disputed, as he was the first person to recognise Crippen and Le Neve as the fugitives, and he had immediately reported his suspicions. Dew had carefully questioned others on board the *Montrose* and was satisfied that Kendall was entitled to the bounty. Indeed, no one else aboard the *Montrose* had claimed the reward for themselves, despite it being well known that it was on offer.

There was an element of doubt, as the deputy coroner had received a letter, signed 'One of the Public', which said that a steward on the *Montrose* who had formerly been a barman at the Brecknock Tavern, Camden Road, which it was suggested Crippen had frequented, had been the first to realise that 'Mr Robinson' was none other than Dr Crippen. Dew had noticed this story appear in a couple of periodicals 'of no particular standing', and dismissed the story. As far as he was concerned the money rightfully belonged to Captain Kendall, who duly collected a cheque at Scotland Yard from Mr Mann of the Scotland Yard Receiver's office.

Dew was also the recipient of a reward. He was commended for 'his conduct of the arrest & subsequent proceedings in Canada, when his work was I know done under trying conditions. The discovery of the remains in the cellar was also an example of this most careful investigation.' Dew received a £4 reward (his wages at the time were £6 14*s* a week).

Now, at long last, the remains found at Hilldrop Crescent could be laid to rest. At the final hearing of the coroner's inquest the jury had concluded that the remains were those of Cora Crippen, otherwise Belle Elmore. It was now late September, and the remains were causing concern to the Public Health Department of Islington, who held them in their mortuary. They soon wrote to Melville Macnaghten explaining that the *disjecta membra* 'are likely to cause a serious nuisance'.

It was up to Dew to sort the matter out. He had received the order for burial from the deputy coroner, and first checked with Dr Pepper, Dr Marshall and the Director of Public Prosecutions, to make sure they had no further need of the remains. They did not. Crippen's solicitor Arthur Newton also had no objection to the burial, but perhaps unsurprisingly 'demurred somewhat to their being buried in the name of Belle Elmore or Cora Crippen'. No doubt it might have helped his cause if the remains had not been positively identified, but the coroner's burial order clearly stated: '[I do] hereby authorise the burial of the remains of the body of Cora Crippen alias Belle Elmore late of 39 Hilldrop Crescent, Islington, age 34 years.'

Cora Crippen's old friends of the Music Hall Ladies' Guild took charge of the funeral. They desired a private ceremony and did not want the press to find out their plans; so they arranged a cortege consisting of a hearse and two mourning coaches, which would leave the undertaker's in Camden Road at 2.45 p.m. on 11 October and take a direct route to St Pancras Roman Catholic Cemetery in Finchley.

15

Rex *v.* Crippen

> The defendant is an extraordinary man.
>
> *Lord Alverstone*

The trial of Hawley Harvey Crippen was held at the Old Bailey, and lasted five days, from Tuesday 18 October to Saturday 22 October 1910. The presiding judge was Richard 'Dicky' Webster, the Right Honourable Lord Alverstone, Lord Chief Justice of England. Alverstone had been made Queen's Counsel in 1878, and then became Attorney General in 1885 under Prime Minister Lord Salisbury, a position he held three times. Alverstone had also been the Member of Parliament for the Isle of Wight, until he became a judge. It was said that it was unlikely that 'in thirty-two years at the bar any man ever had more work to do, or earned more money'. In 1900 he was appointed Master of the Rolls and made a Privy Councillor, before being created Baron Alverstone, and then made Lord Chief Justice of England.[1] He was, according to Dew, 'one of the kindliest of men'. Alverstone's view of the Crippen case was that it was 'an extraordinary one'.[2] Representing the Crown were Richard Muir, Travers Humphreys and Samuel Ingleby Oddie, all acting under instruction from the Director of Public Prosecutions, Sir Charles Mathews.

When Crippen learned that he was to face the ferocious and daunting Richard Muir, he said despairingly, 'It is most unfortunate that he is against me. I wish it had been anyone else but him. I fear the worst.'[3] Thorough, grim and remorseless, Muir worked relentlessly in preparing his cases, leaving nothing to chance. Samuel Ingleby Oddie worked in Muir's chambers, as well as acting as a coroner for West London. He described Muir as

> an indefatigable worker. His work was his life. He had no amusements and no relaxation. He always took work home every night, and after his evening meal and a short snooze over the paper, he drew up his chair to the table and set to work on his briefs, at which he continued nightly up to one and two in the morning. Yet he was always the first to arrive in the chambers and the last to leave.[4]

Muir was sure that Crippen was guilty, and built up an impression of the man:

> He is not the ordinary type of man one would expect to commit a murder and then to cut up the body of his victim and dispose of it. Rather is he the sort of man I would expect to find running a successful swindle. He has a certain amount of craftiness and cunning, as well as considerable self-assurance.
>
> There is no doubt that his life with his wife had been one of unending misery, and apparently he found a good deal of relief and a certain stolen happiness with Ethel Le Neve.
>
> I suppose one cannot look upon the cutting up of his wife's body as being such an outrageous or aggravating feature as it might have been with anyone else. He had more than a passing knowledge of medicine and surgery and to such a person, no doubt, the dissecting of a body would not create such a revolting impression as it would in an ordinary individual.[5]

Travers Humphreys was on holiday in Filey with his wife and two sons when he was summoned back to London by the Director of Public Prosecutions. Humphreys was certain that Crippen had murdered his wife, yet he 'could not help feeling something almost like pity for the henpecked little doctor'.[6] He believed that Le Neve may have had 'an inkling that something serious had happened' when she was asked to disguise herself as a boy, but thought that had she known the full facts she would have immediately left Crippen.[7] Despite the incredible public interest the case was creating, Humphreys thought that the evidence against Crippen was so overwhelming that, from a legal point of view, it would be 'of little interest for the lawyer'.[8]

Ingleby Oddie was given the junior brief for the Crown, chosen over Cecil Mercer because of his medical experience. As it was a poisoning case he did not rate Crippen's chances, for his attitude was that 'the average Englishman is a decent sort of fellow who does not like homicide and looks upon secret poisoning as a low-down dirty game, and indeed it is'.[9]

Muir was unhappy that the police had allowed Crippen to flee England in the first place, and felt that since Dew had brought his prisoners back he had been less than energetic in helping to put together the case against them. He went so far as to suggest Dew 'must be suffering from sleepy sickness'. This view was echoed by Travers Humphreys, who recalled, 'We made more than one attempt through Dew to obtain further information, but without success.' One of Humphreys' biographers wrote that Muir and Humphreys 'did much of the work usually done by the police'. Another wrote that the detective was suffering from an inflated ego upon his return to England.[10]

Humphreys explained his grievances with Dew's investigations. He began by complimenting Dew on his enquiries before Crippen's arrest. The initial statement he had taken from Crippen was admirably done, and was 'thorough and complete; in fact, it took the form of a very effective cross-examination. Moreover, it was probably the fear that further investigation by this highly inquisitive officer would lead to a thorough search of the premises that caused Crippen to lose his nerve and flee the country.' However, Dew's 'subsequent lack of energy must be animadverted upon'.[11] Humphreys visited 39 Hilldrop Crescent, and was surprised to see that Cora Crippen's furs had remained at the house rather than being removed as evidence, and made exhibits for the trial. Humphreys was unsatisfied with Dew's explanation of why he had left the furs at the house, and instructed him to take away the furs, as he was convinced that the jury would see them as evidence that Cora had not left for America, in the middle of winter.[12]

The accusations of Dew's tardiness were disputed by the Director of Public Prosecution's office, who sent Macnaghten a letter on 26 October thanking Dew and Mitchell for 'the unfailing and valuable services which they rendered to my staff, and to my Counsel, both in the investigation of these cases before the Magistrate, and at the trial of them at the Central Criminal Court'. But as both Muir and Humphreys commented on the accusations about Dew's tardiness and supplied specific examples, there may have been something to them.

Acting for Crippen's defence were Alfred Tobin, Huntley Jenkins and Mr Roome, who were instructed by Crippen's solicitor Arthur Newton. Tobin had been called to the Bar in 1880 and joined the Northern Assize circuit. He was clever, industrious and experienced. His 'cheerful and plausible manner made him an effective defender of prisoners',[13] but he was now facing a difficult task in arguing that Crippen was not guilty of the murder of his wife.

As ever, the case was causing huge public interest and excitement. The court had been overwhelmed by applications for tickets to attend the trial. Several thousand letters were received, most requesting two tickets, but as only about one hundred seats were available each day the majority of applicants were disappointed. Among the hopeful applicants were many titled and theatrical people who claimed to have known Cora Crippen.[14]

Crippen and Le Neve were tried separately, and Crippen stood trial first. Day one of the trial began with the Clerk of the Court reading out the charge. 'Hawley Harvey Crippen, you are indicted and also charged on the coroner's inquisition with the wilful murder of Cora Crippen on the 1st February last. Are you guilty or not guilty?' Crippen replied, 'Not guilty, my lord.'

Richard Muir made the opening statement for the Crown. Muir's biographer described him as 'essentially a logician: he had no patience with high-flown rhetoric, and he made it an invariable practice to open his cases so that a man of the meanest intelligence could easily understand what they were about'.[15] In his opening speech the plain-speaking Muir suggested a financial motive for the murder, in addition to a 'romantic' one:

> The position, therefore, was this – his affection fixed upon Ethel Le Neve, and himself desirous of establishing closer relations with that young woman; the physical presence of his wife an obstacle to those relations; the fact that he had no money another obstacle. If Belle Elmore died both those obstacles would be removed, because Belle Elmore's money, and property which could be converted into money, would enable him to keep Ethel Le Neve, which at that time he was unable to do.

Muir continued:

> Her friends said she was a good correspondent; but from the moment that Mr. and Mrs. Martinetti left the house in the early morning of 1st February she passed out of the world which knew her as completely as if she were dead. She left behind her everything she would have left if she had died – money, jewels, furs, clothes, home, and husband. The prisoner made up his mind that she had left never to return. He at once began to convert her property, and on 12th March Ethel Le Neve, who had been seen wearing a brooch and furs belonging to Belle Elmore, went permanently to live with him at 39 Hilldrop Cresent. Crippen was therefore quite certain that his wife would never return.

Muir then raised the question of why Crippen felt the need to flee the country if his statement to Dew had been correct, and his wife were still alive. Crippen had not so far offered any explanation. Then there was the question of who, other than Crippen, had the opportunity to bury the remains in the cellar, and why they would have been buried there if the death had been a natural one.

Most of the first three days of the trial consisted of evidence for the prosecution. An uncomfortable Bruce Miller had been given a first-class

passage from America to England. He testified that he had not seen Cora
Crippen since April 1904, but that they corresponded occasionally. Tobin
hoped to establish that Cora and Miller had been lovers, thus making it
seem feasible that she would have left Crippen to join Miller in America:

Tobin	Did you ever tell her that you loved her?
Miller	Well, I do not know that I ever put it in that way.
Tobin	Did you indicate to her that you did love her?
Miller	She always understood it that way, I suppose.
Tobin	Then you did love her, I presume?
Miller	I did not mean to say that. I did not exactly love her; I thought a great deal of her as far as friendship was concerned. She was a married lady, and we will let it end at that. It was a platonic friendship.
Tobin	Do you know the difference between friendship and love?
Miller	Yes.
Tobin	Were you more than a friend, sir?
Miller	I could not be more than a friend. She was a married lady and I was a married man.

Miller did admit to having kissed Cora, but insisted that he 'always
treated her as a gentleman, and never went any further'. While it is quite
possible, or even probable, that Cora and Bruce Miller had an affair,
there does not appear to be any explicit proof of the true nature of their
relationship. One early writer on the Crippen case neatly explained their
friendship, 'which, if not proved guilty, at least never was proved to be
innocent'.[16] There was, of course, no question about Dr Crippen's
infidelity with Le Neve.

Walter Dew had again been the first of the witnesses to arrive at the
Old Bailey on the second day of the trial, when he was called to give
evidence.[17] A watching journalist described Dew in the witness box as
'a slim, but well-built man, with fresh complexion, rather deeply-set
eyes, iron-grey moustache and hair'.[18] Dew spent more than two hours
in the witness box, and began by detailing the visit to Scotland Yard of
the Nashes, continuing up to his interviews with Crippen and Le Neve
on 8 July. At this point Travers Humphreys read out to the court the
lengthy statements that Crippen and Le Neve had given to Dew and
Mitchell.

As Dew's testimony continued, he explained how he had searched 39
Hilldrop Crescent in the presence of Crippen, and later, in his absence,
how further searching had led to the discovery of the human remains in

the cellar. A press observer described Dew's performance as 'very suave, perfectly cool, and self-possessed. Mr. Dew is scrupulously fair to the prisoner. He not only assents to Mr. Tobin's suggestion that he was not anxious to conceal anything, but he adds to it the perfectly voluntary statement that he did not attempt to.'[19] Dew concluded by briefly mentioning his chase and arrest of Crippen and Le Neve. He felt 'intense relief' when the time came for him to stand down; he had been gently questioned by Travers Humphreys. Despite the fact that he thought Dew had been resting on his laurels too much on his return to London, Humphreys was not about to say anything in court that disparaged the CID or Dew. He said nothing to contradict Dew's testimony, 'which suggested sleepless energy on his part and the highest efficiency'.[20]

Much of the trial was taken up by the detailed discussion of medical evidence – primarily, whether a piece of skin found upon the remains bore the mark of a scar or otherwise. This was a vital point, as it could go towards identifying the corpse as being Cora Crippen, who had an operational scar on her abdomen. This specimen was shown around the court, and was seen by a totally impassive Dr Crippen:

> The hideous moment in which the pieces of his dead wife's skin were handed round in a soup plate for inspection left him, alone of all the people in that crowded Court, quite unmoved. He peered at them with an intelligent curiosity as though they had been mere museum specimens. Not by one word or tremor did this frail little man betray any sign of his terrible position.

The first doctor to give evidence was Dr Pepper. Pepper thought that the remains had been buried in the cellar shortly after death, and that they had lain there for between four and eight months. When asked whether they could have been there prior to 21 September 1905, Pepper emphatically replied, 'Oh, no, absolutely impossible.' That was the date when the Crippens had moved into 39 Hilldrop Crescent, and would prove to be crucial later in the trial.

Pepper thought that the piece of skin in question was from the lower front part of the abdomen. He was convinced that the mark upon it was a scar, and a microscopic examination of it had confirmed his view. Tobin cross-examined Dr Pepper, and tried to establish that whoever dismembered the body was possessed of great anatomical and medical skill – perhaps to suggest that Crippen would not have had the requisite skill to have undertaken such a task. But Pepper would not allow himself to be led:

Tobin	As to the great dexterity you have already told us that was required to remove these organs in the way they were removed, it would require a really practised hand and eye, would it not?
Pepper	Certainly.
Tobin	A man frequently accustomed to dissect bodies or to conduct post-mortem examinations, or matters of that kind?
Pepper	No, a person who had previously done it, but not necessarily continuously. If a person had once learned how to do it he could do it.
Tobin	Suppose a student in the hospitals learnt it, and then there was a long lapse of time afterwards – fifteen years or so – surely the hand and eye have to be pretty well accustomed?
Pepper	I think he could do it quite as well after ten years as he could at the time. It is not a minute dissection; it is a particular kind of work.

On the third day of the trial Dr Bernard Henry Spilsbury, a pathologist at St Mary's Hospital, gave evidence. Spilsbury was later knighted and as Sir Bernard Spilsbury gave medical testimony at many important criminal trials. Spilsbury had also had his holiday interrupted by the Crippen case. He remained in London while his wife and baby went to Minehead without him.

Even from this early court appearance Dew gained the impression that Spilsbury 'was a man who knew what he was talking about'. He was 'a new, dominating voice in the courts of justice . . . Tall, handsome, well-dressed, a red carnation in his buttonhole, his bearing in his first capital case was as detached, imperturbable, and confident as it was when he was at the height of his fame.'[21] Spilsbury had made notes on the case, and concluded that Crippen had 'Skill in evisceration – acquisition of hyoscine – access to textbooks.' Cora Crippen was 'American. 35. Vivacious – good company – attractive – dressed well – jewellery – fast life. Private: very overbearing – bad temper.' As well as being the case that made his name, the Crippen case would be the one that made the most lasting impression on Spilsbury. Years after the trial he read, reread and annotated his copy of the Notable British Trials Crippen volume until the spine broke and the pages became loose.[22]

Spilsbury had been a student of Dr Pepper, but emphatically stated that this would have no bearing upon the evidence he was about to give. Spilsbury also thought the skin was from the lower abdomen, and he

clearly stated: 'that mark is undoubtedly an old operation scar.'
Spilsbury's opinions did differ from those of Pepper on the matter of the
killer's anatomical skill. He answered Tobin's questions coldly and
unemotionally:

Tobin	Dealing with the question of the remains, must the person who removed the viscera have been a person of very considerable dexterity?
Spilsbury	He must certainly have had considerable dexterity, yes.
Tobin	And must that removal have been done by somebody with a very considerable anatomical knowledge, or somebody accustomed to evisceration?
Spilsbury	Certainly some one having considerable anatomical knowledge.
Tobin	And accustomed to evisceration?
Spilsbury	Yes, one who has done a considerable amount of evisceration.

Next to testify was Dr Marshall, the police surgeon for the Kentish
Town Division, which contained Hilldrop Crescent. He concurred that
the skin was from the lower part of the abdominal wall, and stated, 'I
formed the opinion that it was a scar mark, and that is still my opinion.'

Crippen's defence produced their own medical experts, who
contradicted those who had testified that the mark on the skin was a scar.
Dr Gilbert Maitland Turnbull, the Director of the Pathological Institute
at the London Hospital, emphatically stated, 'it cannot possibly be a
scar'; but he conceded that the skin was from the lower abdomen.
Another expert for the defence, Dr Reginald Cecil Wall, said: 'In my
opinion it is not a scar.'

The medical evidence turned to the issue of the cause of death.
Dr William Willcox, the senior scientific adviser to the Home Office,
had tested the viscera of the corpse for poisons, eventually finding
traces of the alkaloid poison hyoscine. Willcox had 'no doubt it was
hyoscine', which was 'gummy syrupy stuff', but used medicinally in the
salt form of hydrobromide of hyoscine. He had found two-fifths of a
grain of the drug in the organs he had examined, which he estimated
would mean that there would have been more than half a grain in the
whole body – easily a fatal dose. Willcox had never known hyoscine to
have been used in a murder case before, but thought that in this
instance it would have been taken by mouth, and that the victim would
have lived for at least one hour but no more than twelve. Dr Arthur
Pearson Luff, the honorary scientific adviser to the Home Office, had

repeated Willcox's tests for hyoscine and come up with the same results.

The next task for the prosecution was to connect Crippen with large quantities of hyoscine, and this proved a simple task. Charles Hetherington, a chemist who, like Crippen, worked in New Oxford Street, was acquainted with Crippen, who was a customer at his shop. Around 17 or 18 January 1910, Crippen had called in at the chemist's shop and ordered five grains of hyoscine hydrobromide, which he said he wanted for homeopathic purposes. Hetherington had to order the drug, which Crippen collected on 19 January. He signed the reason for purchase column in the poisons register as 'homeopathic preparation'. Crippen had often bought drugs from the chemist, including cocaine (for preparing dental anaesthetic), morphia and mercury, but never before hyoscine.

The Crown had finished presenting its case. Now it was the turn of the defence. Mr Tobin pointed out that every witness who knew Crippen described his character in glowing terms. He was, according to people who knew him, 'amiable', 'kind-hearted', 'good-hearted', 'good-tempered', and 'one of the nicest men I ever met'. How could such a man suddenly become 'a fiend incarnate'? Furthermore, Crippen's behaviour did not appear to have changed immediately before Cora's disappearance, and he carried on working as normal immediately afterwards. Tobin continued:

> The position, therefore, was this. There was an illicit intimacy between Mrs. Crippen and Bruce Miller, and an illicit intimacy between Crippen and Le Neve – the latter might be another reason for Mrs. Crippen's departure. Where was she now? Why did she go? She went because she had long disliked Crippen, and her dislike had turned to hate. Who knew where Belle Elmore was? Who knew whether it was Belle Elmore's flesh that was buried in the cellar? Who knew for a certainty whether Belle Elmore was alive to-day or not? Who knew for certain whether she was abroad, whether she was ill or well, alive or dead? In a case of life and death, and in a charge of murder, they had to know, to know beyond all reasonable doubt, before they could find a verdict that would send a fellow-man to death.

Crippen's flight could be explained. 'Feeling there was that high mountain of prejudice which he had erected by his lies against himself, he did what innocent men, threatened with a charge, have done before. He resolved in his folly to fly.' Finally, Tobin reminded the jury that they had to be sure that the remains had not lain in the cellar of 39 Hilldrop Crescent for years, and that they were indeed those of Belle Elmore.

When Crippen took the stand he said that the reason he had made such a large purchase of hyoscine was for 'a nerve remedy in a homeopathic preparation, that is, reduced to extremely minute doses'. He freely admitted purchasing the five grains of hyoscine on 19 January, but claimed to have diluted them into 500 minute doses, two-thirds of which he had already dispensed. He had wanted 'to prepare some special nerve remedies for some very obstinate cases'. Crippen was unable to provide any record of his disposal of over 300 doses of hyoscine; nor could the remainder of the 500 doses be found.

Crippen stuck rigidly to his story about returning home from work one day to find his wife gone, and insisted that the statements he had subsequently made concerning her death had all been false. When examined by Huntley Jenkins, Crippen explained his motives for saying Cora had died:

Crippen	I said that my wife had left me, that she afterwards became ill, and that subsequently her death took place. I admit all that.
Jenkins	Were those statements true or false?
Crippen	The statements that I made were false.
Jenkins	Why did you make those statements?
Crippen	She told me I must do the best I could to cover up the scandal, and I made those statements for that reason; I wanted to hide anything regarding her departure from me the best I could, both for my sake and for hers.
Jenkins	Was the statement that you made to Inspector Dew a false or a true statement?
Crippen	It was quite true. Inspector Dew was very imperative in pressing upon me that I must produce my wife, or otherwise I would be in serious trouble. He also said that if I did not produce her very quickly the statements I had made would be in the newspapers the first thing I knew. I made up my mind next morning to go to Quebec, and, in fact, I did go.

Dew had not told Crippen that he would be in serious trouble if he did not produce his wife, nor did he say anything about publishing details in the newspapers. 'Obviously, this was a thing I should never have dreamed of doing', was the indignant Dew's response.

Crippen also gave an account of his dramatic arrest by Dew:

Jenkins	Was Inspector Dew's coming on board at Father Point a surprise to you?
Crippen	It was at Father Point – well, I did not expect him at all. I thought there had been a cable to the Quebec police; I did not expect Inspector Dew; that was a surprise to me.
Jenkins	Inspector Dew says that you said on arrest, 'I am sorry; the anxiety has been too much.' What were you referring to then?
Crippen	I was referring to this, that I expected to be arrested for all these lies I had told; I thought probably it would cast such a suspicion upon me, and perhaps they would keep me in prison – I do not know how long, perhaps for a year – until they found the missing woman.

Crippen was at pains to point out that all he had told Ethel Le Neve about the affair was that Cora had left him, and that she had died.

On the fourth day of the trial Crippen was recalled, and this time he was examined by Richard Muir. Whispers passed around the court. 'What is Muir like as a cross-examiner?', some one asked. 'Very slow, but very direct,' was the reply, 'with a wonderful way of asking awkward questions.'[23] Muir's incisive questioning was in stark contrast with what Crippen had experienced the previous day with Jenkins:

Muir	On the early morning of the 1st February you were left alone in your house with your wife?
Crippen	Yes.
Muir	She was alive?
Crippen	She was.
Muir	And well.
Crippen	She was.
Muir	Do you know of any person in the world who has seen her alive since?
Crippen	I do not.
Muir	Do you know of any person in the world who has ever had a letter from her since?
Crippen	I do not.
Muir	Do you know of any person in the world who can prove any fact showing she ever left that house alive?
Crippen	Absolutely not; I have told Mr. Dew exactly all the facts.
Muir	But you have made no inquiries?
Crippen	I have made no inquiries.

Muir	It would be most important for your defence in this case on the charge of murder if any person could be found who saw your wife alive after the Martinettis saw her alive; you realise that?
Crippen	I do.
Muir	And you have made no inquiries at all?
Crippen	I have made no inquiries at all.

The crucial evidence of the pyjama top found with the remains made Crippen's already fragile defence seem all but futile. According to Humphreys, he and Muir had to procure the evidence themselves. Dew had told them that Jones Brothers, who had sold the pyjamas to Crippen, could only say that the jacket was similar to those they occasionally sold to Crippen, and that they could not give a precise date as to when Crippen had bought them. Crippen told the court that he had bought all of the pyjamas that Dew had found at Hilldrop Crescent after he and Cora had moved to that address. Crippen thought that the newer pyjama suit had been purchased by himself in September 1909.

Muir and Humphreys felt sure there was more information to be gained from Jones Brothers, and on the eve of Crippen's trial they wrote a series of questions to them explaining why they thought the information was obtainable. The answers showed that they had been sold on 5 January 1909. Regardless of the date of purchase, Muir had established one fact. The material used in the pyjama trousers that Dew found, and its accompanying top found with the remains, was not manufactured and could not have existed before November 1908; therefore the jacket, produced in the court in a sample jar, could not have got among the remains before November 1908, well after the Crippens had moved into Hilldrop Crescent.

It was such a vital piece of evidence for the Crown's case that Muir had been worrying whether he could establish the facts about it in their favour, and hoping that the defence would not find out what he was doing. As the information had not arrived until after the trial had started, the prosecution thought it would be unfair to produce it without giving the defence prior warning. The defence could have asked for the trial to be postponed while they found experts to examine the pyjama evidence.[24]

The evidence of the pyjama top was so conclusive that the Lord Chief Justice could barely contain his incredulity at Crippen's defence. He asked the prisoner, 'Do you really ask the jury to understand that your answer is that, without your knowledge or your wife's, at some time during the five years, those remains could have been put there?' Crippen weakly replied, 'I say that it does not seem possible – I mean, it does not seem probable, but there is a possibility.'

Richard Muir was relentless in his blunt questioning of Crippen, who was becoming less convincing in his answers despite maintaining his composure. Dew was spellbound by Muir's cross-examination, saying that 'Crippen was clever, but not clever enough. There were gaps in his armour which Mr. Muir's skill was able to pierce.'

Muir	When did you make up your mind to go away from London?
Crippen	The morning after Inspector Dew was there – the 8th or 9th.
Muir	Had you the day before been contemplating the possibility of your going away?
Crippen	I would not like to say that I had made up my mind. When Inspector Dew came to me and laid out all the facts that he told me, I might have thought, well, if there is all this suspicion, and I am likely to have to stay in jail for months and months and months, perhaps until this woman is found, I had better be out of it.
Judge	Mr. Crippen; do you really mean that you thought that you would have to lie in gaol for months and months; do you say that?
Crippen	Quite so, yes.
Muir	Upon what charge?
Crippen	Suspicion.
Muir	Suspicion of what?
Crippen	Suspicion of – Inspector Dew said, 'This woman has disappeared, she must be found.'
Muir	Suspicion of what?
Crippen	Suspicion of being concerned in her disappearance.
Muir	What crime did you understand you might be kept in gaol upon suspicion of?
Crippen	I do not understand the law enough to say. From what I have read it seems to me I have heard of people being arrested on suspicion of being concerned in the disappearance of other people.
Muir	And that is why you contemplated on the afternoon of 8th July flying from the country?
Crippen	Quite so – that, and the idea that I had said that Miss Le Neve was living with me, and she had told her people she was married to me, and it would put her in a terrible position; the only thing I could think of was to take her away out of the country where she would not have this scandal thrown upon her.

In the light of Crippen's devotion to Le Neve, this was a considerably more plausible response.

Another point raised by Muir was that Crippen had written letters to Cora's friends and relatives telling them that Cora was dead. How did he know that she would not write to them herself, if indeed she had simply left him to live with Bruce Miller? Dew's final assessment of the cross-examination was that it had ended in the Crown's favour, but he had gained a strange kind of admiration for Crippen, whose composure had not cracked throughout his appearance, which had lasted three hours and forty-eight minutes:

> And so, hour after hour, the cross-examination went on. On the whole, Crippen came out of the ordeal well, but there were times when the penetrative questioning of Mr. Muir laid bare the weaknesses of his case.
>
> No person, with experience of criminal court procedure, could have escaped the impression that the little doctor was seeking cleverly, if unconvincingly, to give innocent interpretations to facts all pointing strongly to his guilt.
>
> A lesser man – that is lesser in education and self-control – would have collapsed completely under the searching cross-examination for the Crown.

The Verdict

For a man with a cool head and some ability to think
he also did many things which simply didn't make sense.

Raymond Chandler

All of the evidence had been presented, but one important question remained unanswered. It was never established what had happened to Cora Crippen's head, bones and other missing parts. Dr Pepper made a passing remark about a limb found in the River Thames at Greenwich, but nothing conclusive came of this. Dew knew of two theories. The first was that Crippen had burnt them in the kitchen grate of 39 Hilldrop Crescent, but none of the neighbours Dew interviewed had noticed any offensive smell around the time of Cora's disappearance, other than Frederick Evans, who made his statement at a later date. The other theory was that Crippen had disposed of the remains in a bag over the side of the cross-channel steamer when he and Le Neve had gone to Dieppe in March. Melville Macnaghten thought this was the likeliest explanation, and admitted that it is what he would have done had he been in Crippen's position.[1]

In Alfred Tobin's closing speech for the defence, he laid out the case in favour of Crippen's innocence. He explained to the jury that 'the burden of proof rested on the prosecution, and if on a single material point there could be reasonable doubt it was not for him to appeal for mercy; he had only to claim what was the right of the prisoner'.

According to Tobin, Crippen's failure to look for his missing wife was simply explained by the fact that he was glad to be rid of her and able to live with Le Neve. 'It was idle to suppose', he pointed out, 'that he would be other than relieved at her departure from Hilldrop Crescent. One would have supposed that he did not care, or that he would prefer her to be away.'

Tobin claimed that Le Neve had spent the night of 2 February at Hilldrop Crescent (although the prosecution refuted this, as there was only Crippen's word for it). It was inconceivable, Tobin said, that Crippen could have murdered Cora on 1 February before spending the whole day at work and then dismembering her corpse, then tidying up and regaining his composure to such an extent that Le Neve noticed nothing the next day.

The prosecution had made a great deal of the fact that Dr Crippen was a liar, as shown by his letters to Cora's friends and relations informing them of her death. Remarkably, Tobin said that these letters were almost an act of kindness on Crippen's part, for 'those friends would have been glad indeed to find that Dr. Crippen's story of her illness and her death was quite untrue, and further, they would have thought none the worse of Dr. Crippen for having told those lies in order to try and cover up his wife's disappearance and his wife's shame'.

The flight of Crippen and Le Neve, in disguise and under false names, was thus explained by Tobin, stoically trying to make the best of a bad job:

[The jury] had to consider what was the reason for his flight, or his folly, if they liked. They had to realise the time of his flight, and what had just been said by Inspector Dew. They had to remember the lies Dr. Crippen had told, and that he had admitted that they were lies. They must not forget what Inspector Dew had said to him, 'I am not satisfied about your wife,' and, 'There will be serious trouble in store for you unless you find your wife' [which of course Dew had never said]. A man who had lost sight of his wife for all those months, who had no notion where she was, and who remembered that he had told lie after lie as to the reason for her disappearance, might be thoroughly alarmed when an officer of the law appeared and said there would be serious trouble in store for him about this disappearance. Dr. Crippen realised the mass of prejudice he had raised against himself by the lies he had told, and was flight, although an act of folly, a clear proof of guilt?

Tobin told the jury that they must be entirely satisfied that the remains were female before they could even address the question of whether they were those of Cora Crippen. 'Suspicion was not enough.' He also raised the question of Crippen's anatomical skill:

There was another thing was admittedly needed, and that was a dextrous hand, well versed in anatomical operations. So far from being dextrous in anatomy, he was, compared with the skill required by an anatomical surgeon, a very commonplace manager for Munyon's remedies. Something else was needed. There was needed the fiend incarnate to do a deed like that; but the prisoner's reputation was that of a kind-hearted, good-hearted, amiable man.

Tobin did not attempt to offer an alternative explanation for how the remains managed to find their way to Crippen's cellar. He asked the jury if they could believe that a man who had committed such a terrible crime could go about his day-to-day business with no one noticing any change in his demeanour. 'Were they to be told that during the doctor's close intimacy with his friends in London, and with his business people in London, they would never have detected any trait such as cruelty or something of that kind in his nature? The characteristics of the man who would do a deed like this were absolutely absent.' Edward Marshall Hall had visited the court during the trial. He later told a journalist, 'When I took the opportunity of snatching that hour at the Old Bailey, and hearing the line which the defence had taken to try to save Crippen, I walked out appalled.'[2]

The fifth and final day of the trial heard the closing speech for the Crown, presented by Richard Muir. Muir had been staggered by Tobin's assessment of Crippen as a kind man:

> Let me examine the foundation for that theory. The prisoner had admitted that over a long series of months he had led a life of studied hypocrisy, utterly regardless of the pain which the lies which he was telling and was acting would inflict upon friend or sister of his wife. Letters full of grief of a bereaved husband were written to Mrs. Martinetti, to Dr. Burroughs to be seen by Dr. Burroughs' wife, to Mrs. Mills, the half sister of Cora Crippen. There was that letter of his carrying the sobs of the bereaved husband across the ocean to harrow the feelings of his wife's relations. He put on mourning, wrote on black-edged paper, mocked the grief of his wife's dearest friends, who thought they were sympathising with him, when they wished to lay a last tribute of love upon the far-off grave of their dead friend. He said, 'A wreath is no use; she is not being buried, she is being cremated; her ashes will soon be here' – and then with his tongue in his cheek – 'you may have your little ceremony then.' Ashes to be fetched across the sea! They were asked to say then that he was too kind-hearted to have done this deed.

In addition to Crippen's lies, there was also his rank hypocrisy. He had told Dew that Cora had been unfaithful to him with Bruce Miller, despite the fact that they 'had never cast eyes on each other for six years'. Besides this, 'the man who brought those accusations against his wife was the man who was himself carrying on an intrigue with Ethel Le Neve, extending over three years, and who said in the witness-box that he believed his wife knew nothing about it'.

Muir admitted that there was no conclusive evidence that the remains were those of Cora Crippen, or even those of a woman. However, the evidence had overwhelmingly pointed to the fact that Cora Crippen was dead. The hair found amongst the remains was naturally dark brown, but had been bleached to a lighter colour, and 'Belle Elmore had dark brown hair bleached to a lighter shade. It was true that other women had dark brown hair bleached to lighter colour, but there was no suggestion that any woman with hair of that sort was missing in London within the limits of the time which were involved in that case.' Muir reiterated the prosecution's claim that the mark on the piece of skin was an abdominal scar, and reminded the jury that 'Belle Elmore had been operated upon in that region in the year 1892 or 1893.'

In addition, and most damagingly, the remains had been riddled with hyoscine, and Crippen had purchased large quantities of the drug. Summing up, Muir said:

Ask yourselves in this most important case these questions. Where is Belle Elmore? Is your answer to be that she is dead? Then, whose remains were those in the cellar? Is your answer to be Belle Elmore's? If not Belle Elmore's, what conceivable explanation is there? None in the world. Who mutilated her body and put the remains there? Who but the prisoner had the opportunity, the skill, the access to the pieces of pyjama jacket which were found in the grave? How did she die? Is your answer to be of hyoscine poisoning? If not, how did that person die? No sign upon the internal organs which were left, no sign on post-mortem examination, of any cause of death at all except hyoscine poisoning. If your answer is to be that she died of hyoscine poisoning, where did she get it and who administered it? Crippen bought it – it was not much known – on 19th January, and Belle Elmore disappeared from this world on 1st February.

Lord Alverstone lucidly summed up the case to the jury: 'That is the crime of murder charged here against Dr. Crippen, that he wilfully and intentionally killed his wife, poisoned his wife, and that he mutilated the body, and buried the remains in the cellar at 39 Hilldrop Crescent in order to conceal his crime.' The jury had to consider two questions. The first:

Were the remains found at 39 Hilldrop Crescent the remains of Cora Crippen? If they were not, there is an end of this case. If you find that they were the remains of Cora Crippen, then you have got to ask yourselves, was her death occasioned by the wilful act of the defendant Crippen? If not, again the defendant is entitled to be acquitted. Those are the two issues that you have got to consider, and those are the issues upon which I shall ask you in a short time to concentrate your attention.

Dew had found Crippen to be an enigmatic character, saying, 'There will never be another Crippen. There were two distinct sides to the man.' Alverstone had been similarly intrigued by Crippen:

Whatever the truth in this case, the defendant is an extraordinary man. He has committed a ghastly crime; he has covered up that ghastly crime, or endeavoured to, in a ghastly way, and he has behaved with the most brutal and callous indifference after the crime has been committed. If he is an innocent man, it is almost impossible, as you may probably think, to fathom his mind or his character, again absolutely indifferent to the charge made against him of murder; having, according to him, I will not say a ready means, but at any rate the means of doing his utmost to establish his innocence, no step taken of any sort or kind by him.

It was the judge's opinion that 'the fact that Dr. Crippen has lied on material points in this case is a very important matter for your consideration'. Another 'very serious matter' was why, if Cora had left Crippen on 1 February, she did not take the bulk of her jewellery and furs with her.

As to the matter of whether Cora Crippen was still alive, Alverstone thought there were two problems with this. Firstly, how could Crippen have written the mourning letters

except with the knowledge that the wife could not appear? Friends in America, gone to America, friends at home making inquiries; put off, hoodwinked – we need not care about the dates, but hoodwinked in a disgraceful way by mourning black-edged paper, and so forth. Do not consider it from the point of view of taste. Consider it from the point of view of upon which side the truth lies. If you come to the conclusion that the game was so enormously dangerous that Dr. Crippen could not have possibly carried it out if he thought his wife might appear again, you will

ask yourselves, can you believe the story that his wife left him on
1st February.

Cora may even have come forward herself:

> The man was arrested, as you know, in consequence of the agency of
> this new invention, wireless telegraphy; there is no doubt about that;
> it is a matter that could not have been established but for that
> invention; that part is common knowledge; he is arrested in Canada,
> and then the story is known all over the world. It is a very serious
> suggestion to make to you, as it is made by the counsel for the
> defence, that Belle Elmore may still be alive. If Belle Elmore is alive,
> is it possible to think that this has not come to her knowledge? Does
> that man in the dock mean to suggest that so bad is this woman who
> was his wife for eighteen years, and whom, apart from her being
> angry and bad tempered, he does not make any serious complaint
> against – that she is so mean and so abominably wicked as to allow
> this man to stand his trial in the dock without making any
> communication or anything of the kind? That is what you have got to
> consider in this part of the case.

After a brief adjournment Alverstone continued his summing up. He
addressed the issues of how long the remains had been buried, saying
that 'perhaps the most important thing is the pyjama jacket'. Were the
remains those of Cora Crippen? Alverstone asserted: 'that they are the
remains of a woman now is really not seriously disputed', as they were
partially clothed with a woman's vest and found with hair curlers. There
were suggestions that it was Cora Crippen on account of the hair
colouring and pyjama top, but the evidence was 'not so certain' as was
the evidence suggesting the remains were those of a woman.

Alverstone described the alleged scar on the piece of skin as 'the
battleground in this case'. 'Now is that a scar or not?' he asked, before
warning the jury, 'In order to satisfy you that it is not Cora Crippen, the
defence must have satisfied you that there is no scar there. Coupled with
the pyjama and the camisole and the combinations and the vests, you
have to ask yourselves have you any doubt that that is the body of Cora
Crippen?'

The penultimate point was 'what was the cause of death, who put that
body there, was it the same person who killed her or not?' Alverstone
thought that the jury would be 'of the opinion that the person who
caused the death of Cora Crippen took steps to get rid of the body. That
is the natural thing a man would do who had committed a great crime.' If

she had not been poisoned, could the jury account for her death by any natural cause? The defence had not put forward an alternative suggestion to hyoscine poisoning, so the only explanation of her death was that '[s]ome one gave Belle Elmore hyoscine, and she became unconscious, comatose, and died, and there was the dead woman in the house'.

Finally, Alverstone addressed the jury on the subject of Crippen's behaviour, which he considered to be 'a most important part of the case'.

Now, you have had Inspector Dew's statement put before you, and you heard it read more than once. The only important thing in Dew's statement for the present consideration is, not the lies that the accused told, which he admits now were lies, namely, the letters and all the statements about his wife being dead – but the things he said were true were not consistent with the facts as proved. He was at trouble to show Inspector Dew the jewels, and those are the same that were found sewn in his undervest when he was arrested at Quebec; he was at trouble to show Dew that his wife must have taken the other jewels with her. Now, one has to make every allowance for a man in a difficult position; he says, 'She had other jewellery, and must have taken that with her,' but, when you are dealing with a man who is supposed to be speaking the truth, and who is asking you to believe that his wife had gone away, you cannot forget the fact that he had pawned a very considerable portion of that jewellery on 2nd February, the day after she disappeared, and on 9th February, seven days afterwards. He says, 'I have never pawned or sold any jewellery belonging to her before or after I left her.' He says afterwards, 'I thought it was my property.' It may be that that taken by itself may be so construed; it may be so understood; but the important thing is that he said that she had taken it with her and he follows that up by the statement about pawning. Then he says, and I suggest to you that it is one of the most important things, 'I shall, of course, do all I can to get in touch with her and clear this matter up.' Gentlemen, on that day he, with the assistance of Inspector Dew, drafts an advertisement offering a reward, to be published in the papers, to endeavour to find Belle Elmore. He never sent it. If he believed that his wife could be found, why should not he have sent it?

Alverstone then told the jury of 'a test applied in these Courts'. That test was 'How did the man behave when the charge was brought against him?'

You have it that, living there in the same name, carrying on his business, consorting with Ethel Le Neve for practically six months, the day after the inspector goes to his house he alters his name and flees – goes to Antwerp, appears under the name of Robinson, induces Le Neve to disguise herself as a boy, passes Le Neve off as his son, and endeavours to escape to Canada; and he would no doubt have got there but for Inspector Dew being able to catch him.

When Dew arrested Crippen the fugitive told his captor, 'It is only fair to say she knows nothing about it.' Alverstone wondered, 'What did that "it" mean?' The judge concluded by reiterating that '[t]here has been ample opportunity for getting hold of Cora Crippen if she is really alive'.

After the judge's summing up, the jury retired to consider their decision at 2.15 p.m., and returned just twenty-seven minutes later. Dew rated Crippen's chances as being 'slender in the extreme', and suspected that Crippen knew as much himself. The jury had unanimously found Crippen to be guilty of the murder of his wife. Crippen responded to the verdict by saying, 'I still protest my innocence.'

Lord Alverstone passed the dread sentence:

Hawley Harvey Crippen, you have been convicted upon evidence, which could leave no doubt on the minds of any reasonable man, that you cruelly poisoned your wife, that you concealed your crime, you mutilated her body, and disposed piece-meal of her remains; you possessed yourself of her property, and used it for your own purposes. It was further established that as soon as suspicion was aroused you fled from justice, and took every measure to conceal your flight. On the ghastly and wicked nature of the crime I will not dwell. I only tell you that you must entertain no expectation or hope that you will escape the consequences of your crime, and I implore you to make your peace with Almighty God. I have now to pass upon you the sentence of the Court, which is that you be taken from hence to a lawful prison, and from thence to a place of execution, and that you be there hanged by the neck until you are dead, and that your body be buried in the precincts of the prison where you shall have last been confined after your conviction. And may the Lord have mercy on your soul!

Dew had been surprised at the speed with which the jury returned their verdict, as it was a murder case; but it was a verdict he agreed with wholeheartedly. The case had caused a sensation although, with perhaps the exception of the medical arguments, it had not been one of any great legal importance. Travers Humphreys admitted as much, and his junior Cecil Mercer described it as a 'dead case', meaning that Crippen had never stood a chance. The case against Crippen was so overwhelming that the prosecution never bothered to call the man who delivered the lime to Crippen. One of the few things to impress Mercer about the trial was Tobin's vigorous defence of his client. He thought Tobin 'put up an excellent show. How he contrived to do it, I have no idea, but he appeared to have convinced himself of Crippen's innocence.'[3] Alverstone concurred, thinking that Crippen had been 'ably defended' by Tobin.[4]

Dew summed up his view of Dr Crippen as follows:

Dr. Crippen was in many ways a modest man. In others he was egotistical. I shall always believe that he was vain enough to think he had the cleverness to commit the perfect crime. But murderers, however clever, invariably make fatal blunders. Crippen made many. I have never entertained a doubt as to his guilt. He was, as he was proved at the Old Bailey, a callously calculating murderer.

There were several positive aspects of Crippen's character. He was generally well liked by everyone who knew him, he was exceptionally courteous and considerate, and his love for Ethel Le Neve cannot be doubted (although he also appeared to have loved Cora in the early years of their marriage). One early writer on the case correctly pointed out that Crippen 'would seem to have been a man of many minor virtues and of one monstrous crime'.[5] Bernard Spilsbury dryly observed that Crippen was 'always considerate – even in the weapon he used to kill his wife'.[6] However likeable Crippen may have been, Dew was absolutely correct. Crippen was a liar and a cold-blooded murderer who lived quite happily with his mistress at 39 Hilldrop Crescent for months, knowing that the mutilated remains of his wife were buried in the cellar beneath their feet.

Dew thought he knew Crippen as well as anyone by now, and had watched him closely throughout his trial. Despite this he was really none the wiser about the enigma of Dr Crippen:

To me he was still a puzzle. In my whole dealings with him I saw nothing which by the wildest stretch of the imagination could be said to suggest that he had in his make-up the capacity for so terrible a crime.

I noticed one curious thing about Crippen when he was giving evidence. He never once referred to the dead woman as 'my wife', or 'Mrs. Crippen'. Throughout, he spoke of her as 'this woman', or 'that woman'.

There never has been an adequate motive for murder. There certainly was no reason for Crippen to kill his wife. He had no strong ties to keep him in England, so he could have taken all he wanted in the way of jewellery and left for any part of the world, taking Miss Le Neve with him. If he had done this, I doubt if anyone would have tried to stop him or to bring him back.

I believe he harboured an intense hatred for his wife. The cause does not matter. It was, however, sufficient to cause him to take her life, and to do so in a way which he hoped would escape discovery.

Rex *v.* Le Neve

She denied all knowledge of the crime, and I am convinced that she told the truth.

F.E. Smith

With Dr Crippen awaiting his appointment with the hangman, Ethel Le Neve now stood trial at the Old Bailey. On Tuesday 25 October 1910 she was tried with being an accessory after the fact in the murder of Cora Crippen at 39 Hilldrop Crescent. She would have been found guilty if the jury could be satisfied that she had helped Crippen escape knowing that he was a murderer.

Once again Richard Muir, Travers Humphreys and Samuel Ingleby Oddie were the counsel for the Crown, but Le Neve had a different team defending her from that which had defended Crippen. Appearing for her was Winston Churchill's best friend Frederick Edwin Smith, whom Dew described as a 'brilliant lawyer and orator'. Smith, popularly known as 'F.E.', cut a singular figure. He was

> strikingly handsome, six feet one inch in height, of a distinguished figure, slightly marred by sloping shoulders. His clothes, although not in any one particular out of the ordinary, gave the impression that he was over-dressed. The hat worn on the back of his head, the red flower in his button-hole, the very long cigar always carried in his mouth, made him a ready subject for the caricaturist.[1]

Arthur Newton had wished to brief Smith for Crippen's defence, but F.E., who would later have the reputation of being 'the cleverest man in the kingdom', quickly realised what the outcome of that trial would inevitably be. He pointed out that, as Crippen and Le Neve would be tried separately, it would be necessary to employ separate counsel, and shrewdly opted to defend Le Neve instead, assisted by Mr Barrington Ward.

Richard Muir began by explaining that Le Neve was charged 'in effect, with assisting Hawley Harvey Crippen to escape from justice at a time when she knew that he had been guilty of the murder of his wife'. There was no question on either side that Crippen had been rightly convicted of the murder. Muir elaborated what the prosecution aimed to prove:

> What was the state of knowledge that prisoner had, and what was her intention with regard to the acts which she undoubtedly committed. Guilty knowledge and guilty intention are issues in this case, and upon such issues a jury can rarely have direct evidence at all. It hardly ever happens that the state of a person's mind can be judged by anything but that person's actions, and, therefore, you will look at the facts in this case with a view to discovering what was the knowledge of the prisoner at the time that the acts in question were done, and what was her intention with regard to the acts which she herself did.

According to Muir, a vital point in the case was Le Neve's behaviour around the time of Cora Crippen's death. Le Neve had been lodging with a Mrs Emily Jackson in Camden Town since September 1908, and the pair enjoyed a close relationship. In correspondence Le Neve called Jackson 'My dearest Mum' and 'My dear Ma'. Muir explained:

> Mrs. Jackson says that about January last prisoner began to look ill and troubled, and that one night towards the end of January, or in the beginning of February – she did not fix any date – prisoner came home very ill. She would take no supper, and went to bed. Her appearance, according to Mrs. Jackson's description, was the appearance of somebody who had suffered a great shock, who was stricken with horror at something that had happened. Prisoner was asked for an explanation, but little or none was forthcoming that night. The next morning, again, this young woman was in the same condition. She was practically unable to eat her breakfast, and her condition was such that Mrs. Jackson saw she was quite unfit to go to her work as a typist, and persuaded her to remain at home.
>
> That was no ordinary illness. It was something which seemed to strike the prisoner with horror. Whatever it may have been, it was contemporaneous, or nearly contemporaneous, with the murder of Mrs. Crippen. This is a fact which cannot be disputed.

Muir told the jury that they would have to decide what caused Le Neve's state of horror. He obviously wanted them to think that it was the knowledge of Cora's murder. Le Neve's state of horror was soon replaced with cheerfulness:

She says that 'the doctor' has promised to marry her. She comes home wearing Mrs. Crippen's clothes and jewels, and makes presents to Mrs. Jackson of enormous quantities of clothing that Mrs. Crippen had left behind her. She says that Mrs. Crippen has gone to America, and she and Crippen visit Mrs. Jackson on more than one occasion. She also had the knowledge that Crippen for a large sum of money had been pawning some of Mrs. Crippen's jewellery. You must ask yourselves, 'What is the explanation of this?' Is it likely that any woman would suppose that the wife was going away from the husband leaving behind her furs, jewels, and everything practically that she had in the world, to be worn by any woman to whom Crippen liked to give them?

According to the prisoner, Crippen never told her, so far as she could remember, whether Mrs. Crippen was coming back or not. But immediately she began to wear Mrs. Crippen's jewels and go out in public in them – wearing the brooch at a dinner and ball of the Music Hall Artiste's Benevolent Fund, a place where all Mrs. Crippen's friends would be gathered together. You will have to ask yourselves whether there was not in her mind such knowledge that Mrs. Crippen would never come back as this indictment imputes to her, otherwise she never would have gone about with Mrs. Crippen's husband, [worn] Mrs. Crippen's clothes and jewels, and give[n] away some of Mrs. Crippen's clothing to friends.

Muir then discussed the Atlantic flight:

What was it the prisoner knew which induced her to cut off her hair and masquerade as a boy, and condemn herself practically to perpetual silence, because she dare not speak in public in the hearing of any person lest her voice should betray her? The explanation which lies on the surface of those facts is that the prisoner knew that Crippen was flying from justice for the murder of his wife. What other explanation is there? Absolutely none.

Walter Dew appeared at the trial and was examined by the prosecution, for whom he repeated yet again the story of the Crippen case from the Nashes' statement at Scotland Yard until the arrest of Crippen and Le Neve. He was then cross-examined by Smith:

Smith   Have you enquired about her past life?
Dew   Yes. For ten years she has been a shorthand typist. I understand that she has not been living with her father and mother for some years.

Smith   What is her father's position in life?

Dew   He is of the lower middle class. He is a canvasser for coal orders.

Smith   You know he wrote some articles for a paper called *Answers*?

Dew   He did, but I did not read them.

Then Emily Jackson was called to the stand, where she gave her account of Le Neve's strange behaviour around the end of January:

> During the latter part of January I observed that there was something strange about Miss Le Neve's manner. She became very miserable and depressed. Upon one occasion in the latter part of January Miss Le Neve came home looking very tired and strange. She was greatly agitated and went to bed without supper. I went into the bedroom after her. I could see that her whole body was trembling, and that she was in a terrible state. I asked her what was the matter, but she did not seem to have the strength to speak. I asked her again, and she said she would be all right in the morning.
>
> I said to her that I was sure there was something dreadful on her mind, and that if she did not relieve her mind she would go absolutely mad. She said, 'I will tell you the whole story presently.' A little while afterwards she said, 'Would you be surprised if I told you it is the doctor?' I said, 'What do you mean; do you mean he was the cause of your trouble when I first saw you?' She said 'Yes.' I said, 'Why worry about that; it is past and gone?' She burst into tears again, and said, 'It is Miss Elmore.' Up to that time I had never heard the name of Miss Elmore in my life. I wondered what she meant, and asked her, and she said, 'She is his wife, you know. When I see them go away together it makes me realise what my position is.' I said, 'My dear girl, what is the use of worrying about another woman's husband?' and she said, 'She has been threatening to go away with another man, and that is all we are waiting for, and when she does that the doctor is going to divorce her and marry me.'

F.E. Smith was so confident that the Crown's case against Le Neve was groundless that he announced to the court that he did not propose to call any evidence for the defence. He knew that it was up to Muir to prove that Le Neve was guilty and not for him to argue her innocence. Smith undermined the prosecution's case when he cross-examined Emily Jackson. He established that Le Neve was frequently ill, and that the illness Muir had referred to actually took place at the beginning of

January 1910, well before Cora Crippen's disappearance. It also emerged that Le Neve had suffered a miscarriage shortly after she moved in with Jackson.[2]

Muir proceeded with the prosecution's closing speech. He reminded the jury of Le Neve's behaviour at Emily Jackson's house and her flight under a false name. Then he said:

> Le Neve was arrested on 31st July. She was told of the charge made against her – the charge of murder, and the charge of being accessory after the fact. She made no reply. On 21st August on her way home she was told the charge, and made no reply. On 27th August, at Bow Street Police Station she was told of the charge, and made no reply; and when committed for trial, with every opportunity for making a statement she made none.

Then Smith made the closing speech for Le Neve's defence, which was all the evidence he would present. Dew described it as 'an eloquent and feeling speech'. He put forward the suggestion that Le Neve was a naive innocent who fell under Crippen's spell:

> What was the misfortune of this girl, little more than a child, when it became necessary for her to earn her living? She had the extreme misfortune to come across the path, at the age of seventeen, of one of the most dangerous and remarkable men who have lived in this century; a man to whom in the whole history of psychology of crime a high place must be given as a compelling and masterful personality.

Smith attributed the Atlantic flight to the fact that 'Crippen had acquired this enormous power over her, and she was utterly ignorant of the laws of England. She was confronted with the problem as to whether she would stay in England or go with him.'

He criticised Muir's suggestion that Le Neve knew of the murder. 'Does any one believe', Smith asked, 'that the girl went back to live at Hilldrop Crescent towards the end of February, the month that this murder was committed – went to live in this house knowing that its last tenant had been murdered by the man she was going to live with?'

Lord Alverstone was again the presiding judge. In his summing up he told the jury, 'The only matter upon which you have to concentrate your attention is, "Did Ethel Le Neve know when she fled with Crippen that Crippen was a murderer and had murdered his wife?"' Among the things that they had to consider were:

what is the probability of this scoundrel having told her. So far as the evidence is concerned, it stands this way. When he was arrested he said, 'It is only fair to say she knows nothing about it. I never told her anything.' It is perfectly plain that that was a most serious statement so far as he was concerned. There is no secret about it. Crippen was most seriously cross-examined upon it, and he was asked to what it could refer except his wicked deed towards his wife.

The fact of this woman living with him and going with him to Dieppe, wicked and immoral as it is, is not evidence that he told her he committed the murder.

Upon that part of the case you are entitled to take into consideration what Mr. Smith has said to you about her being gentle, sympathetic, and loving and affectionate towards Crippen. If he had told her, not only might it have been dangerous to himself, but do you not think that it might have changed her feelings towards him?

Dew thought that Smith's closing speech would have relieved Le Neve of any anxieties she would have had about the outcome of her trial. It came as no surprise to Dew that the jury found Ethel Le Neve not guilty. She was immediately liberated. Dew felt the outcome was correct and felt 'satisfied that justice had been done. Poor Miss Le Neve had suffered enough. Her association with Crippen had cost her many weeks of mental torture and doubt.'

After the trial Lord Alverstone said to Smith, 'I think you ought to have put her in the box.' Smith replied, enigmatically, 'No. I knew what she would say. You did not.' Smith had been convinced throughout of Le Neve's innocence. 'Frail she was, and of submissive temperament, but not an accomplice in murder, or an ally in its concealment.'[3]

Smith never changed his view of Le Neve's innocence. In his account of her trial, years later, he wrote:

> I am convinced that she was innocent in every sense of the word. I had the advantage of a close study of the case, including a great deal that was never in evidence.
>
> She was a girl whose character for truthfulness had never been questioned. She denied all knowledge of the crime, and I am convinced that she told the truth . . . I was told that after the trial she left for America. But I never heard of her again.

Smith's assessment of Crippen was that he had been guilty of 'a murder callous, calculated, cold-blooded, a murder which I say, in the whole annals of crime it would be hard to match for cold-blooded deliberation', but 'he was at least a brave man and a true lover'.[4] Dew agreed, saying, 'Whatever may be said and thought about Crippen, one can only admire his attitude towards the girl who had shared his great adventure.'

Ethel Le Neve always convincingly denied any knowledge of Cora Crippen's murder. She stood by Crippen until the end, and would never say a word against him. Le Neve eventually concluded that Crippen had killed Cora accidentally, and could not be considered to be a murderer. In her opinion the only viable theory as to what happened on the night Cora died was that Crippen had mistakenly given her an overdose of hyoscine to calm her down when she was in a fit of rage.[5] This overlooked the fact that Crippen had purchased such an enormous quantity of hyoscine soon before Cora's disappearance, making it almost inconceivable that he just wanted it to sedate her.

Le Neve visited Dew at Scotland Yard shortly after her trial to thank him for his 'kindness and consideration to her through her ordeal', adding that Crippen, whom she had visited at Pentonville Prison where he had been sent awaiting execution, wished to add his thanks too. While Dew was pleased that they bore him no animosity despite the fact that he had tracked them down and arrested them, he did not consider that he had done anything out of the ordinary in his dealings with them, even though he had, like many other people, found Crippen an agreeable character. Dew admitted that 'detached from the crime, there was something almost likeable about the mild little fellow'.

It appeared that Le Neve was genuinely grateful to Dew, and in a series of newspaper articles published in 1920 she told the story of her involvement in the Crippen case. In them she recalled Dew's first visit to Hilldrop Crescent:

> The visit of Detective-Inspector Dew, of Scotland Yard, was no shock to me. On the contrary it rather amused me. At first he must either have thought me terribly stupid or a very guilty person. What I thought about him was that he was very hard to convince and very persistent in his manner.
>
> Walter Dew turned out to be a very nice man and a real friend to a poor girl in distress, but when he first came to Hilldrop Crescent I was not greatly impressed with him.[6]

As Le Neve told her story to the readers of the tabloid she paid further tribute to Dew, saying:

Mr Walter Dew is a detective with a sixth sense.

After he arrested me on board the s.s. Montrose I saw a great deal of him. In course of time I grew to like him. He is one of the straightest, kindliest men I ever met, but if you saw him you would never dream for a moment that he was a detective.

Tall and quiet-looking, there is nothing out of the common about his appearance, and, looking into the kindly brown eyes [in fact Dew had grey eyes], you would never dream that behind them the brain of the man pulsates with human voltage.

I think that Walter Dew gave Dr Crippen the idea that he was not worth a great deal of powder and shot.

Walter Dew, however, never loosened his grip on the case from the moment he left our house at Hilldrop Crescent.[7]

She also recalled another example of Dew's kindness when in Quebec:

I was longing to get out of my boy's clothes and be a girl again. Mr Walter Dew came to see me and when I told him how miserable I felt he said there was no reason in the world why I should not purchase anything I wanted. He was very kind, and not only advised me what to get, but went out himself and saw that they were purchased.

It was his idea that I should buy a black bonnet and veil so that I could easily cover up my face from the gaze of the crowd.[8]

After the excitement and magnitude of the trials of Crippen and Le Neve, Dew had to deal with more mundane matters. Crippen's former landlord, Mr Lown, was trying to extract one quarter's rent for 39 Hilldrop Crescent from the police for the period from 29 September to 25 December. Dew protested that he had returned the house keys to Lowns on 29 October, and Lown's claim was an unreasonable one. After some parley Lown agreed to the payment of one quarter's rent, to cover both the cost of the rent and compensation for the damage done to the property when the police searched it. Dew was secretly pleased with the outcome of the negotiations, knowing that Lown was perfectly entitled to claim for one quarter's rent, and quite likely to put in an inflated estimate for damages.

Appeal and Execution

You can't help liking this guy somehow. He was one murderer
who died like a gentleman . . .

Raymond Chandler

Immediately after he was sentenced to death, Crippen's steely composure
gave way. Arthur Newton saw him after he had been taken down from the
dock, and found that his client had 'completely collapsed [though the
more reliable Oddie said Crippen did not break down], and sat there in a
huddled heap, crying with his head between his hands, utterly broken
and dejected.' 'We shall appeal', Newton assured him, but Crippen's
thoughts were only with Ethel Le Neve.[1]

On 5 November 1910 Crippen did appeal against his death sentence, at
the Court of Criminal Appeal before Mr Justice Darling, Mr Justice
Channell and Mr Justice Pickford. The grounds of appeal rested upon
the following points, signed by Crippen:

1. That one of the Jurymen, after I had been given in charge of the
Jury absented himself from the rest of the Jury without either he or
the rest of the Jury being given in charge of the proper Officer of the
court.

2. That the identity of the remains found at 39 Hilldrop Crescent was
not established.

3. That the Judge did not sufficiently place before the Jury the
question of there being no navel upon the piece of skin measuring
seven inches by six inches.

4. That the Judge misdirected the Jury in telling them that the onus
of proof that the mark upon the piece of skin, measuring seven
inches by six inches was not a scar, rested upon me.

5. I desire to be supplied free of charge with a shorthand note of the
proceedings at the Central Criminal Court to be forwarded forthwith
to my solicitor.

The member of the jury who absented himself during the trial was George Craig, who had fainted around midday on 19 October, the second day of Crippen's trial. He was taken from the court by an usher and two doctors, while the judge adjourned the case until 2 p.m. Craig had sufficiently recovered within fifteen minutes to be reunited with the eleven other jurors in their private room. During his fifteen minutes' absence, Craig did not see anyone other than the doctors and court usher.

Crippen attended the court looking 'little the worse' for his recent ordeal. Crippen's appeal failed on every point, and the judges considered that 'there was ample evidence to support the verdict of the jury'. Crippen 'turned round like an automaton and walked quickly out of the dock'.[2]

Undeterred, Newton drafted a petition for mercy, in the hope that Crippen's death sentence would be commuted to one of life imprisonment. He made several hundred copies of the petition and sent them to cities and major towns throughout England to collect signatures from sympathetic members of the public. Newton quickly raised 150 signatures for the copy of the petition in his office alone; many of those signing it were women.[3] The petitions raised over 15,000 signatures by the time they were submitted to the Home Secretary.

During his spell as Home Secretary Winston Churchill oversaw forty-three capital sentences. He granted reprieves in twenty-one of them, but not in Crippen's case. Churchill took the matter of deciding the fate of condemned prisoners very seriously, and personally studied each case in great detail before making his burdensome decision. He would leave his verdict until the last possible moment, lest any new evidence came to light. Despite being a supporter of the death penalty, Churchill found such decisions very painful to make.[4] On 19 November he announced that he had 'failed to discover any sufficient ground to justify him in advising His Majesty to interfere with the due course of law' (the prerogative of commuting death sentences belonged to the monarch, but in practice the Home Secretary dealt with the matter). Crippen was informed of the decision at 9.15 a.m. that day.

Churchill did make one concession in Crippen's favour. He had received a memo from his assistant under-secretary at the Home Office, Ernley Blackwell, and Home Office adviser Sir Edward Troup, indicating that if Le Neve and Crippen wanted to kiss each other at their final meeting at Pentonville they should be kept apart to prevent a weapon or poison being passed, and they thought 'it is kinder to the parties themselves to keep such interviews as formal and unemotional as possible'. Churchill disagreed. He would not instruct the prison governor to keep Le Neve and Crippen apart, as long as every precaution was taken to prevent Crippen obtaining any poison.

Ethel Le Neve's reaction to the news of Crippen's appeal failing was bizarre. The actor/manager Seymour Hicks was visiting a detective at Bow Street police station. Hicks was told that Le Neve was in the building to ask if she could borrow the pair of boy's trousers that she had worn on the *Montrose*, because she had been offered money by a newspaper to pose as a boy for a photograph. The news of Crippen's failed appeal came through while Le Neve was still there. When she heard the news all she said was 'Oh!'

Coincidentally, Seymour Hicks was a cousin of Alfred Tobin and had previously met Dr Crippen. The pair had enjoyed a 'long and pleasant chat together'. Hicks found Crippen to be a man of a gentle nature, whose most striking feature was his strong spectacles, which gave the impression that he had bulging eyes. Like many others, he admitted, 'I don't know why, I always had a sneaking pity for the wretched man Crippen'.[5]

Now that the normal courses of action had failed to save Crippen, desperate measures were being taken. Crippen's former employer, Dr J.H. Munyon, offered a £10,000 reward for the reappearance of Cora Crippen, or for anyone who could prove that she was still alive.[6] Francis Tobias, a Philadelphia lawyer, claimed to have proof that Cora Crippen was alive and in hiding in Chicago, 'in order to carry out the most diabolical plan of revenge in the annals of crime'. However, Tobias failed to produce any evidence to support his story. In Cambridge an old soldier applied to the Borough justices offering himself to be hanged in place of Crippen, as a doctor should not be executed.[7]

While Crippen was languishing in Pentonville Prison awaiting his fate, the prison's governor, Major Owen Mytton Davies, was paying close attention to his notorious charge:

> Crippen was another prisoner who remains impressed on my mind, chiefly, I must admit, owing to the notoriety surrounding his case, as there was nothing heroic about him. He was a sordid, mean, avaricious little man, whose one redeeming feature was his extraordinary devotion to Ethel Le Neve.
>
> My first glimpse of him in prison garb was in the central hall at Pentonville; in his drab convict clothes, stamped with a broad arrow and ill-fitting, he looked more than unprepossessing.
>
> I was very suspicious concerning Crippen, and even had the rims and ear-pieces of his spectacles examined for concealed poison.[8]

The prison's chief warder, Mr H.T. Boreham, had a more sympathetic attitude towards the prisoner. He recalled Crippen as being 'a very pleasant little man'.[9] Another warder, J. Alan Shields, was similarly impressed by Crippen's demeanour. Upon his arrival at Pentonville, Crippen asked for the prison's regulations to be explained to him so that he could conform to them and be as little trouble as possible. Shields said that it was rare for a murderer to elicit any sympathy from the warders, but 'there was about Crippen something that made it possible to forget for the time being . . . the crime he was accused of'.

Shields noticed that Crippen was not sleeping at night. Crippen explained that he was seeing visions of the scaffold and of Cora passing through his cell. Crippen told Shields that this was not the first time he had figured in an execution:

> Years ago when I was living in Cleveland, Ohio, my wife and I both took part in private theatricals for the benefit of a local charity, and I played the part of a man falsely accused of murder and cut down from the gallows at the last moment on the arrival of the heroine, my wife, with proof of my innocence.[10]

With all hope of a reprieve gone, Crippen published a statement that appeared in the *Daily Mail* and clearly showed the depth of his feelings towards Ethel Le Neve, as well as declaring her total innocence in the whole affair. Crippen took full responsibility for her plight, but not for the murder of Cora:

> About my unhappy relations with Belle Elmore I will say nothing. We drifted apart in sympathy; she had her own friends and pleasures, and I was rather a lonely man and rather miserable. Then I obtained the affection and sympathy of Miss Le Neve. I confess that, according to the moral laws of Church and State, we were guilty, and I do not defend our position in that respect. But what I do say is that this love was not of a debased and degraded character. It was – if I may say so to people who will not perhaps understand or believe – a good love. She comforted me in my melancholy condition; her mind was beautiful to me; her loyalty and courage and self-sacrifice were of a high character. Whatever sin there was – and we broke the law – it was my sin, not hers . . .
>
> In this farewell letter to the world, written as I face eternity, I say that Ethel Le Neve has loved me as few women love men, and that her innocence of any crime, save that of yielding to the dictates of the heart, is absolute. To her I pay this last tribute. It is of her that my last thoughts have been. My last prayer will be that God may protect her and keep her safe from harm, and allow her to join me in eternity.

Despite his moving words, there was still the stench of hypocrisy when Crippen claimed 'that the love of Ethel Le Neve has been the best thing in my life – my only happiness – and that in return for that great gift I have been inspired with a greater kindness towards my fellow beings, and with a greater desire to do good'. Clearly this kindness had not extended to his murdered wife's family and many friends.

Crippen wrote to Le Neve every day. One letter read:

How can I find the strength and heart to struggle through this last letter? God indeed must hear our cry to Him for Divine help in this last farewell.

How to control myself to write I hardly know, but pray God help us to be brave to help to face the end so near.

The thoughts rush to my mind quicker than I can put them down. Time is so short now, and there is so much that I would say.

There are less than two days left to us. Only one more letter after this can I write you, and only two more visits – one to-night before you read this letter, and one tomorrow.

When I wrote to you on Saturday I had not heard any news of the petition, and though I never at any time had hope, yet deep down in my heart was just a glimmer of trust that God might give us yet a chance to put me right before the world and let me have the passionate longing of my soul.

Your letter, written early Saturday, came to me last Saturday evening, and soon after the Governor brought me the dreadful news about ten o'clock.

He was so kind and considerate in telling me, in breaking the shock as gently as he could. He was most kind, and left me at last with 'God bless you! Good night,' so that I know you will ever remember him most kindly.

When he had gone I first kissed your face in the photo, my faithful, devoted companion in all this sorrow.

Oh, how glad I am I had the photo. It was some consolation, although in spite of all my greatest efforts it was impossible to keep down a great sob and my heart's agonised cry.

How am I to endure to take my last look at your dear face? What agony must I go through at the last when you disappear for ever from my eyes? God help us to be brave then.

Prison governor Mytton Davies recalled how Crippen took the letter from Le Neve, read it and then kissed it again and again. His last request to Mytton Davies was for Le Neve's letters and photograph to be buried with him.

Crippen's executioner was John Ellis, the public hangman. As soon as the death sentence was passed on Dr Crippen, Ellis's tribulations began. In addition to carrying out executions Ellis ran a barber's shop, which was inundated with people coming in, not for haircuts, but to ask Ellis about Crippen. People stopped in the street and pointed excitedly at him, saying to their friends, 'That's him! That's the man who is going to hang Crippen!' To add to his woes, Ellis had to carry out an execution both the day before and after he hanged Crippen. Ellis said that the execution of Dr Crippen 'was about the only time in my life that I really almost regretted the office I held'.

Ellis arrived at Pentonville Prison on the afternoon of 22 November:

I learned that the condemned murderer had been deeply disappointed when he found that all hope of a reprieve must be dismissed from his mind. He seemed to have convinced himself that he would never be hanged, and when the truth came home to him he was on the verge of total nervous collapse.

Terrible though the shock was, he soon controlled his feelings once more and became his old cool, calculating self, a fact of which we were to have startling evidence that very night.

The peephole in his cell door provided me with means of observing him, and as I gazed in at the man who had set the whole world by the ears I marvelled at his calmness. He sat there writing, and would occasionally break off to chat pleasantly and in most affable fashion with the warders whose duty it was to watch him night and day until the scaffold claimed him.

Like all those who came into contact with Crippen, Ellis was struck by his amiable and helpful nature, which always came to the fore despite his awful predicament. He said that Crippen, 'execrated murderer though he was . . . had a natural amiability and innate gentlemanliness that seized the affections of even his warders'. There must have been some inner turmoil under the calm façade, for Crippen attempted to commit suicide on the eve of his execution:

Crippen undoubtedly committed a hideous crime which admits of no excuse but he had two sides of his nature, and it was the pleasant only that was uppermost during my contact with him.

Yet that very night he showed that behind his suave graciousness lay power to make firm life and death decisions. Just before midnight one of the warders in that silent cell made a thrilling discovery.

Crippen was in bed, and the men watching his progress through his last night on earth felt uneasy at Crippen's restless motions. The strain on warders in such a position is a most intense one, and these men would have been superhuman if they had not felt overweighted with the responsibility that was resting upon their shoulders.

At last one of them went to Crippen's bedside to satisfy himself that the latter's movements were nothing more than the usual restless tossings of a condemned man on his last night, but to his amazement found he was just in time to prevent the scaffold being cheated of its victim!

For some reason never explained, Crippen had been allowed to retain his glasses, and the determined man had deliberately broken one of the lenses with the intention of using the jagged edge to cut his throat. This was discovered when the warder, seeing that Crippen's glasses were not in their usual place, asked him where they were.

'They are here,' he replied, pointing under the bedclothes.

He was at once ordered to get out of bed and then the frame, with one of the lenses broken out of it, was then found – just in time.

This act was about the only one Crippen ever did that caused his custodians any trouble, for he was a most considerate prisoner, never making unnecessary trouble, and always doing exactly as he was told.[11]

William Willis, Ellis's assistant, confirmed the story. Willis thought that Crippen had planned to puncture an artery and slowly bleed to death while he slept.[12] In addition, there was another incident two days earlier which the prison governor had noted in his diary: 'Broke off rim of glass whilst retiring to lavatory with the presumed idea of attempting self-injury.'

Hawley Harvey Crippen barely touched his final breakfast, which consisted of a pot of tea, bread and butter, and two eggs.[13] He was hanged at Pentonville Prison at nine o'clock on the dark, cold and foggy morning of 23 November. Ellis had correctly determined that a drop of 7ft 9in would be sufficient to instantly dispatch Crippen, who stood 5ft 4in tall, and weighed 142lb clothed the day before the execution. The character of Crippen's neck was recorded as being 'normal'. Dew was relieved that he was not there to witness it: 'How he met his death I do not know. Happily it was not part of my duties to be present at that grim scene. But knowing the man as I had learned to know him, I have no doubt that he bore himself bravely, and that his self-control never deserted him on that cold November morning when he breathed his last.' Despite Crippen's earlier suicide attempt, Dew was right in his guess. Ellis described Crippen's last hours:

> His face throughout wore a set, calm expression. His warders looked more distressed than he was and nobody glancing at him would have realised that this was the man who had committed a fearful murder, had attempted to commit suicide a few hours ago, and who, in an hour and a half would have to walk to the gallows from which he would never return alive.
>
> As I stood on the scaffold I could see the procession come into view twelve yards distant. Behind the praying priest came the notorious Dr. Crippen, no longer a murderer to fear but rather a man to be pitied. Yet his attitude was not that of one who asks for sympathy. If he had ever shown cowardice or collapse he displayed none now.
>
> I could see him smiling as he approached, and the smile never left his face up to the moment when I threw the white cap over it and blotted out God's light from his eyes for ever.
>
> In a trice he was on the trap-doors with his legs strapped together and a rope round his neck. One swift glance round to be assured that all was right and my hand shot to the lever.
>
> Thud! The fatal doors had fallen. The slack rope tightened, and in an instant was still. Dr. Crippen was dead.[14]

All rumours of a last-minute confession made by Crippen were flatly denied. As with all executed criminals, a coroner's inquest was held to establish the cause of Crippen's death. Walter Schroder, who had been the coroner at Cora Crippen's inquest, oversaw this formality. Dew knew that Crippen went to his death safe in the knowledge that his beloved Ethel had been set free. He wondered 'if Crippen died with Miss Le Neve's name on his lips?' He probably suspected that he did, and was probably correct.

POSTSCRIPT: THE MYSTERY OF CRIPPEN'S CONFESSION

While reliable sources state that Crippen made no confession to the murder of his wife, the possibility that a confession did exist led to dramatic scenes the day before Crippen's execution. On 22 November a young man entered the offices of the London *Evening Times*, a newspaper that had only been in existence for twenty days. He told the editor that Arthur Newton had a confession from Crippen, and was prepared to sell it.

The *Evening Times*'s crime reporter, Arthur Findon, hurried to Marlborough Street magistrates' court, where he found Newton. After much bartering Newton settled on a price of £500 in cash for the confession, and an assurance that his name would not be mentioned. They agreed to meet at 8 p.m. at the Langham Hotel, where Newton would hand the confession over. Findon took Newton at his word, and told his editor that it would be safe to announce in that evening's 'Stop Press' column that the next day's issue would contain the confession.

Findon, along with reporter James Little, met Newton at the Langham, but the solicitor said he was reneging on the deal, fearing that he would be struck off the rolls by the Law Society if they ever found out what he had done. Findon threatened to print a story of how Newton tried to sell the confession. Newton backed down and said that an associate of his named Low would bring the confession to Findon's house at 2 a.m. on 23 November (the day of Crippen's execution). Low would show Findon the confession and then burn it. That way, Newton could say that he had not given it to Findon.

Low duly arrived and read the confession to Findon and Little, who took notes. He then threw the papers on the fire; but as soon as his back was turned, Little plucked the half-burned confession from the grate. From this and their notes the two journalists pieced together Crippen's confession.

The *Evening Times* ran the story of Crippen's confession on 23 November,[15] and the paper sold close to a million copies that evening. The newspaper's problems started when another London evening paper ran a story the same day that they had interviewed officials at the prison and the Home Office who denied that there had been a confession. They had also interviewed Newton, who had refused to comment. These denials were circulated by press agencies and appeared in the final editions of the evening papers.

The next day the *Evening Times* staff held a meeting to decide what to do to protect their reputation. According to Findon they decided to say nothing, to preserve Newton's reputation. Furthermore, Findon did not reveal any of this until immediately after Newton's death in 1930. This remarkable altruism seems a little unlikely, as Newton had pocketed £500 of the *Times*'s money and humiliated them in front of their Fleet Street rivals. Findon said that he went to see Newton for an explanation and a statement. An unrepentant Newton told him, 'I can say nothing about the confession. I personally know of no confession, but beyond this I cannot discuss the matter except to say that it is not within the right of any man to throw doubt on the confession.' It was too little, too late. By 26 November the *Evening Times*'s circulation had fallen from 1 million to 30,000, and it went out of business after just over a year.[16]

If Findon's story is to be believed, then that was not the only occasion that Newton profited from an alleged Crippen confession. In 1922 he sold his memoirs to *Thomson's Weekly News*, and these included the claim that Crippen had signed a confession in Brixton Prison before his trial.

According to Newton, Crippen revealed that he had been driven to murder by Cora's infidelity, nagging, drinking and jealousy. The murder was premeditated, for Crippen had bought a dissecting knife for the purpose of dismembering Cora. He had hidden the knife under his mattress, safe in the knowledge that Cora would not find it, 'for she never even bothered to make my bed'. He burned the missing remains in the kitchen stove, but could not finish the job as the fumes were overpowering and he did not want to arouse the suspicions of his neighbours. Newton added that the confession was either lost or destroyed by the time he gave up his practice.[17]

Retirement and Libel Cases

. . . an absolute lie from beginning to end.

The Times, *1 April 1911*

Walter Dew was now probably the best known and most celebrated detective in the world, and it came as a surprise to many when he announced his retirement from Scotland Yard after 'nearly 29 years' strenuous and exciting service',[1] which received wide press coverage, coming as it did on the day that Crippen's appeal failed. The popular tabloid *Lloyd's Weekly News* paid Dew the following tribute:

On the Continent, as in this country, his astuteness and tact have won him fame. His quiet, unassuming disposition secured him considerable popularity among his colleagues, and the intimation of his ensuing resignation has been received with universal regret.

The newspaper stated that the fact that Dew had announced his retirement immediately after the conclusion of the Crippen case was merely a coincidence, because '[h]e had already seriously considered his resignation before he was concerned in [the Crippen case], but consented to remain in office until its completion'.[2] Dew himself described it as 'a fitting moment to retire', adding that the decision came as a surprise to his superiors and the Director of Public Prosecutions, Sir Charles Mathews, who asked Dew to reconsider.

Dew would not be turned, as there were unspecified 'special private reasons which compelled me to stick to my resolution'. He was quite content with the achievements of his career. As he would later recall, 'Looking back at my nearly 30 years' service in the police, and forgetting the black side of it, I could well describe it as a life of thrills and adventures rarely given to one man to experience.'[3]

Dew noted a 'strange and gruesome coincidence' at the end of his career:

As a young officer, just appointed to the Criminal Investigation Department, I was stationed in the Whitechapel Division. This was at the height of the 'Jack the Ripper' terror. My inquiries in connexion with that unsolved mystery brought me to the notice of the higher authorities at Scotland Yard, and helped my advancement.

My last job as a chief inspector at the 'Yard' was the capture of Crippen.

Mutilation of the bodies was a feature of both crimes.

In the course of his career, Dew had received some 130 commendations and rewards from the Metropolitan Police Commissioner, judges and magistrates.[4] He left the Metropolitan Police on 5 December 1910 with an exemplary certificate,[5] indicating that not a single complaint had ever been made against him. Dew's pension papers revealed that he was 47 years old, and had served a total of 28 years and 176 days, during which he had only spent two or three weeks off sick with influenza and other minor complaints. He was entitled to an annual pension of £238 5s 8d (as opposed to his previous weekly wage of £6 14s). He was 5ft 9in tall, had brown hair which was turning grey, grey eyes and a fresh complexion.[6]

Detective Inspector Tom Divall was transferred from Bethnal Green Division to fill Dew's position at Scotland Yard.[7] Coincidentally, Divall was also a former railway employee, who had worked on the Whitechapel murder investigations.[8]

Just before his departure Dew played a small part in the sale of 39 Hilldrop Crescent to the Glaswegian comedian Sandy McNab. The frugal Scot had correctly guessed that the owner of the property would be keen to be rid of it, as it now had a gruesome reputation. He may also have taken into account the publicity value of the story of his purchase, which saw his photograph splashed across the front page of a weekly tabloid with a circulation of over 430,000. McNab's letter to the house's owner had been returned undelivered, so he wrote to Dew, who passed on the letter to the property's agent, who subsequently agreed to the sale. McNab was well satisfied with the property, having acquired a house worth more than £1,000 for £500.

McNab described his new property as follows:

When I went through it as I did from top to bottom, I felt fully convinced that the authorities had left not the slightest trace of the terrible crime behind them. Every wall had been stripped of its wallpaper and here and there the plaster and lath had been removed. Floor boarding had been taken up, and ceilings had been pierced during the search for clues.

On my first visit I made my way all over the premises, and at last I came to the fatal cellar. I will not attempt to hide the fact that as my

163

foot stepped upon the concrete floor, hardly yet dried, I felt a queer sensation at the pit of my stomach and a choking sensation in my throat. In my mind's eye I could see again the culprit working with feverish haste to bury the last trace of the crime from the eyes of man. Then I imagined the officers of the law examining the dark, damp, dungeon-like cellar, while the culprit stood calmly upon the steps behind them. The detectives were probably wise to leave the cellar at that time without making farther examinations, and I felt I could do no better than follow their example.[9]

McNab exploited his connection to the Crippen case, billing himself as 'The Man Who Made Crippen's Cat Laugh'.[10]

Walter Dew's pension was soon to be substantially supplemented. In 1911 he would bring libel actions against nine newspapers for comments they had made about him during the Crippen investigation. Some of the cases were settled out of court, but others were not. At the end of March 1911 the High Court of Justice heard the case of *Dew* v. *Edward Lloyd (Limited)*, the publishers of the *Daily Chronicle*. Dew's grievance against the *Chronicle* related to the following passage published on 4 August 1910, which claimed Dew had informed their correspondent that Crippen had confessed to the murder of his wife:

Crippen Tells Police the Whole Story
[From Our Special Correspondent]

There is no longer any doubt that Crippen has made a confession to Inspector Dew regarding the crime of which he is charged, and the news which I sent you as a rumour last night can now be stated as a fact.

I not only have the very best authority for saying this, but I also have the admission of Inspector Dew, made to me this afternoon, that Crippen has told him the complete story of the killing of Belle Elmore. Inspector Dew said when I asked him: 'Yes, Crippen has now told me the complete story of the crime and how her body was disposed of. He also related to me exactly how the murder occurred.'

This is all the inspector would say, and when asked for further particulars said: 'I cannot say any more. If you want to know any more about the case I must refer you to Scotland Yard.'

I asked him if he would confirm or deny the report that Crippen also said that he was not a murderer and would escape conviction. Mr Dew replied: 'I would be very glad to oblige you, but I cannot. My mouth is closed for the present.'

In the next column the correspondent added:

> She [Le Neve] is unaware that Crippen has made any confession, and Inspector Dew has told the Canadian police that he is firmly convinced that she has been kept in ignorance of all the facts of the murder.

Dew contested that

> the words imputed to the plaintiff [Dew] that he was guilty of grave misconduct as a police officer; that he had deliberately violated his duty, and was no longer fit to remain a police officer or to be placed in any position of confidence or responsibility.

The *Chronicle* readily admitted that they had published the words (for how could they deny it?), and conceded that the words were indeed libellous, but denied that they should be interpreted as severely as Dew had. The paper had already faced action for contempt of court for the article the previous year. They had published a lengthy apology to Dew in mitigation of damages, which ran thus:

> On August 4 last year there was published in the *Daily Chronicle* a cable from our Special Correspondent at Quebec in reference to the Crippen case. In it our Correspondent made a statement to the effect that Crippen had confessed to Inspector Dew that he had killed Belle Elmore and that the inspector had stated that Crippen had told him the complete story of the crime, how the murder occurred, and how the body was disposed of. The message also gave an account of an alleged interview with and alleged statements by Inspector Dew relating to the matter.
>
> At the time this was published in our columns we had no intention of casting any reflection whatever upon Inspector Dew.
>
> We had always considered, and still consider, that Inspector Dew was a capable and zealous officer, and that he had performed his extremely difficult duties in connexion with the investigation of the Crippen affair with ability and discretion.
>
> Recently our attention has been called to the original publication, and it has been pointed out to us that the words which were published were capable of being read as casting a reflection on Inspector Dew in the performance of his duties.
>
> In these circumstances we desire to state publicly that we did not intend to publish anything derogatory to Inspector Dew. We printed

the cable in good faith as an item of news, believing it to be true. We now fully withdraw the statements in question and offer to Inspector Dew an apology and an expression of our deep regret that we should have been the means of circulating such statements or have been the cause of any annoyance to him.[11]

But the apology was not enough. Dew's lawyer, Mr Charles Gill, said that as a libel had already been admitted the issue now was the amount of damages Dew was entitled to. Gill pointed out that the press's hunger for information about the Crippen case had made them troublesome and hampered Dew's investigation. The *Daily Chronicle* in particular had 'made themselves notorious'.

Dew had been under orders from his superiors and 'had to carry out obvious instructions that he was not to betray the trust and confidence reposed in him. He was not authorised to make any communication to any members of the public, least of all to members of the press. Those instructions were well known, and a breach of them would bring upon the man serious consequences.' Gill pressed this point home to the jury. He told them, 'On no account was he to give information with regard to the progress of a case. He had express instructions to make no communication, except as a witness, upon the trial of the case.'

Then Dew's career was reviewed. It was explained that there 'was never a suggestion against his conduct'. Dew jealously guarded his reputation, for 'he contemplated that when the time arrived, and with the very exceptional character he had earned, he might get employment by banks and other public authorities'.[12] Dew was at this time working as a confidential enquiries agent, and successfully carried on in this profession for some years.[13]

Mr Gill really made the most of the opportunity to build up a case against the *Chronicle* and the extent of their libel. He continued by saying that if Dew had spoken about the case to the press, he would have been 'absolutely unfit for his post. For a man to make a disclosure of a confession would [make him] guilty of the grossest misconduct and contempt of Court.' The libel had been 'an absolute lie from beginning to end, and the defendants dared not say there was a word of truth in it'.

Gill concluded with the following tirade against the *Chronicle*:

. . . the words meant that [Dew] was not fit to remain a member of the force or to be placed in any position of confidence or responsibility. How could the plaintiff at 47, if he had been guilty of misconduct, be entrusted with any work in which an honourable man had to be trusted? The imputation upon him was that no one would have been guilty of such misconduct unless money had been paid to him.

To finish off, Gill explained that Dew had delayed the libel action because he could not have taken it while still a serving police officer, and had to tie up the Crippen case before he could sue for damages. Dew then gave evidence, saying that he had never made any communication to either the press or the public with regard to Crippen.

The *Chronicle* defended itself as best it could. It considered that its earlier apology had been action enough, as 'the plaintiff was not injured and there was no need to bring this action'.[14] The jury disagreed, and their verdict was in favour of Dew. He was awarded a hefty £400 in damages.

Another libel case soon followed, this time against the weekly newspaper *M.A.P.* (*Mainly About People*). The offending article was one published on 13 August 1910, 'which cast reflections upon the capability of the plaintiff [Dew] in dealing with the Crippen case'.[15] This was an understatement. The piece, quoted here in full, was an outrageous vilification of Dew's character and his handling of the Crippen case:

Dew, the Sleuth-hound
SOME PLAIN QUESTIONS ABOUT HIS LATEST CASE

There are various amazing figures in the Crippen case.

There are the principals themselves, a commonplace man and a commonplace girl who suddenly become the centre of the world's attention.

There is Captain Kendall, of the s.s. *Montrose*. Or, at least, Captain Kendall would be an amazing person had he said or written a tithe of the things attributed to him. But then no sane person for a moment believes that any British sea captain would be guilty of the melodramatic boasting, the inhuman crowing over a man who is down that has been foisted upon Captain Kendall by journalists of the baser sort.

But one figure stands out supreme. The solitary unapproachable figure of Detective-Inspector Dew.

With Inspector Dew in his private capacity the public is not concerned. The information recently given to the world that he is domesticated and musical leaves the world still breathing. But Inspector Dew stands for the Criminal Investigation Department, New Scotland Yard, and their methods, and as such he is an absorbing picture, the more so that he has cost the country almost the price of an Old Master.

Very briefly to recapitulate the facts of the case, Mrs. Crippen disappeared on or about January 31st 1910. To her friends, her husband told an unconvincing story of her death in America.

On June 28th [*sic*] these friends communicated their suspicions to Scotland Yard. Scotland Yard apparently were not much impressed. Anyway, the actual conduct of the case was handed over to Inspector Dew, an officer of good record but of no particular distinction.

Acting with almost dazzling rapidity, Inspector Dew calls on Crippen on July 8th – ten days later.

To an ordinary man the advantage to be gained by putting Crippen on his guard is not quite plain. A sense of fair play is all very well, but to indicate to a man that he is suspected of murder is, perhaps, carrying our idea of 'giving a man a chance' too far.

Crippen has a pleasant chat with Dew, tells him another, and a more plausible tale to account for 'Belle Elmore's' disappearance, shows him over the house, and even takes him down to the fatal cellar, where the eagle eyes of the sleuth-hound of the law – do sleuth-hounds have eagle eyes? – detect nothing suspicious.

Crippen promises not to run away, but, in a very caddish manner, breaks his word and bolts next day, accompanied by Miss Le Neve.

Crippen bolted on July 9th; it was not until July 11th that Inspector Dew, by a brilliant piece of detective work, discovered that the bird had flown.

Apparently the police had a touching faith in Crippen, and expected him to return.

Then, nearly a week after Crippen had disappeared, the hue and cry was raised.

Meanwhile, Dew, the indefatigable, was here, there, and everywhere that the wanted couple were not.

It does not seem to have occurred to the authorities that Brussels, during Exhibition time, would be a likely hiding-place for a fugitive.

Crippen played the game. He did everything that untrained intelligence might expect him to do. He went to Brussels.

It is an axiom in criminology that a hunted man usually makes for the scenes of his childhood.

Crippen followed the rule, and tried to return to his native America by way of Canada, and he very nearly succeeded.

True, he came on board at Antwerp; but a mere layman may be pardoned for thinking that within two days Scotland Yard might have had every port by which Crippen could join a boat bound for

North or South America effectively watched. Then the captain of the *Montrose* sent a message to the effect that Crippen was on board his ship.

At last Inspector Dew got going. Apparently acting under the instructions, he hurled himself into a train and caught the *Laurentic*. Hundreds of business men do this sort of thing every week; but Scotland Yard detectives are not business men.

'Dew's dash' for Liverpool stirred the country. The public felt that they were getting their money's worth out of the C.I.D.

Crippen had hoodwinked Dew; obviously therefore, Dew was the man to send after him. If there be any flaw in this logic, I can't find it – I am not a detective-inspector.

Sherlock Holmes could hardly have effected the capture in neater fashion. The pilot disguise was worthy of the highest moments of Arsene Lupin; but here, again, the credit of it is due, not to Dew, but to Captain Kendall.

Crippen has now been caught (thanks mainly to his own stupidity), after an expenditure of some £5,000 of public money, all of which could have been saved if Inspector Dew had taken the very ordinary precaution of having Crippen shadowed when he was first suspected. Why such precautions were not taken must be explained, or public faith in the capacity of Scotland Yard will be seriously shaken.

The newspaper conceded that Dew's grievance against them was justified; unlike the *Chronicle* they did not argue. They 'desired to withdraw in the fullest possible way any and all imputations upon the character of the plaintiff'. They further expressed regret for having published the article, and paid Dew an undisclosed sum in damages.

The case ended with some light-hearted banter between the judge, Mr Justice Darling (who had rejected Dr Crippen's appeal) and *M.A.P.*'s barrister, Mr Hugh Fraser, after Fraser had apologised for his client's actions:

Darling   They will exercise more care in the future?

Fraser   No doubt every one who has figured as a defendant in a libel suit becomes more careful.

Darling   I express no opinion on Mr Fraser's latest dictum.[16]

Shortly afterwards Dew took action against *John Bull* and others for stories which included the words, 'Inspector Dew has resigned'. Dew was once again represented by Mr Gill, who argued that the words suggested that Dew 'had been compelled to resign and that he had not entered into voluntary retirement'.

Mr Justice Darling again presided. He agreed with Gill that '[t]he words would certainly bear the interpretation put upon them; indeed, if that were not the meaning, I cannot see what they did mean'. *John Bull's* barrister was F.E. Smith. F.E., fresh from his triumph of defending Ethel Le Neve, quipped that 'they had offered a prize to any one who could suggest what the words did mean'. Darling dryly responded that if there was a prize, it was Dew who had won it, for the ex-Chief Inspector had been awarded a 'small solatium' by the paper.[17]

The Wee Hoose

Ask the average person who Walter Dew is, and he will answer, 'The
man who arrested Crippen.' Some will cut down the answer to
'Crippen Dew.' Such is fame.

Saturday Post, *29 January 1916*

The Dews left Allfarthing Lane in Wandsworth in 1911 after living there
for over ten years, and moved to Perrivale Lane in Greenford, Middlesex.
Dew paid 200 guineas for a house called 'The Nook',[1] where he spent
much of his time gardening.[2]

On 22 May 1913 Dew's eldest son Walter, who was living in France at
the time, married Gertrude Florence Gifford at Southampton. His father
believed that the younger Walter was the only other member of the
family to have set foot inside a police station. He had joined the
Metropolitan Police in June 1908, and eventually became an inspector in
the Special Branch before retiring in 1933.[3] Walter jnr had spent twenty-
four of his twenty-five years' service at Scotland Yard, and had
accompanied the Prime Minister to America and Canada in 1929.[4]

Tragedy struck in 1915 when, on 26 May, the Dews' young son Stanley
(known as Tom), a private in the 23rd Battalion of the London Regiment,
was killed in action at Givenchy, France. This calamity came soon after
the death of Dew's mother Eliza, who had been living in Fulham, and
passed away at St George's Hospital at Hyde Park Corner on 21
September 1914. His father had died in 1884 of renal disease.

In 1916 Dew was featured in a series of newspaper profiles of 'The
Twelve Greatest Detectives of the World', which reviewed his career. Dew
told the newspaper's representative that being a detective 'is the finest
profession in the world, and if I could start life all over again I would
rather be a detective than anything else'. The journalist described Dew's
appearance as follows:

Mr Dew suggests the retired army officer rather than the detective.
Imagine a man just above medium height, with a dark moustache,
hair turning grey, a strong face tempered by a pair of kindly eyes, a
clear-cut figure reminiscent of the barracks, and you have Mr Dew as
he is to-day at the age of fifty-three. A major in mufti is as good a

description as any. You will find many like him in the famous military clubs in West End London.[5]

In 1920 the Crippen case was added to the series of Notable British Trials volumes. These excellent books contained transcriptions of the trials of famous criminals, with introductions to the cases and appendices. The editor, Filson Young, included Walter Dew in his acknowledgements, and he referred to receiving information about the case from Dew in his introduction. This included Dew telling Young that after searching 39 Hilldrop Crescent on 8 July in Crippen's presence and finding nothing, the investigation 'was to all intents and purposes finished', indicating that if Crippen had not fled, then perhaps the murder of Cora Crippen might have remained a missing person case.[6] Years later Dew contradicted this statement. His new version of events put him in a better light:

> Yet it has been stated in print that following the happenings of that day my inclination was to drop the inquiry on the ground that I was satisfied with the doctor's explanation.
>
> What actually happened completely disproves any such suggestion.
>
> Next day – Saturday – one of the first things I did was to circulate a description of Mrs. Crippen as a missing person to every police station in London. I spent the remainder of the day on further inquiries, and on the Sunday occupied myself by analysing in detail the statement Dr. Crippen had made.
>
> As a final proof that I was far from satisfied, I went early on the Monday morning to Albion House with the object of seeing Crippen again.

By now the Dews had moved again, to a house called 'Hollywood' at 3 Vincent Road, Croydon. On 15 July 1924 Dew's youngest daughter Ethel married accountant Albert Martin at the parish church of St James in Croydon. It was in Croydon that Dew's wife Kate died on 12 July 1927, from cancer, at the age of 61. One year after the death of his wife Dew moved house for the final time. He went to the southern coastal town of Worthing in West Sussex. Dew bought an attractive small bungalow at 10 Beaumont Road named 'The Wee Hoose'. Ironically its previous inhabitants had been a family called Hawley. Dew retained the house's name and shared the Wee Hoose with two women: a widow called Florence Idle (née Beadle), and her spinster sister-in-law Iris.[7] On 10 December 1928 Dew married Florence, who was twelve years his junior, at Broadwater in Sussex.

Although Dew would soon start writing on criminological matters, he admitted that he seldom read detective novels as he had seen too much of the real thing during his long career.[8] In his retirement years Dew was occasionally consulted by newspapers and asked to give his views on the sensational events and crimes of the day. While he had always remained tight-lipped when approached by journalists during the Crippen case, he readily gave his opinions when asked during his retirement. Even decades after his retirement from the Metropolitan Police, the name of Dew was still recognised by the tabloid-reading public as being that of the man who had caught Crippen.

In December 1926 the well-known author of detective stories Agatha Christie mysteriously disappeared. The newspapers made much of the disappearance of the writer, whose work was so closely associated with crime and mystery. The *Sunday Express* asked Dew what his opinion was of the incident, and he was forthcoming:

Foul play is possible, but I do not think there has been foul play. It is just conceivable that she has been murdered, and that her body will soon be discovered, hidden, say, in some spot near the house, or perhaps where her car was found.

Those who support this theory say that it must be the secret belief of the police, or they would not have carried out such a thorough search in the case of a missing woman. They point out that this is not usual in all cases of disappearance.

Even if the missing woman is safe and well, and, as some think, laughing in hiding at the hullabaloo she has caused, I think the police are justified in the course they are taking. They would look ridiculous if they had given up on the search and the body of the woman – possibly murdered – were found subsequently.

I cannot subscribe to the theory of foul play, however. I have had experience of one famous case of a woman's disappearance – that of Belle Elmore – and of her murderer, Crippen. This case is altogether different.

Agatha Christie has been writing detective stories, and one suggestion is that the publicity of a disappearance would be good for the sales of her books. That might be the view of an unknown actress out for publicity, but no clever woman novelist of her standing would believe that to disappear for publicity's sake would be of service to her in her work.

I reject the theory of voluntary disappearance for pecuniary advantage, as I do the murder theory.

She may have had other motives for disappearing besides publicity, such as that of causing annoyance to some one else. That time may prove or disprove.

I am content to accept loss of memory or hysteria as the likeliest reason for her absence.

Agatha Christie is a woman whose work focussed her attention on crime and things sinister. She wrote detective stories, thought about crooks and murder all day, and possibly her subconscious brain was at work on these subjects all night.

These reflections might affect the minds of strong men; even public executioners have gone crazy. Agatha Christie may have had other, possibly smaller, things than plotting novels to worry her. Those together may have brought on a condition of hysteria.

All women are subject to hysteria at times. If Mrs Christie's mind became hysterical she may have gone wandering over the country, on and on, with the false strength of the half-demented, until she dropped in some spot miles away from where she is being sought now.

She even may have found her way to London, or some other town.

It is said there had been so much publicity that it would be impossible for her to hide in London. I do not believe it. London is still one of the easiest places in which to hide.[9]

Dew had certainly hedged his bets over what had happened to Christie. The writer had indeed had other matters on her mind: her mother had recently died and she had also discovered that her husband Archibald had fallen in love with a friend's secretary, named Nancy Neele. Christie had booked into a hotel in Harrogate under the name of Neele, and was recognised nine days after her disappearance. The Christies divorced in 1928.

The year after Agatha Christie's disappearance Dew was once again asked by the *Sunday Express* to comment on a headline-grabbing story. This time it was the murder of PC George Gutteridge on the Romford-to-Ongar road in Essex on 27 September. The murder was particularly shocking, as the killer had shot Gutteridge in the head several times, including in both eyes. James Berrett, whom Dew had worked with on the case of Conrad Harms eighteen years earlier, was investigating the case:

Were the murderers of Police Constable Gutteridge, the Essex rural policeman who was shot dead in the lonely lane between Stapleford Abbots and Romford, desperate and experienced criminals, or were they comparatively inexperienced men, one of whom shot the constable under the nervous tension of fear and apprehension caused by his unexpected appearance and probable questions?

Why were these men in the neighbourhood, and why did they stop their car in that lonely road just before dawn?

These are the questions which present themselves to my mind in connection with this, the latest murder mystery, which the police have to unravel.

I have no actual experience of this crime or of the clues which are being followed, but as an interested member of the public, and as one who has assisted to unravel many murder mysteries – from that of the notorious Dr. Crippen to many lesser-known 'lights' of crime – I feel inclined to put forward my own hypothesis of the probable cause of the crime.

But, it must be remembered, it is only a hypothesis. I do not pose as an authority on this latest mystery, or even as one possessing any inside information.

My theory, then, for what it is worth is this. We may assume that the murderers were out for robbery on a far more important scale than the mere theft of the car itself. Strangers would not travel to an obscure county town merely to steal a small car.

Many large houses in the neighbourhood contain objects of considerable value, and one or more of these houses may have been the object of the projected raid. We will assume for the sake of argument, that it was either Lord Lambourne's house, Bishop's Hall, or that of a woman who is known to possess a valuable object of art.

I do not believe that they stopped because the murdered constable called on them to do so. No desperate man in a car at night would be likely to stop for a pedestrian.

My view is either that in the fog they missed a side turning – there is such a lane leading to Lord Lambourne's house, I believe – or that they halted for some adjustment to the car.

Then the constable came on the scene. He saw the stationary car and stopped to examine it. Possibly he recognised it.

Again, his suspicions may have been aroused by the mere appearance or demeanour of the men in it.

Whatever the reason he apparently thought that the circumstances warranted his taking a note of the car and the passengers.

He stood well in the light of the lamps and pulled out his notebook and pencil to do so. Then some one shot him.

He staggered, clutched at the car for support, and fell forward. The murderer or murderers realised that desperate circumstances needed desperate measures, turned him over on his back and shot him again twice, through the head. They wanted to make sure that he was dead. Then they fled.

Why was the constable shot?

Every sort of theory has been advanced, but mine is simply that he was shot by a man in a bad state of nerves, whose fears and apprehensions were doubled by the sudden appearance of a policeman and the production of a notebook.

The murderer, I believe, was a young and possibly inexperienced man, jumpy and nervous, and so obsessed with the further crime which he and his companions had in view that the appearance of Police Constable Gutteridge acted on him like a shock.

He shot the policeman in blind fear.

This theory, is, I think, borne out by the fact that many criminals, particularly burglars, are in a highly nervous condition while they are committing their crimes.

The public conception of the criminal as a man of callous, cold-steel nerves and unshakeable calm is by no means correct.

He is often in a state of bine [*sic*] funk the whole time. I have known case after case of this description. I have even known men who had committed a burglary almost faint with fright when the policeman's hand fell on their shoulders to arrest them.

Crippen was one of the rare exceptions, but he was a man of great intellectual qualities and iron self-control.

When I stepped aboard the ship to arrest him on his arrival in America, six months after he had committed his crime, I said, 'Good morning, Dr. Crippen.'

He replied, 'Good morning inspector,' but, although he must have known that I had come for him, he never flickered an eyelid. The only sign of emotion was that his Adam's apple moved convulsively up and down, as though he was gulping.

But I do not assume that the man or men in this case are criminals of the calibre of Dr. Crippen.[10]

Early in 1928 two violent car thieves, Frederick Guy Browne and William Kennedy, were arrested. It had been Browne who had shot Gutteridge after he had stopped them in a stolen car but at their Old Bailey trial both were sentenced to death. They were executed on 31 May 1928.

In 1929 Dew was interviewed by the *Sunday Express* and asked to give his views on the Croydon poisoning mystery which was enthralling the nation. Three members of the same family living in Birdhurst Rise had died from poisoning within a period of eleven months.[11] The murders in Dew's former home-town were never officially solved. The retired detective inspector had a great deal of sympathy for the Scotland Yard officers engaged on the case. Having been involved in perhaps the most famous poisoning case of all, Dew knew just what they had to contend with. His comments on the case contained echoes of his feelings towards the Whitechapel murders and the Crippen case:

Scotland Yard – in the Croydon poison mystery – is faced with a problem which might have been staged by the creator of Sherlock Holmes, and it is a problem which will require the assistance of a good many Dr. Watsons, if it is to be solved.

Poison is elusive – particularly so far as a criminal investigation is concerned. The bullet or the knife finds its mark, but must leave behind the source of its origin, and therefore provide a clue to the murderer – a clue which incidentally seldom fails to reveal the culprit.

The poisoner, however, is the most difficult murderer with whom the police have to contend. He is subtle and cunning, and he is aided by the fact that his crime is rendered comparatively easy.

The victim may be attacked in a thousand different ways. I believe, in fact, it is on record that a subtle poison has even been impregnated into a glove, by which means the person who wore it met with an untimely death.

Now, what is the problem which presents itself to Scotland-yard? The accusing finger has failed to point itself to any particular individual.

The coroner, in his particular careful analysis of the cases to the juries, bore on the point that it might be 'this, that, or the other person' who had committed the crimes.

And as there was not a scrap of evidence to point to a murderer or a suggestion of motive the verdicts do not help the police in the slightest.

One is tempted to the conclusion, however, that one hand must have been responsible for the deaths of all three members of the family.

Whose hand then? Assuming that since at the inquests no new facts have come into the possession of the detectives in charge of the case, then, indeed, it looks as if the police are faced with such an unfathomable mystery that no blame could possibly be attached to them if it passed into the lists of unsolved crimes.

The public little dream of the enormous amount of work entailed in endeavouring to solve such a mystery as this – of the heartbreaking disappointments in following clues which breathe success, and which are shattered after sleepless nights of investigation.

In all cases of poisoning, however, the chief difficulty is to prove, not that the person was poisoned, but that the accused person possessed the poison, had the opportunity and actually administered it.

The apparent absence of motive in the Croydon case might lead to the supposition that the crimes have been the work of some person with the poison mind – that mysterious individual who kills without motive or idea of gain.

We shall see.[12]

In May 1936 Dew wrote an article for *Thomson's Weekly Newspaper* after the murder by strangulation of two young women in the Soho district of London. Dew dismissed the suggestion that the murders were part of a series, like the Jack the Ripper murders. He said that murders of this kind occurred periodically among women 'of a Bohemian character [who] invite strange men sometimes to their rooms or flats'.

While Dew did not think a serial killer was at large in Soho, he did digress and recall the cases of two multiple murderers. His thoughts on them may give some further indication of the type of person he thought his old adversary Jack the Ripper may have been:

Personally, I have never come in contact with a person of weak intellect who committed murders on a wholesale scale.

There have been a series of murders committed by one individual in the past.

I recollect, and the public will remember, the notorious Neil [*sic*] Cream. This man was convicted and executed for a series of murders of women in South London, to whom he gave pills containing poison.

Another well known case is Smith, of the Brides in the Bath murders. These two will suffice for the point I wish to make.

The point is this. Could either of these two men be looked upon as maniacal or insane? On the contrary. Neil [*sic*] Cream was a person of intelligence and cunning.

He certainly had a vein of cruelty in him, but I think notoriety more than anything else moved him to carry out his designs. I saw this man several times. From my study of him, I wish to emphasise that there was nothing whatever of the madman about him.

And so far as Smith is concerned, his murders were committed for the purpose of becoming possessed of his poor victims' property. He married them, got their money and drowned them.

It was systematic but, above all, the act of a man who could think out his schemes very cleverly.[13]

To his credit, Dew did not engage in any speculation that prostitute poisoner Dr Thomas Neill Cream (1850–92) had been Jack the Ripper. He had dismissed the theory in his memoirs, saying 'Various men who were hanged for subsequent murders [to those of Jack the Ripper], notably Neil [*sic*] Cream, came under the suspicion of the public, but there were never any real grounds for believing that any one of them had had anything to do with the Whitechapel crimes.' There had been suggestions over the years that Cream (who was executed in 1892) and the Ripper were one and the same. However, Chief Inspector Mulvaney, who had worked on the Cream case, easily dismissed Cream's candidature on the grounds that he was in an American prison at the time of the murders, and of his belief that such criminals do not vary their method of killing.[14]

The Smith of the Brides in the Bath murders whom Dew had referred to was George Joseph Smith (1872–1915). Smith was a bigamist who murdered three women between 1912 and 1914 by drowning them in baths. He was executed in 1915 at Maidstone.[15] John Ellis, who had hanged both Crippen and Smith, thought that Smith failed miserably to match the dignity of Dr Crippen, 'though he tried so hard to ape the gentleman'.[16]

Memoirs

He was a good detective, and he's a good story-teller.

Daily Telegraph *(Sydney)*

Over twenty years after his successful libel trials, Dew was once again provoked into defending his conduct in the Crippen case. The perceived slight appeared in July 1934, when the *Daily Mail* printed an article entitled 'What a Big Crime Costs the Nation', in which it said that the cost of the Crippen case was £10,000, not to mention the cost of the trial.[1] Dew wrote an angry letter to the editor of the *Mail* the same day the paper had run the story. The letter does not appear to have been published. It read:

I was interested to read the above mentioned article in to-days 'Daily Mail'.

I was more than interested, and indeed staggered, at the statement therein as follows:

'Dr. Crippen, the murderer of Belle Elmore, his actress wife made a dash for Canada with a woman companion. Before the first wireless used in crime reached England – it revealed the whereabouts of Crippen – something like £10,000 had been spent in the search for him.'

As the officer in charge of the inquiries, and the one who chased and captured him in Canada, I should know something about the expenses incurred up to the time stated. I am puzzled indeed to know how £10,000 was spent?

Not one extra police officer was recruited and the pay of those engaged would still have gone on, whether Crippen had committed a crime or not, so it cannot be said that that was an extra charge on the nation, and I doubt if my own expenses for cab fares up to the time the wireless was received, exceeded £2, and the extra costs, whilst I was making inquiries, as a Chief Inspector, for food allowance, would be 4/- per day, always supposing I could not reach home in time for a meal for a continuous period of nine hours, other officers of less rank would be paid in proportion.

Of course, there was the printing of the Reward bills and other expenses, such as medical men, etc. and I should have thought I was exaggerating if I had suggested that up to the time of the wireless being received the cost would not have exceeded £500.

Maybe, Mr. Hugh Brady [the author of the article] has some information as to the expenses incurred which I am ignorant of, but oh! £10,000 extra cost to the Nation before the famous wireless was received and that in 1910, too!

I really should be glad to be enlightened, and doubtless, so would the taxpayers.[2]

Shortly after the appearance of the *Mail* article, Dew's full-length account of the Crippen case first appeared in the Saturday newspaper *Thomson's Weekly News* as a well illustrated series that ran between September and October 1934. It was entitled 'The Whole Truth About the Crippen Case', and dramatically promised that 'nothing more intense and thrilling has been published than the battle of wits between the shrewd police officer and one of the cleverest and most amazing personalities in the history of crime'. Dew gave his reason for writing his memoir straight away:

Many stories have been written about Dr. Crippen and his crime.

Some of them have approached the truth. Others have grossly misrepresented the facts.

As the Scotland Yard officer who handled the case from the beginning to the end, I am the only person who knows every detail of what happened, from the moment the disappearance of Belle Elmore was first reported to Scotland Yard until Crippen was condemned to death at the Old Bailey.

All these years, while others have been giving their versions from second-hand knowledge, I have remained silent.

My reason for speaking now is that I feel I should leave behind an authoritative record of the biggest case I was privileged to handle while an officer at the Yard.[3]

The Crippen serialisation was the first part of Dew's memoirs. The following year *Thomson's* printed 'My Hunt for Jack the Ripper', between January and March 1935, and finally, 'From Pitch-and-Toss to Murder' (a reference to the wide variety of crimes Dew had investigated), between July and August 1936, in which Dew recounted several of his more interesting cases, on which he commented: 'It is not always the most sensational case which gives the biggest kick to the detective.'

These cases included those of Conrad Harms and Harry the Valet. In addition there were also episodes of blackmail, counterfeiting, fraud, theft and manslaughter. Incidents in the various cases reinforce elements of Dew's character that emerged during the Whitechapel and Crippen murder cases. He showed sympathy and concern to one woman he arrested for theft from dwelling houses. Whenever he saw her, 'I talked to her and tried to persuade her to lead an honest life'. Then there was his usual refusal to accept criticism of himself or his fellow officers. In the case of a swindler who had been at large for twenty years, 'the blame, in most cases at any rate, has to be laid at the door of the public rather than of the police'.

Dew's memoirs were published in their entirety in one volume in 1938, by Blackie & Son, under the title *I Caught Crippen: Memoirs of Ex-Chief Inspector Walter Dew C.I.D.* They were dedicated to his late son Stanley and his daughters Ethel, (Kate) May and Dorothy, but not to his other son Walter. It was further dedicated to 'F. for encouragement and help' – no doubt a reference to his second wife, Florence. The book was a word-for-word retelling of the newspaper serialisation. It included a short additional prologue and afterword, but contained far fewer illustrations than the newspaper version.

When compared with contemporary records the memoirs are revealed to be broadly accurate, but also to contain significant discrepancies, contradictions and errors. But these did not spoil the book, which was a colourful and highly entertaining read and is now a valuable and sought-after item. The irregularities may be partly explained by the fact that the memoirs were originally written for a tabloid newspaper that was perhaps more concerned with sensationalism than accuracy. Dew's account of the Crippen case was, however, significantly more accurate in some parts than in others, possibly as the result of the availability of the Notable British Trials volume on the case, first published in 1920, which contained a transcription of Crippen's Old Bailey trial. Despite this, Dew's memoirs still contained glaring errors. For example, he wrote that the Martinettis had dined with the Crippens on 10 January, when it had been 31 January. He also spells Melville Macnaghten's name incorrectly throughout as 'Macnaughton'.

Dew's memory may have been a factor. When he wrote about the Whitechapel murders he excused himself by saying, 'it must be remembered that they took place fifty years ago, and it may be that small errors as to dates and days may have crept in'. Despite this, he also stated that during his police career one of his chief assets was a 'splendid memory'. Dew's daughter Kate said at the time of the book's release, 'To-day his memory is still faultless. I think it is remarkable that a man of 75

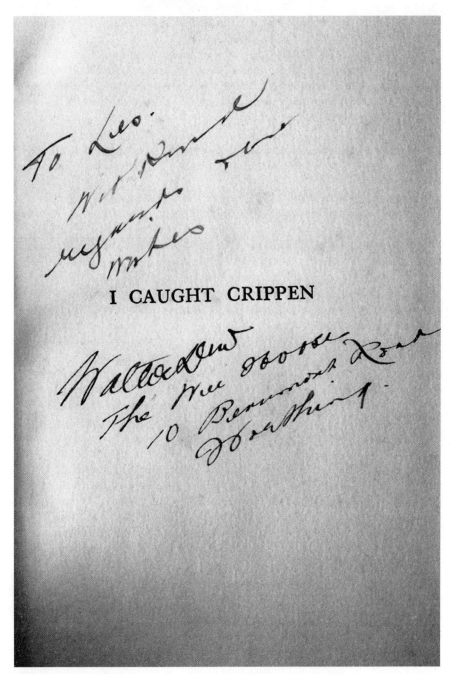

I CAUGHT CRIPPEN

Autographed frontispiece to Dew's autobiography. *(Stewart P. Evans)*

who has led a life so varied and exhausting should be able to recall so many details of his experiences.'[4]

Some of his contradictions are too obvious to ignore. He described Flower and Dean Street in the East End of London as being so rough that constables were forced to go down there in pairs, because a 'single constable would have been lucky to reach the other end unscathed'. Just two pages later, Dew angrily wrote:

> I have seen it stated that there were some parts of the East End the police themselves were afraid to penetrate.
> Rubbish!
> I could recount story after story of single police officers walking calmly into the very dens of gangs and claiming their men.

Again, Dew mixed up his dates, saying, 'Three days only had elapsed since the death of Annie Chapman – the date was 30 September, 1888.' Annie Chapman had died on 8 September.

A good example of the difference between Dew's autobiographical version of events and that contained in official records is in the story of the arrest of Conrad Harms. In Dew's words, he could not 'definitely remember if I arrested him myself or not . . . My recollection is that Berrett and I arrested him at an hotel in Northumberland Avenue.' The minutes of the Central Criminal Court stated that the arrest was made by DS Crutchett and DC Bishop at the Crown Emporium. However, Dew did add that this was 'one of those instances when one cannot remember an important detail, of thirty years ago, and so, to be on the safe side, raise the doubt, as I don't wish to claim credit for something I have not done.'

The book also contained what appears to be an episode of blatant fiction. Dew told the story of Crippen asking him the favour of being allowed to see Le Neve while on the deck of the *Megantic* on their return to England. In his autobiography Dew said the following:

> The next day I went to see Miss Le Neve and told her of the request her fellow prisoner had made. Her eyes lit up as she eagerly replied: 'Oh, yes, please arrange it, Mr. Dew. I should like it very much.'
> And so it came about that there was staged somewhere in mid-Atlantic one of real life's strangest little dramas.
> Crippen was brought to the doorway of his cabin, Miss Le Neve stood in hers. The distance between them was probably thirty feet. There for a minute or so this tragic pair remained with eyes only for one another.
> I had to be present. But somehow as I looked on I felt an interloper.

Not a word was spoken. There were no hysterics on either side. Just a slight motion of the hand from one to the other. That was all.

Then back to their impoverished cells to await what fate had in store for them both.

I have often wondered what passed through Crippen's mind during those tense moments when his little dream was realized, and he was able to gaze again on the face of the woman he loved so devotedly. Perhaps he guessed even then that the association for which he had risked so much would never again be resumed.

This seems to be the first time Dew told this tale. It did not appear in his official, contemporary reports, in one of which Dew stated, 'They were arrested on 31 July. And I have kept them – as far as I was concerned – apart from one another ever since.' Dew had allowed Crippen a surreptitious glance at Le Neve on the train from Liverpool to London, which was noted in *The Times* and in Muir's opening statement for the Crown at Crippen's trial. Neither of these mentioned a sighting on the ship's deck, nor did the story appear in one of the earliest full-length book accounts of the case, in 1935.[5] Of course it may have happened. Sergeant Mitchell reported that 'Mr. Dew promised to see Le Neve if there was an opportunity.' Dew's phrase, 'as far as I was concerned', is a little ambiguous, and Dew may have chosen to withhold the full story from his report, but it seems unlikely. Dew was known to be a compassionate man, but he also wanted to return his prisoners with as little disruption as possible.

Ethel Le Neve did not speak about the incident when she wrote her accounts of the case for *Lloyd's Weekly News* in November 1910, and for *Thomson's Weekly News* in November 1920, in which she said that Dew only agreed to pass a message from her to Crippen. Le Neve's story was told once more by Ursula Bloom in her mushy 1955 'factual novel', *The Girl Who Loved Crippen*, as told to the author by Le Neve. The book was published after Dew's *I Caught Crippen*, and repeats Dew's story. In it Dew allows Crippen to see Le Neve, who was on a lower deck:

She walked as in a dream, no longer a prisoner, but a girl in love! She looked like some sylvan elf with her cropped hair curling wistfully round her face, her eyes shining, and she held out her arms.

'Hawley? Hawley?'

But that could not be! It was the Inspector who barred the way. He said, 'One moment. One moment only, please.'

They looked at each other, she drinking in every detail of his dear face, and the newly grown moustache. She was glad that he looked again like the man she loved so much. He said nothing. Had he not promised not to speak a word? And he was a man who kept his promises. His eyes said everything.[6]

Another feature of the autobiography was Dew's discretion. He frequently concealed names, and stated that he would not give any details regarding two of the cases he worked upon, saying, 'I refrain from going into the details of these lest it should give pain and annoyance to some of the relatives, or those associated with the cases.'

One of these was the Druce–Portland inheritance case. This had involved a bogus claim to the deceased Duke of Portland's fortune. In a bizarre and long-drawn-out affair, relatives of a London upholsterer called Thomas Charles Druce argued that Druce was in fact the Duke of Portland, and leading a double life as the eccentric 5th Duke of Portland. Their story of Druce staging a fake funeral in 1864 was disproved when his body was exhumed in December 1907.

After the Druce case had collapsed, Dew arrested Mary Robinson in January 1908 for committing perjury during the Druce–Portland case. Robinson hoped to profit from the case, and had claimed that she knew Druce and Portland were one and the same. If the Druce family's claim had been successful they would have rewarded Robinson handsomely for helping their cause. In her Clapham flat Dew found many incriminating papers, including a diary purporting to cover the years 1861, 1862 and 1868–70. Dew thought it had been written in Robinson's hand, but in one sitting rather than over a period of years. She pleaded guilty and received a four-year sentence. The newspapers were full of the story at the time, so Dew's reticence to write about it is a little mystifying. His excuse that it might cause pain to the relatives could easily apply to some of those cases he did cover.

Perhaps Dew was over-zealous in his withholding of names. When writing about Dr. Crippen's statement, Dew held back the name of the Criterion Restaurant, where Crippen and Le Neve attended the Guild's benevolent dinner, writing 'the C____ Restaurant', despite the restaurant having been named in Notable British Trials. Neither did he name Crippen's business partner, Dr Rylance, whom he described as 'Dr ____'.

Upon the publication of *I Caught Crippen*, Dew's local newspaper, the *Worthing Gazette*, interviewed their resident celebrity at the Wee Hoose. Dew reminisced:

Twenty-eight years ago to-day Crippen was already safe inside the gaol on the Heights of Abraham. As for myself, I was simply sweltering in the hot and humid atmosphere of the city.

Much of my time was spent evading reporters and cameramen –
who knew all about my arrival in spite of our efforts to keep it secret,
and who frequently became personal when I did not give them a
statement – visiting Crippen in gaol (he was continually asking for
new books to read), and making arrangements for the return to
England.

Old Crippen took it quite well. He always was a bit of a
philosopher, though he could not have helped being astounded to
see me on board the boat . . . He was quite a likeable chap in his way.

The *Gazette* also found another connection that their town had with the
Crippen case, albeit a much looser one. The memorial stone for Belle
Elmore was constructed by the father of the monumental mason who had
a workshop in North Street, Worthing.[7]

The book received favourable reviews in newspapers all over the world.
The *Daily Mail* called it 'very readable', while the *News Chronicle* described
it as 'an absorbingly interesting book'. Additional praise came from the
Daily Telegraph's reviewer, who wrote, 'Inspector Dew tells these stories
amusingly, and well . . . I enjoyed his book immensely', and Dew's other
local paper, the *Worthing Herald*, said 'Mr. Dew has an admirable style,
easy, natural and completely free from catch-words or the strain of
literary affectation.'

While the book did not appear to receive any bad reviews, there were
some that were a little more critical. The *Western Morning News*'s reviewer
enjoyed the 'From Pitch and Toss to Murder' section of the book, but
thought that it needed more on the pathological side of the Crippen
investigation, and also on the finer points of detection. The *Sunday Times*
praised the book for killing a few of the minor myths about the Crippen
case, but thought it added little to the reader's understanding of
Crippen's character.

Dew's daughter Kate was living in South Africa with her husband Jack,
supposedly a prominent member of the African Labour party, and when
her father's book was published a local paper spoke to her about it. The
newspaper stated that Kate had helped Dew in compiling the book. Not
so, Dew retorted: 'No such assistance was ever given or asked for.'
Furthermore Dew 'was not aware my daughter's husband was a member
of the Labour party, of whom I am not in sympathy'.[8]

Around the time that *I Caught Crippen* was published, the *Bromley and
Kentish Times* ran an article entitled 'Dream Solved Mysteries'. According to
this story, a friend of Cora Crippen had dreamed of Cora's demise, and if it
had not been for this vision the police would not have found Cora's remains
under the hearthstone, and the crime would never have been revealed.

Dew subscribed to a press cutting association who supplied him with cuttings relating to him and the Crippen case. He soon learned of the 'Dream Solved Mysteries' article, and wrote to the newspaper. Dew said (somewhat unconvincingly) that 'under ordinary circumstances, I should have taken no notice', but as his autobiography had just been released he was concerned that people would ask him why the dream incident had not been included in the book. He therefore wanted to set the record straight:

> I hasten to say that the remains were not buried under the hearthstone, but under the bricks in the coal cellar. The search was not instituted and insisted upon by a person who had a grim dream concerning Belle Elmore. It was my own perseverance which led to the discovery of the remains and capture of Crippen.[9]

A brief comment in the 'London Playgoers' Club' column of *The Times* newspaper, in October 1938, led to Dew's next public defence of the handling of the Crippen Case. The column contained a review of the play *Dearly Beloved Wife* by Jeanne de Casalis, which was based upon the Crippen case. The reviewer remembered Crippen as 'the brave and gentle little dentist who yet murdered the termagant who was his wife'. The offending phrase in the review was 'the murderer's successful disarming of police suspicion'.

Dew had not mellowed since his 1911 libel victories. His heated response to the editor of *The Times* was published three weeks later:

> I am the officer who had sole charge of the case from the moment it was reported to police that Mrs. Crippen was missing. It was I who discovered the remains and later chased and captured Crippen in Canada. Therefore it must refer to me when it said: 'Crippen successfully disarmed police suspicion.'
>
> Will you permit me to say that from the moment I took up the inquiries concerning the missing Mrs. Crippen I never for one minute (except for a few hours sleep) relaxed my efforts to clear this matter up, until on the Wednesday I dug up the remains of this unfortunate woman in the cellar at Hilldrop Crescent. This was all within a few days of my undertaking the inquiry, and the very day after I interviewed Crippen I circulated the description of Mrs. Crippen far and wide.
>
> It is strange that if police suspicion was disarmed that I should have done this and persisted in my efforts until I succeeded in discovering the gruesome remains in the cellar, and all within such a

short time, and it must be remembered that until those remains were found there was no suggestion of Crippen having committed any crime whatever.

I do not for a moment suggest that your critic intends to cast any reflection on me – in all probability he does not know me – but some who read it might take it in a different light.[10]

Coincidentally, another play on the Crippen theme was put on at Worthing some years later. It was called *They Fly by Twilight*.[11] Dew does not appear to have commented on the play, but it was performed just one month after the death of his resident sister-in-law Iris. Dew fell ill soon afterwards. He died at the Wee Hoose on 16 December 1947, from haemapericardium due to the rupture of his heart muscle. He was eighty-four years old. His funeral was held three days later. Dew was buried in the same plot as Iris Idle, at Worthing Cemetery. Obituaries appeared in both of Worthing's local newspapers,[12] as well as in *The Times*.[13]

Without Dr Crippen, Dew could have been just another Scotland Yard man who, like so many of his contemporaries, spent his well-earned years of retirement by the sea. Despite his rise from being a humble seed merchant's clerk to Chief Inspector at Scotland Yard, and his flawless professional reputation, earned through nearly thirty years of hard work, he would not have enjoyed the celebrity that capturing Crippen had brought him. But Dew had caught the most infamous murderer of his generation. He had risked his reputation by pursuing Crippen across the Atlantic without knowing for sure if his quarry was the fugitive doctor. Furthermore, he had brought his prisoner safely back to face justice in England under the scrutiny of the world's media. He would forever more be remembered as the man who caught the infamous Dr Crippen.

Aftermath of the Crippen Case

39 HILLDROP CRESCENT

In November 1888 Hilldrop Crescent played a small part in the Jack the Ripper saga. A letter was sent to a Mr MacKean, who lived in the street. It was signed 'Jack Ripper' and the author threatened to pay a visit to MacKean either at his house or shop. After the Crippen case there was some talk of renaming Hilldrop Crescent. Among the suggestions proposed were Dewdrop Crescent and Filleted Place. The Crescent retained its name (as it does to this day), but bears little resemblance to how it looked in 1910. It was bombed twice in September 1940. No. 39 is now a block of flats named Margaret Bondfield House, after the first British woman Cabinet member (1873–1953).

SUPERINTENDENT FRANK CASTLE FROEST

Froest retired from Scotland Yard after thirty-three years' service on 30 September 1912, at the age of fifty-four. He would later write several fictional crime stories. King George V sent him the following message: 'Good-bye, Mr. Froest, and God-speed. The detective and police organization in which you have served so long is, in my opinion, the best in the world.'

Froest moved to Weston-super-Mare, Somerset, where he became a Justice of the Peace and an alderman. He died on 7 January 1930 at the General Hospital, Weston-super-Mare, after a long illness, and was buried at Uphill Old Church.

JOHN NASH AND LIL HAWTHORNE

In February 1911 the Nashes politely sought compensation from Scotland Yard for loss of earnings incurred through their involvement in the Crippen case, which had led to Lil Hawthorne having to cancel three weeks of engagements in London, Stockton and Glasgow. They estimated that they had lost £125 in fees.

The Treasury office looked upon their claim sympathetically, saying that 'these two people have rendered very signal service to the cause of justice, and Inspector [sic] Froest, of New Scotland Yard, is of opinion that, but for their efforts, it is quite possible that this grave crime might never have been discovered'. Consequently they were awarded £100.

CAPTAIN HENRY GEORGE KENDALL

Kendall retired from his post as marine superintendent for Canadian Pacific at Surrey Commercial Docks in 1939. He died aged ninety-one in a London nursing home in November 1965. In 1974 the original telegrams he had sent during Crippen's voyage on the *Montrose* were sold at auction for £1,600.

The *SS Montrose* was sold to the Admiralty in 1914. They intended to fill her holds with concrete and sink her outside Dover harbour as a block ship to deter German U-boats. However, the *Montrose* broke free from her moorings, drifted and foundered on the Goodwin Sands, where she remained until breaking up in June 1963.

ETHEL LE NEVE

Immediately after her acquittal Ethel Le Neve gave her account of the Crippen case to *Lloyd's Weekly News*, for which she even dressed up as a boy to be photographed. A transcription of these articles was quickly published in a pamphlet. She gave further accounts of the case in *Thomson's Weekly News* between September 1920 and February 1921, and an account of what had happened to her since in the same paper in 1928. Her story was again told in 1955, in a 'factual novel' by Ursula Bloom called *The Girl Who Loved Crippen*.

Ethel Le Neve was the sole executrix and benefactor of Dr Crippen's will. His estate was worth £268 6s 9d, and included his gold-rimmed spectacles. Winston Churchill permitted Le Neve to have a farewell letter Crippen wrote to her on the back of the photograph of her that Crippen had in his cell. This was against the wishes of some of Churchill's colleagues, who considered it to be an unauthorised communication and feared she may sell the contents to a newspaper. She sailed to America on the *Majestic* three hours after the execution of Crippen, again using a false name. This time she was 'Miss Allen'. Le Neve went from New York to Montreal and worked as a typist. She returned to England in 1914, where she got a job as a typist at Hampton's furnishing store in Trafalgar Square. There she met and married a clerk, Stanley Smith. In 1928 she wrote in *Thomson's Weekly News*, 'I am happy now; happy in the love, the devotion, above all the trust, of an honest man who knows all about my past.' They had a son and a daughter together. She died in 1967 at Dulwich hospital, aged eighty-four.

SIR MELVILLE MACNAGHTEN

Macnaghten remained at Scotland Yard as Assistant Commissioner CID until his retirement in 1913, after two years of declining health. He wrote his memoirs, *Days of My Years*, in 1914, and died in May 1921.

PAUL MARTINETTI

Paul Martinetti died on Boxing Day, 1924, at the British College Hospital. He had been staying at the Mustapha Hotel in Algiers on account of his health.

RICHARD DAVID MUIR

Muir was appointed Recorder of Colchester in 1911, and knighted in 1918. In January 1924 he was attacked by a bout of influenza, which developed into double pneumonia, from which he died at his London home. He was buried at Norwood cemetery on 16 January 1924.

ARTHUR NEWTON

After the trial of Dr Crippen, Newton was found guilty of professional misconduct by the Law Society and struck off for twelve months. In 1913 he was sentenced to three years' penal servitude for fraud, and struck off the rolls as a solicitor. Arthur Newton died in 1930 at the age of seventy.

FREDERICK EDWIN SMITH

After the acquittal of Ethel Le Neve, Smith's career flourished. In May 1915 he became Solicitor-General, and in November of that year Attorney-General. The year was capped with his knighthood. Three years later he was made Baron Birkenhead, and created a peer the following year, sitting regularly as Speaker of the House of Lords as Lord Birkenhead. In October 1924 he accepted the office of Secretary of State for India. He died, aged fifty-eight, at London, on 30 September 1930.

ALFRED TOBIN

Tobin became Member of Parliament for Preston in 1910 and held the seat until 1915. He received a knighthood in 1919, the same year that his friend F.E. Smith arranged his appointment as Judge of Westminster County Court. Tobin held that position until his retirement from judgeship in 1935. He died at Montreaux on 30 November 1939, aged eighty-three.

RICHARD EVERARD WEBSTER (LORD ALVERSTONE)

During the Crippen trial a joke was doing the rounds that was attributed to Alverstone. 'Oh, the Crippen Case. Tried for the murder of his wife – and she was in court all the time.' 'Nonsense.' 'She was, indeed. But she was too cut up to say anything.' Alverstone retired in 1913 on account of ill health, and was made a Viscount. In 1914 his memoirs, *Recollections of Bar and Bench*, were published. He died in 1915.

Dew's Appearances in Films and Fiction

Walter Dew has been portrayed several times on film, television and radio, as well as appearing as a character in works of fiction.

FILMS

Dr Crippen an Bord (Germany, 1942)
Oberinspektor Duwell   René Deltgen
Dr Crippen   Rudolf Fernau

There was another German film featuring Crippen, *Dr Crippen Lebt* (1958), but Dew does not appear in it.

Dr Crippen (Great Britain, 1962)
Walter Dew   John Arnatt
Dr Crippen   Donald Pleasance

(Arnatt had previously played Dew in a 1960 stage play, *The Little Doctor*. Edward Woodward played Dr Crippen.)

TELEVISION

The Case of Dr Crippen – 1956, Associated TeleVision Ltd (ITA)
Walter Dew   Philip Lennard
Dr Crippen   Eric Portman

'Investigating Murder', *Horizon* – 1968, BBC
Walter Dew   Philip Webb
Dr Crippen   John Cazabon

Jack the Ripper – 1973, BBC
Walter Dew   Norman Shelley

The Ladykillers: Miss Elmore – 1981, ITV
Walter Dew   Alan Downer
Doctor Crippen   John Fraser

Tales From the Black Museum – 1999, Discovery Channel
The parts of Walter Dew and Crippen were both non-speaking, so unknown extras were used. The production company has no record of who played them.

The Last Secret of Dr Crippen – 2004, Channel 4
Walter Dew   David Broughton Davis
Doctor Crippen   Terry Francis

BROADCASTS AND RECORDINGS

Dr Crippen's Trial – 12 December 1986, BBC Radio 4
Walter Dew   John Church
Dr Crippen   Bob Sherman

Saturday Night Theatre: Crippen (Based upon *Dr Crippen's Diary* by Emlyn Williams)
– 13 November 1993, BBC Radio 4
Walter Dew   Ivor Roberts
Dr Crippen   Charles Kay

Great British Trials: Dr Crippen – London, Mr Punch, 1999
Walter Dew   Howard Ward
Dr Crippen   Andrew Sachs

BOOKS

Doctor Crippen, by Michael Hooker (adapted from the screenplay by Leigh Vance), London, Digit Books, 1963.
The Private Life of Dr Crippen, by Richard Gordon, London, Heinemann, 1981.
The False Inspector Dew, by Peter Lovesey, London, Macmillan, 1982.
The Adventures of Inspector Lestrade, by M.J. Trow, London, Macmillan, 1985.
Dr Crippen's Diary, by Emlyn Williams, London, Robson Books, 1987.
Lestrade and the Leviathan, by M.J. Trow, London, Macmillan, 1987.
Lestrade and the Ripper, by M.J. Trow, London, Macmillan, 1988.
All-Consuming Fire, by Andy Lane, London, Doctor Who Books, 1994.
Crippen: A Novel of Murder, by John Boyne, London, Penguin, 2004.

VERSES

The notoriety of the Crippen case led to a number of verses being written, a couple of which mentioned Walter Dew.

> Miss Le Neve, old Dew is waiting
> On the wall for you at Liverpool,
> And he says he saw you sitting
> On the knee of Dr Crippen,
> Dressed in boy's clothes,
> On the Montrose,
> Miss Le Neve.

The antiquarian book dealer J.C.G. Hammond recalled that when he was a boy his mother sang him to sleep with the following verse, sung to the tune of 'Let's All Go Down the Strand'.

> On came Inspector Dew,
> He said 'I want you two.
> Come back again to England's shore
> For the murder of Belle Elmore,
> Crippen and Miss Le Neve.'

Notes

Note: Any PRO references refer to Public Record Office documents held at the National Archives.

PREFACE

1. In his autobiography Dew said his mother was a Norfolk woman, but she gave her place of birth as Ireland on the 1871, 1881, 1891 and 1901 census.
2. *Police Review and Parade Gossip*, 30 December 1910.
3. *Ibid.*
4. Unfortunately I have been unable to find anything of substance about Kate Morris. Dew wrote next to nothing about her.
5. *Police Review and Parade Gossip*, 30 December 1910.
6. All material from the section on Jack the Ripper, unless otherwise stated, taken from Stewart P. Evans and Keith Skinner, *The Ultimate Jack the Ripper Sourcebook*, London, Constable & Robinson, 2000, and Walter Dew, *I Caught Crippen*, London and Glasgow, Blackie & Son Ltd, 1938.
7. *Pall Mall Gazette*, 12 September 1888.

CHAPTER ONE

1. *Star*, 10 September 1888.

CHAPTER TWO

1. *Star*, 5 September 1888.
2. *Morning Advertiser*, 10 September 1888.
3. *Star*, 8 September 1888.

CHAPTER FOUR

1. University College London Chadwick Collection.
2. Leonard Archer Collection (Stewart P. Evans Collection).

CHAPTER FIVE

1. PRO CRIM 10/79.
2. Joseph Hall Richardson, *From the City to Fleet Street*, London, Stanley Paul & Co., 1927, pp. 277–9.

CHAPTER SIX

1. Philip Sugden, *The Complete History of Jack the Ripper*, London, Constable & Robinson, 2002, pp. xx–xxi.
2. *Morning Advertiser*, 23 April 1910.
3. *East London Observer*, 20 May 1893.
4. *East London Observer*, 1 June 1901. Reid would also state erroneously that the Ripper never took away any parts of his victim's body.
5. *East London Observer*, 14 May 1910.

CHAPTER SEVEN

1. *Saturday Post*, 29 January 1916.
2. *The Times*, 15 December 1898.
3. Dinnie would later become Chief Commissioner of the New Zealand police. He was the brother of the famous Highland Games athlete Donald Dinnie, and had been something of a sportsman himself in his youth before joining the police. Froest had worked on the Whitechapel murders as a sergeant, and later worked with Dew on the Crippen case.
4. *The Times*, 5 January 1899.
5. *The Times*, 15 December 1898.
6. *Lloyd's Weekly News*, 25 December 1898.
7. *Illustrated Police News*, 7 January 1899.
8. *The Times*, 22 December 1898.
9. *The Times*, 5 January 1899.
10. *Ibid.*
11. *The Times*, 30 November 1898.
12. *Ibid.*
13. *The Times*, 5 January 1899.
14. *Lloyd's Weekly News*, 8 December 1898.
15. *The Times*, 15 December 1898.
16. *Ibid.*
17. *Illustrated Police News*, 7 January 1899.
18. *Lloyd's Weekly News*, 25 December 1898.
19. *Illustrated Police News*, 7 January 1899.
20. *The Times*, 19 January 1899.

CHAPTER EIGHT

1. *The Times*, 2 November 1906.
2. All information from PRO CRIM 10/99, unless otherwise stated. For the purpose of simplification Clifford/Harms/Friedlauski is referred to throughout as Conrad Harms.
3. He was named as Newbold in the minutes of the Central Criminal Court, instead of Hugo.
4. *The Times*, 22 July 1909.
5. *Ibid*. Berrett would eventually become a Chief Inspector, and wrote his memoirs, *When I Was at Scotland Yard* (London, Sampson Low & Co.), in 1932.
6. *Lloyd's Weekly News*, 12 September 1909.
7. *The Times*, 7 July 1909.
8. *The Times*, 29 June 1909.
9. *The Times*, 22 July 1909.
10. *The Times*, 13 September 1909.
11 *The Times*, 3 July 1922.

CHAPTER NINE

1. Unless otherwise stated, the information contained in the Crippen section of this book was obtained from PRO CRIM1/117, PRO DPP 1/13, PRO MEPO 3/198, PRO P/COM 8/30 and Filson Young (ed.), *The Trial of Hawley Harvey Crippen* (Notable British Trials, 2nd edition), Edinburgh and London, William Hodge & Company Ltd, 1933; Walter Dew, *I Caught Crippen*, London and Glasgow, Blackie & Son Ltd, 1938.
2. *Sunday News*, 12 January 1930.

CHAPTER ELEVEN

1. Sir Melville Macnaghten, *Days of My Years*, London, Edward Arnold, 1914, p. 195.
2. *Ibid.*
3. *Islington Daily Gazette and North London Tribune*, 15 July 1910.
4. Gooch later became a Chief Inspector and head of the Flying Squad. He died in a car crash in 1936.
5. *Pall Mall Gazette*, 15 July 1910.
6. *Pall Mall Gazette*, 14 July 1910.
7. *The People*, 17 July 1910.
8. *The Times*, 19 July 1910.
9. *The Times*, 16 July 1910.

CHAPTER TWELVE

1. *The Times*, 19 July 1910.
2. *The Times*, 20 July 1910.
3. *The Times*, 21 July 1910.
4. *Daily Mail*, 29 July 1910.
5. *The Times*, 20 July 1910.
6. *The Times*, 22 July 1910.
7. Macnaghten, *Days of My Years*, p. 189.
8. The controversy over Crippen's title was later discussed in the letters column of *The Times*, on 2 November 1938 and 5 November 1938.
9. *Daily Mail*, 20 July 1910.
10. *The Times*, 22 July 1910.
11. *Islington Daily Gazette and North London Tribune*, 21 July 1910.
12. Macnaghten, *Days of My Years*, pp. 199–200.
13. *Durban Daily News*, 12 November 1938.
14. *Liverpool Courier*, 25 July 1910.
15. *Montreal Daily Star*, 30 July 1910.
16. *The Umpire*, 27 July 1910.
17. *The Times*, 29 July 1910.
18. *Montreal Daily Star*, 30 July 1910.
19. *Ibid*.

CHAPTER THIRTEEN

1. *Daily Mail*, 12 August 1910.
2. Macnaghten, *Days of My Years*, p. 189.
3. *Reynold's Weekly Newspaper*, 7 August 1910.
4. *The Times*, 1 August 1910.
5. *The Times*, 2 August 1910.
6. *Islington Daily Gazette and North London Tribune*, 4 August 1910.
7. *Cleveland Plain Dealer*, 4 August 1910.
8. *Liverpool Courier*, 3 August 1910.
9. *The Times*, 6 August 1910.
10. *Daily Chronicle*, 8 August 1910.
11. *The Times*, 9 August 1910.
12. *San Francisco Chronicle*, 9 August 1910.
13. *The Times*, 5 August 1910.
14. *Montreal Daily Star*, 15 August 1910.
15. *The Times*, 16 August 1910.
16. Dornford Yates, *As Berry and I Were Saying*, London and Melbourne, Ward, Lock & Co., 1952, p. 240.

17. *Liverpool Daily Post*, 22 August 1910.
18. *The Times*, 29 August 1910.
19. *Cleveland Plain Dealer*, 22 August 1910.
20. Yates, *As Berry and I Were Saying*, p. 243.
21. *Ibid.*, pp. 255–6.
22. *Lloyd's Weekly News*, 13 November 1910.
23. *Daily Mail*, 29 August 1910.
24. *Liverpool Courier*, 29 August 1910.
25. *Reynold's Weekly Newspaper*, 28 August 1910.

CHAPTER FOURTEEN

1. *Thomson's Weekly News*, 6 November 1920.
2. Travers Humphreys, *A Book of Trials*, London, William Heinemann Ltd., 1953, p. 162.
3. Travers Humphreys, *Criminal Days*, London, Hodder & Stoughton, 1946, p. 112.
4. *Sunday Express*, 31 December 1923.
5. Tom Cullen, *The Mild Murderer*, London, The Bodley Head, 1977, p. 146.
6. *Sunday Express*, 6 January 1924.
7. *Lloyd's Weekly Newspaper*, 4 September 1910.
8. *Reynold's Weekly Newspaper*, 4 September 1910.
9. *The Times*, 1 August 1910.
10. *Pall Mall Gazette*, 14 September 1910.
11. The drug hyoscine is spelt both hyoscine and hyoscin in the various documents and books concerning the Crippen case. Here the spelling hyoscine is used throughout.
12. *The Times*, 7 September 1910.
13. *The Times*, 9 September 1910.
14. *The Times*, 13 September 1910.
15. *Pall Mall Gazette*, 14 September 1910.
16. *The Times*, 15 September 1910.
17. *The Times*, 17 September 1910.
18. *The Globe*, 21 September 1910.
19. *Ibid.*
20. *Dictionary of National Biography*.
21. Edward Marjoribanks, *The Life of Sir Edward Marshall Hall*, London, Victor Gollancz Ltd, 1929, pp. 281–3. Travers Humphreys denied that this was the case. In his *A Book of Trials*, he wrote that Marshall Hall 'declined to accept it for reasons which seemed good to him and which had nothing to do with the suggested defence of manslaughter' (pp. 62–3).

22. *Islington Daily Gazette and North London Tribune*, 20 September 1910.
23. *Penny Illustrated Paper*, 1 October 1910.
24. *The People*, 23 April 1933.
25. *The Times*, 27 September 1910.

CHAPTER FIFTEEN

1. *Dictionary of National Biography*.
2. Rt Hon. Viscount Alverstone, *Recollections of Bar and Bench*, London, Edward Arnold, 1914, p. 274.
3. Douglas G. Browne and E.V. Tullett, *Bernard Spilsbury: His Life and Cases*, London, White Lion Publishers Ltd, 1951, p. 48.
4. S. Ingleby Oddie, *Inquest*, London, Hutchinson & Co., 1941, p. 74.
5. Sidney Felstad, *Sir Richard Muir: A Memoir of a Public Prosecutor*, London, John Lane, 1927, p. 116.
6. Stanley Jackson, *The Life and Cases of Mr Justice Humphreys*, London, Odhams Press, 1952, p. 74.
7. Travers Humphreys, *Criminal Days*, London, Hodder & Stoughton, 1946, p. 113.
8. *Ibid.*, p. 106.
9. Ingleby Oddie, *Inquest*, p. 13.
10. Douglas G. Browne, *Sir Travers Humphreys: A Biography*, London, George G. Harrap & Co. Ltd, 1960, p. 69.
11. Travers Humphreys, *A Book of Trials*, London, William Heinemann Ltd, 1953, p. 55.
12. *Ibid.*, p. 59.
13. *The Times*, 4 December 1939.
14. *The Globe*, 17 October 1910.
15. Felstead, *Sir Richard Muir*, p. 88.
16. Max Constantine-Quinn, *Doctor Crippen*, London, Duckworth, 1935, p. 45.
17. *Pall Mall Gazette*, 19 October 1910.
18. *Lloyd's Weekly News*, 23 October 1910.
19. *Pall Mall Gazette*, 19 October 1910.
20. Felstead, *Sir Richard Muir*, p. 73.
21. Douglas G. Browne and E.V. Tullett, *Bernard Spilsbury: His Life and Cases*, London, George G. Harrap & Co. Ltd, 1951, p. 51.
22. *Ibid.*, pp. 38–9.
23. *Pall Mall Gazette*, 21 October 1910.
24. Travers Humphreys, *Criminal Days*, London, Hodder & Stoughton, 1946, pp. 108–9.

Chapter Sixteen

1. Macnaghten, *Days of My Years*, p. 201.
2. *Sunday Express*, 27 February 1927.
3. Yates, *As Berry and I Were Saying*, p. 258.
4. Alverstone, *Recollections of Bar and Bench*, p. 274.
5. Harold Eaton, 'Crippen and the Belle Elmore', in *The Fifty Most Amazing Crimes of the Last 100 Years*, London, Odhams Press Ltd, 1936, p. 119.
6. Browne and Tullett, *Sir Travers Humphreys*, p. 43.

Chapter Seventeen

1. *Dictionary of National Biography*.
2. *The Times*, 26 October 1910.
3. Earl of Birkenhead, *Frederick Edwin, Earl of Birkenhead*, vol. 1, London, Thornton Butterworth, 1933, p. 300.
4. *Ibid.*, p. 297.
5. *Thomson's Weekly News*, 8 January 1920.
6. *Thomson's Weekly News*, 16 October 1920.
7. *Thomson's Weekly News*, 30 October 1920.
8. *Thomson's Weekly News*, 20 November 1920. Contemporary reports state that Le Neve was given women's clothes by the wardresses from Holloway.

Chapter Eighteen

1. *Sunday Express*, 6 January 1924.
2. *Globe*, 5 November 1910.
3. *Islington Daily Gazette and North London Tribune*, 11 November 1910.
4. Randolph S. Churchill, *Young Statesman: Winston S. Churchill 1901–1914*, London, Heinemann, 1967, p. 418. Churchill does not appear to have written anything about his involvement in the Crippen case, nor have his biographers. This seems a little odd, as he was so closely involved in the case, as was his best friend F.E. Smith. It may be an indication that, despite its notoriety, the Crippen case was of little historical significance compared to other events in Churchill's monumental life.
5. *Sunday Express*, 23 June 1935.
6. *Daily Mail*, 17 November 1910.
7. *The Umpire*, 13 November 1910.
8. *Sunday Express*, 27 February 1921. Another, more sympathetic account of Mytton Davies's feelings towards Crippen can be found in Tom Cullen's book on the Crippen case, *The Mild Murderer*, published in 1977. Cullen spoke to

Mytton Davies's son Cynric, who recalled that his father 'found Crippen to be a very mild, inoffensive little man who never gave anyone any trouble. He believed that Crippen was covering up for the real culprit, and was going to his death on that person's behalf' (p. 178).

9. *The Leader*, 17 June 1930.
10. *Thomson's Weekly Newspaper*, 1 March 1919.
11. *Thomson's Weekly News*, 19 July 1924.
12. *Sunday Dispatch*, 26 February 1956.
13. *Reynold's Weekly Newspaper*, 27 November 1910.
14. *Thomson's Weekly News*, 19 July 1924.
15. Unfortunately, there is no copy of this edition at the British Library Newspaper Library.
16. *The Leader*, 14 October 1930.
17. *Thomson's Weekly News*, 16 September 1922. Newton once again made the claim that Crippen had confessed to murdering Cora in the *Sunday Express*, 6 January 1924.

CHAPTER NINETEEN

1. *Police Review and Parade Gossip*, 30 December 1910.
2. *Lloyd's Weekly News*, 6 November 1910.
3. Dew wrote that '[a]part from "Jack the Ripper" case, I was never associated with what is described as "An unsolved murder"'. However, in 1908 he arrested Flora Haskell for the murder of her son at Salisbury. Haskell was reluctantly found guilty by a coroner's jury, but acquitted after a second assize trial. Dew was probably of the opinion that she was guilty, hence his assertion that he worked on only one unsolved murder case.
4. *Police Review and Parade Gossip*, 30 December 1910.
5. PRO MEPO 4/343.
6. PRO MEPO 21/39.
7. PRO MEPO 7/72.
8. Tom Divall, *Scoundrels and Scallywags*, London, Ernest Benn, 1929.
9. *Thomson's Weekly News*, 19 November 1910.
10. *Saturday Post*, 24 August 1912.
11. *Daily Chronicle*, 25 January 1911.
12. *The Times*, 4 April 1911.
13. Wandsworth volume of London Suburban Directory, 1911/1912.
14. *The Times*, 1 April 1911.
15. *The Times*, 2 May 1911.
16. *Ibid.*
17. *The Times*, 12 May 1911.

CHAPTER TWENTY

1. Jonathan Goodman, *The Crippen File*, London, Allison & Busby, 1985, p. 90.
2. A photograph of Dew in his garden was published in the *Weekly News* (aka *Thomson's Weekly News*) on 30 August 1913.
3. PRO MEPO 21/69.
4. *Police Review and Parade Gossip*, 17 November 1933.
5. *Saturday Post*, 29 January 1916.
6. Filson Young (ed.), *Trial of Hawley Harvey Crippen*, 2nd edition, Edinburgh and London, William Hodge & Company Ltd, 1933, p. xxx.
7. Again, as with Kate Morris, I have been unable to find anything substantial about the Idle sisters.
8. *Worthing Herald*, 19 December 1947.
9. *Sunday Express*, 12 December 1926.
10. *Sunday Express*, 2 October 1927.
11. The fullest and best account of this case is in Richard Whittington-Egan, *The Riddle of Birdhurst Rise*, London, George G. Harrap & Co. Ltd, 1975.
12. *Sunday Express*, 1 September 1929.
13. *Thomson's Weekly News*, 16 May 1936.
14. *Lloyd's Weekly News*, 31 December 1911.
15. The story of the Smith case was part of the Notable British Trials series. It was published in 1922 and edited by Eric R. Watson. Cream's case also appeared in 1923, edited by W. Teignmouth Shore.
16. *Thomson's Weekly News*, 19 July 1924.

CHAPTER TWENTY-ONE

1. *Daily Mail*, 10 July 1934.
2. The letter is contained in a scrapbook of Walter Dew's containing cuttings relating to him and reviews of his biography. The scrapbook is in the possession of the crime historian Jonathan Goodman.
3. *Thomson's Weekly News*, 15 September 1934.
4. *Durban Daily News*, 12 November 1938.
5. Constantine-Quinn, *Doctor Crippen*.
6. Ursula Bloom, *The Girl Who Loved Crippen*, London, Hutchinson & Co., 1955, p. 162.
7. *Worthing Gazette*, 10 August 1938.
8. These reviews and many more are contained in Walter Dew's scrapbook.
9. *Ibid.*
10. *The Times*, 21 November 1938.
11. *Worthing Herald*, 8 March 1946, 15 March 1946.
12. *Worthing Gazette*, 17 December 1947; *Worthing Herald*, 19 December 1947.
13. *The Times*, 17 December 1947.

Bibliography

Alverstone, Rt Hon. Viscount, *Recollections of Bar and Bench*, London, Edward Arnold, 1914.

Birkenhead, Earl of, *Famous Trials of History*, London, Hutchinson & Co., 1926.

Birkenhead, Earl of, *Frederick Edwin Earl of Birkenhead*, London, Thornton Butterworth, 1933.

Bloom, Ursula, *The Girl Who Loved Crippen*, London, Hutchinson & Co., 1955.

Browne, Douglas G. and Tullett, E.V., *Bernard Spilsbury: His Life and Cases*, London, White Lion Publishers Ltd, 1951.

Browne, Douglas G., *Sir Travers Humphreys: A Biography*, London, George G. Harrap & Co. Ltd, 1960.

Churchill, Randolph S., *Young Statesman: Winston S. Churchill 1901–1914*, London, Heinemann, 1967.

Constantine-Quinn, Max, *Doctor Crippen*, London, Duckworth, 1935.

Cullen, Tom, *Crippen: The Mild Murderer*, London, The Bodley Head, 1977.

Dew, Walter, *I Caught Crippen*, London and Glasgow, Blackie & Son Ltd, 1938.

Divall, Tom, *Scoundrels and Scallywags*, London, Ernest Benn, 1929.

Eddy, J.P., *Scarlet and Ermine*, London, William Kimber, 1960.

Ellis, John, *Diary of a Hangman*, London, True Crime Library, 1996.

Evans, Stewart P. and Skinner, Keith, *The Ultimate Jack the Ripper Sourcebook*, London, Constable & Robinson, 2000.

Evans, Stewart P. and Skinner, Keith, *Jack the Ripper: Letters From Hell*, Stroud, Sutton, 2001.

Felstead, Sidney, *Sir Richard Muir: A Memoir of a Public Prosecutor*, London, John Lane, 1927.

Gilbert, Michael, *Doctor Crippen*, London, Odhams Press Ltd, 1953.

Goodman, Jonathan, *Bloody Versicles: The Rhymes of Crime*, Newton Abbot, David & Charles, 1971.

Goodman, Jonathan, *The Crippen File*, London, Allison & Busby, 1985.

Harris, Melvin, *ITN Book of Firsts*, London, Michael O'Mara, 1994.

Humphreys, Sir Travers, *Criminal Days*, London, Hodder & Stoughton, 1946.

Humphreys, Sir Travers, *A Book of Trials*, London, William Heinemann Ltd, 1953.

Jackson, Stanley, *The Life and Cases of Mr Justice Humphreys*, London, Odhams Press, 1952.

Le Neve, Ethel, *Ethel Le Neve: Her Life Story*, Manchester, Daisy Bank, 1910.

Macnaghten, Sir Melville, *Days of My Years*, London, Edward Arnold, 1914.

Bibliography

Marjoribanks, Edward, *The Life of Sir Edward Marshall Hall*, London, Victor Gollancz Ltd, 1929.

Oddie, Samuel Ingleby, *Inquest*, London, Hutchinson & Co., 1941.

Parrish, J.M. and Crossland, John R. (eds), *The Fifty Most Amazing Crimes of the Last 100 Years*, London, Odhams Press Ltd, 1936.

Richardson, Joseph Hall, *From the City to Fleet Street*, London, Stanley Paul & Co., 1927.

Shore, W. Teignmouth (ed.), *Crime and its Detection*, London, The Gresham Publishing Company Ltd, 1931.

Sugden, Philip, *The Complete History of Jack the Ripper*, London, Constable & Robinson, 2002.

Yates, Dornford, *As Berry and I Were Saying*, London and Melbourne, Ward, Lock & Co., 1952.

Young, Filson (ed.), *Trial of Hawley Harvey Crippen*, Edinburgh and London, William Hodge & Company Ltd, 1933.

Index